Standard
BIBLE DICTIONARY

with the popular "How to Say It" Guide featured
in the Standard Lesson Commentary

PUBLISHING
Bringing The Word to Life™

Cincinnati, Ohio

Printed in the United States of America.

ISBN 0-7847-1873-3

13 12 11 10 09 08 07 06   9 8 7 6 5 4 3 2 1

Introduction

For more than 50 years the *Standard Lesson Commentary* has helped Sunday school teachers prepare thorough lessons to help their students gain a working understanding of the Scriptures. One of the popular features of this lesson commentary is a simple pronunciation guide to help teachers correctly pronounce Bible names and other difficult-to-pronounce words. This dictionary has grown out of those lists.

We have taken the "How to Say It" lists and added simple definitions to create a concise Bible dictionary for teachers and students. This is no Bible encyclopedia. The definitions are brief, designed to give the user a working knowledge of who or what the subject is. If the student wishes to know more about these subjects, there are plenty of dictionaries and encyclopedias available. Most, however, do not provide any help with pronunciation. This dictionary helps the teacher correctly pronounce and identify some of the most common names and other words that may come up in a Sunday school class or other Bible study.

This is not an exhaustive list of every word or name to appear in the Bible. It does, however, cite the names most likely to come up in a Sunday school lesson because it comes from actual Sunday school lessons. Nor do the definitions provide an exhaustive list of every Scripture where each word or name appears. The examples are representative only.

Sometimes a word will include a notation of an alternate spelling. Two reasons may account for this. Sometimes the same person may have a name that is spelled in different ways. King Jehoram of Judah is also known as Joram. The two spellings reflect slight differences in the Hebrew original, and so the translations generally try to reflect those differences. This is made more complicated by the fact that there was also a King Jehoram of Israel, and he, too, was also known as Joram. The second reason comes about because the different manuscripts on which the translations are based sometimes have different readings. Thus, one translation may have "Jehoram" and another "Joram" in the same passage. In 2 Chronicles 22:5, the *King James Version* has, "He walked also after their counsel, and went with *Jehoram* the son of Ahab king of Israel to war against Hazael king of Syria at Ramothgilead: and the Syrians smote *Joram*." In the same passage the *New International Version* has, "He also followed their counsel when he went with *Joram* son of Ahab king of Israel to war against Hazael king of Aram at Ramoth Gilead. The Arameans wounded *Joram*." It can be confusing!

Because of these differences in translations, sometimes a definition or pronunciation in this dictionary will cite a particular Bible version. Usually this will be either the *King James Version* or the *New International Version*. This is so because the *Standard Lesson Commentary* is available in two editions, one based on each of these translations. The availability of a growing number of translations makes the production of a Bible dictionary ever more challenging. References to particular Bible versions, however, are merely representative. No attempt has been made to locate every Bible version and to consult the spelling. Usually the *KJV* and *NIV* are noted, and sometimes some other versions, but never have we tried to list every version, or even every spelling.

This concise *Standard Bible Dictionary* is offered as one more help for teachers who want to present the Word of God. Coupled with the *Standard Lesson Commentary*, in either the *King James* or *NIV* edition, it will help the serious Bible teacher to be well prepared for comprehensive Bible teaching. May God bless your efforts to share His Word completely and accurately.

Aa

Aaron *Air*-un\\
Brother of Moses. First high priest of Israel.

Aaronic \\Air-*ahn*-ik\\
Related to Aaron, as in "Aaronic priests," who were priests descended from Aaron.

Ab \\Ab\\
Fifth month on the Jewish calendar, roughly equivalent to July–August. See CALENDAR CHART.

Abaddon *(Hebrew)* \\Uh-*bad*-dun\\
Place of destruction or angel of destruction. Used as a synonym for death in the Old Testament. In Revelation 9:11 Abaddon (APOLLYON) is the angel of the bottomless pit or Abyss.

Abana *Ab*-uh-nuh or Uh-*ban*-uh\\
A river in Damascus.

Abba *(Aramaic)* *Ab*-buh\\
An endearing term for "father."

Abdeel *Ab*-dee-el\\
The father of Shelemiah, mentioned in Jeremiah 36:26.

Abdon *Ab*-dahn\\
1. A judge who ruled in Israel for eight years (Judges 12:13-15).
2. Shashak's son; a family from the tribe of Benjamin that lived in Jerusalem (1 Chronicles 8:23-25).
3. Ancestor of King Saul (1 Chronicles 8:30; 9:35, 36).
4. An official that King Josiah sent to the prophetess Huldah (2 Chronicles 34:20-22; called Acbor in 2 Kings 22:12).
5. A town for Levites in the tribal territory of Asher (Joshua 21:30; 1 Chronicles 6:74).

Abednego \\Uh-*bed*-nee-go\\
Originally called Azariah, he was one of Daniel's three friends whom God saved from Nebuchadnezzar's furnace (Daniel 1:7; 3:25, 26).

Abel *Ay*-buhl\\
Second son of Adam and Eve; murdered by his brother Cain (Genesis 4:1-8).

Abel Meholah *Ay*-buhl-muh-*ho*-lah\\ (strong accent on *ho*) (Also spelled Abel-meholah)
Located in the Jordan valley in the tribal territory of Manasseh, it is the place where Elisha was born (1 Kings 19:16).

Abi *A*-bye\\
Short for Abijah, King Hezekiah's mother (2 Kings 18:2).

Abiah \\Uh-*bye*-uh\\ (Also spelled Abijah)
1. The second son of Samuel (1 Samuel 8:2; 1 Chronicles 6:28).
2. A wife of Hezron, father of Caleb, whom he married after the death of Caleb's mother; she was the mother of Asshur (1 Chronicles 2:24).
3. A son of Becher, descendant of Benjamin (1 Chronicles 7:8).
See ABIJAH.

Abiathar \\Ah-*bye*-uh-thar\\
1. Son of Ahimelech, he escaped and took refuge with David when Doeg, at Saul's command, murdered the priest's family (1 Samuel 22:20, 22; 23:6, 9; 2 Samuel 8:17).
2. A joint high priest with Zadok during the time of King David (2 Samuel 15:24-29, 35, 36; 17:15; 19:11; 20:25). He conspired with Adonijah in an attempt to make Adonijah king after David (1 Kings 1, 2).

Abib *A*-bib\\
Pre-exilic name of the first month of the year on the Jewish calendar; changed to Nisan after the exile. Roughly equivalent to March–April. See CALENDAR CHART.

Abiel *Ay*-be-el\\
1. Saul and Abner's grandfather (1 Samuel 14:51)
2. An Arbathite, one of David's mighty men (1 Chronicles 11:32).

Abiezer \\Ah-by-*eez*-er\\
1. A son of Manasseh and grandson of Joseph (Joshua 17:2). Gideon was descended from his clan (Judges 6:11).
2. One of David's mighty men, from Anathoth (1 Chronicles 11:28).

Abiezrite *A*-by-*ez*-rite\\ (strong accent on *ez*)
Related to, or descended from, Abiezer. Warriors descended from Manasseh's tribe (Judges 6:11, 12; 8:2, 32).

Abigail *Ab*-ih-gale\\
1. Wife of Nabal who married David after Nabal's death (1 Samuel 25:14, 39-42).
2. Wife of Jether (Ithra), and mother of Amasa (1 Chronicles 2:16, 17).

Abihu \\Uh-*bye*-hew\\
Son of Aaron. Died when he offered a displeasing sacrifice to God (Leviticus 10:1, 2; Numbers 3:2-4; 26:61; 1 Chronicles 24:1, 2).

Abijah \Uh-*bye*-juh\ (Sometimes spelled Abiah, especially in *KJV*.)
1. One of Samuel's sons who reigned as judge for three years. Became corrupt (1 Samuel 8:2; 1 Chronicles 6:28).
2. Son of Jeroboam I who died as a child in fulfillment of a prophecy by Ahijah (1 Kings 14:1-18).
3. A wife of Judah's grandson Hezron (1 Chronicles 2:24).
4. Hezekiah's mother (2 Chronicles 29:1).
5. The seventh son of Beker from the tribe of Benjamin (1 Chronicles 7:8).
6. Aaronic priest; the eighth ancestral head of the 24 priestly groups that King David established (1 Chronicles 24:10). John the Baptist's father belonged to this group (Luke 1:5).
7. A priest during Nehemiah's time who returned to Babylon with Zerubbabel (Nehemiah 10:7).
8. Son of Rehoboam, second king of Judah (2 Chronicles 12:16–14:1). In 1 Kings 14 and 15 he is typically called Abijam (except in *NIV*). See Kings of Israel and Judah Chart.
See Abiah.

Abijam \Uh-*bye*-jum\
See Abijah, #8.

Abilene \A-bi-*lee*-neh\ or \Ab-i-*lee*-neh\
A tetrarchy northwest of Damascus, which eventually became part of Syria (Luke 3:1).

Abimelech \Uh-*bim*-eh-lek\
1. King of Gerar (probably a title, as Pharaoh was for the king of Egypt), who took Sarah when Abraham said she was his sister instead of his wife. Abimelech was warned of God in a dream and returned Sarah to Abraham. Abimelech later signed a treaty with Abraham concerning a well at Beersheba (Genesis 20; 21:22-34).
2. King of Gerar who was deceived when Isaac claimed Rebekah, his wife, was his sister (Genesis 26:1-11).
3. Son of Gideon by a concubine; murdered 70 sons of Gideon in an effort to become king in Shechem (Judges 8:31; 9:1-57). See Judges of Israel Chart.
4. Philistine king mentioned in the title of Psalm 34.
5. Abiathar's son; a priest during the reign of David (1 Chronicles 18:14-16).

Abinadab \Uh-*bin*-uh-dab\
1. A relative of King Saul. The ark of the covenant was placed in his home when it was returned by the Philistines (1 Samuel 7:1; 2 Samuel 6:3; 1 Chronicles 13:7).
2. King David's brother; a soldier in Saul's army against the Philistines (1 Samuel 16:8; 17:13; 1 Chronicles 2:13).
3. A son of King Saul who died with Saul at Mt. Gilboa (1 Samuel 31:2; 1 Chronicles 8:33; 9:39; 10:2). He is called Ishvi in 1 Samuel 14:49. See Ishvi.
4. The husband of a daughter of King Solomon (1 Kings 4:11).

Abinoam \Uh-*bin*-o-am\
Barak's father (Judges 4:6; 5:1).

Abishai \Uh-*bish*-ay-eye\
King David's nephew from his sister; a most loyal and brave commander in King David's army (1 Samuel 26:6-9; 2 Samuel 2:18, 24; 3:20; 10:10, 14; 16:9, 11).

Abishalom \Uh-*bish*-uh-lum\
See Absalom.

Abraham *Ay*-bruh-ham\
The father of Isaac and grandfather of Jacob (Israel). His name means "father of a multitude." The Jews often referred to themselves as children of Abraham (cf. John 8:33, 39). In the New Testament, Christians are referred to as children of Abraham (Romans 4:11, 12).

Abram *Ay*-brum\
The name given to Abraham by his parents. It means "exalted father" (Genesis 12:1).

Absalom *Ab*-suh-lum\
Third son of King David (2 Samuel 3:2, 3). His name is also spelled Abishalom (1 Kings 15:2, 10).

Accho *Ak*-oh\
A major seaport occupied by Israel during the reigns of Saul, David, and Solomon. Centuries later it was renamed Ptolemais, after Ptolemy the king of Egypt who rebuilt it about 100 BC. Paul stopped here on his way to Jerusalem (Acts 21:7).

Achaia \Uh-*kay*-uh\
Southern province of Greece; its capital was Corinth (Acts 18:12, 27; 19:21; Romans 15:26).

Achan *Ay*-kan\
Israelite who disobeyed God's orders by taking spoils from Jericho; Achan and his family were stoned in the valley of Achor (Joshua 7).

Acbor *Ak*-bor\
See Abdon, #4.

Achbor *Ak*-bor\
Father to a king of Edom named Baalhanan (also spelled Baal-Hanan) (Genesis 36:38, 39; 1 Chronicles 1:49).

Achish *Ay*-kish\
A Philistine king; David fled to him for protection from Saul (1 Samuel 21:10-15).

Achmetha \Ock-*mee*-thuh\ (Also known as Ecbatana.)
The ancient capital of Media. The decree of Cyrus, which gave permission to the Jews to rebuild the temple, was found in a palace there (Ezra 6:1-3).

acropolis \uh-*krop*-uh-lus\
A high, fortified part of an ancient Greek city. The Parthenon is located on the Acropolis in Athens.

Acts \Ax\
"Acts of Apostles," the fifth book of the New Testament, giving details about the history of the church from the time immediately after Christ's resurrection until Paul's first imprisonment in Rome. It was written by Luke. See BOOKS OF THE BIBLE CHART.

Adaiah \Add-uh-*eye*-uh\ or \A-*day*-yuh\
1. Josiah's maternal grandfather, from the land of Bozkath (2 Kings 22:1).
2. One of Shimei's sons from the tribe of Benjamin (1 Chronicles 8:21).
3. A Levite descendant of Gershon (1 Chronicles 6:41-43).
4. Aaronic priest after the exile; a head of family living in Jerusalem (1 Chronicles 9:10-12; Nehemiah 11:12).
5. Maaseiah's father; helped Jehoiada put Joash on the throne (2 Chronicles 23:1).
6. A son of Bani guilty of marrying a foreign woman (Ezra 10:29).
7. Another man guilty of marrying a foreign woman (Ezra 10:39).
8. A descendant of Judah by Perez; lived in Jerusalem after the exile (Nehemiah 11:4, 5).

Adam *(Hebrew)* \uh-*dahm*\
The first man created by God. Also the Hebrew word for "man."

Adamah *(Hebrew)* \Ad-uh-*mah*\
A walled city that belongs to the tribe of Naphtali (Joshua 19:35, 36).

Adar *Ay*-dar\
Twelfth month on the Jewish calendar, roughly equivalent to mid-February to mid-March. See CALENDAR CHART.

Admah *Ad*-muh\
A city near Sodom that was destroyed by God. (Deuteronomy 29:23)

Adonai *(Hebrew)* \Ad-owe-*nye*\
Hebrew word for "lord."

Adonijah \Ad-o-*nye*-juh\
King David's fourth son; though next in line after Absalom, he was passed over in favor of Solomon, who succeeded the throne (1 Kings 1:5–2:27).

Adoniram \Uh-*don*-ih-ram\
A prominent overseer of labor during the reigns of David, Solomon, and Rehoboam (1 Kings 4:6; 5:14). Also spelled Adoram (2 Samuel 20:24; 1 Kings 12:18) or Hadoram (2 Chronicles 10:18) in some translations.

Adoram \Uh-*doe*-rum\
See ADONIRAM.

Adramyttium \Ad-ruh-*mitt*-ee-um\
A port on the western coast of Asia Minor. Paul's trip to Rome began on a ship from Adramyttium (Acts 27:2).

Adriatic \Ay-dree-*at*-ic\
A sea that is located between Italy and Greece.

Adullam \A-*dull*-lum\
A place in the hill country of Judah. The limestone caves there were used as places of refuge. David hid there to escape King Saul (1 Samuel 22:1; 2 Samuel 23:13; 1 Chronicles 11:15).

Aegean \A-*jee*-un\
A sea that is located between Greece and Asia Minor.

Aeneas \Ee-*nee*-us\
A paralyzed man who was healed by the apostle Peter (Acts 9:33-35).

Aenon *Ee*-nun\
A place west of the Jordan near Salim where there was "much water" and was used by John the Baptist to baptize people (John 3:23).

Agabus *Ag*-uh-bus\
A prophet who predicted a famine in Judea (Acts 11:28) and Paul's arrest in Jerusalem (Acts 21:10, 11).

Agag *Ay*-gag\
Title of the king of Amalek; two are mentioned in the Old Testament:
1. King in Balaam's prophecy (Numbers 24:7).
2. King spared by Saul but killed by Samuel (1 Samuel 15:7-33).

Agagite *Ay*-guh-gite\
A title given to Haman as an enemy of the Jews (Esther 3:1, 10; 8:5; 9:24).

agapao *(Greek)* \ah-guh-*pah*-oh\
One of the Greek verbs for "love." See AGAPE.

agape *(Greek)* \uh-*gah*-pay\
Greek word for "love" (the noun). It describes an active, intelligent goodwill toward another without regard to the

response. (It is sometimes described as love "in spite of" as opposed to "because of.")

agate *a*-gut\ (*a* as in *at*)
A precious stone, a multi-colored chalcedony. The term translates two Hebrew words in the *King James Version.* Other versions have "agate" for one (Exodus 28:19; 39:12) and "ruby" for the other (Isaiah 54:12; Ezekiel 27:16). The *New Living Translation* also lists *agate* in Revelation 21:19, where most versions have "chalcedony."

agonia *(Greek)* \ag-o-*nee*-uh\
The Greek word for "agony." Used to describe Jesus' pain in the Garden of Gethsemane (Luke 22:44).

agora *(Greek)* *ag*-uh-ruh\
Greek word for "marketplace." A city's gathering place in Bible times.

Agrippa \Uh-*grip*-puh\
1. Herod Agrippa I. Grandson of Herod the Great (the king who tried to kill the infant Jesus). He is the Herod who had the apostle James killed (Acts 12:2). Herod's death (in AD 44) is recorded in Acts 12:20-23.
2. Herod Agrippa II. Son of Agrippa I, he is the King Agrippa who heard Paul in Acts 25:23–26:32.

Agur *Ay*-gur\
Collector of proverbial sayings; inspired by God to write Proverbs 30. Some students believe it to be a pseudonym for Solomon.

Ahab *Ay*-hab\
1. Seventh king of Israel, after Omri. He ruled for 22 years (1 Kings 16:29). His wife was Jezebel (1 Kings 16:31). See KINGS OF ISRAEL AND JUDAH CHART.
2. A false prophet, son of Kolaiah (Jeremiah 29:21, 22).

Ahasuerus \Uh-haz-you-*ee*-rus\
King of Persia in the *King James Version;* otherwise known as Xerxes.
1. King of Persia in the book of Esther.
2. King of Persia mentioned in Ezra 4:6.
3. The father of Darius the Mede in Daniel 9:1.

Ahaz *Ay*-haz\
Eleventh king of Judah, after Jotham; father of Hezekiah. It was to him Isaiah made his famous prophecy about the virgin's conception of, and giving birth to, Immanuel (Isaiah 7:10-14). See KINGS OF ISRAEL AND JUDAH CHART.

Ahaziah \Ay-huh-*zye*-uh\
1. Eighth king of the northern kingdom of Israel, son of Ahab and Jezebel; he ruled just two years (1 Kings 22:51). See KINGS OF ISRAEL AND JUDAH CHART.
2. Sixth king of Judah, son of Jehoram of Judah and Athaliah, who was related to Ahab of Israel (2 Kings 8:24-26); also known as Jehoahaz. When he was killed in the coup of Jehu (2 Kings 9:27), his mother attempted to destroy the kingly line, usurping the throne and ruling six years before being deposed (2 Kings 11). See KINGS OF ISRAEL AND JUDAH CHART.

Ahiah \Uh-*high*-uh\
See AHIJAH.

Ahijah \Uh-*high*-juh\ (Also spelled Ahiah.)
1. Ahitub's son; priest who brought the ark of the covenant to Saul to seek God about a war against the Philistines (1 Samuel 14:3, 18).
2. Shisha's son, a scribe under Solomon (1 Kings 4:3).
3. A prophet of Shiloh who prophesied Jeroboam's role as king of Israel (1 Kings 11:29-39; 2 Chronicles 10:15).
4. Father to Israel's king, Baasha, from the tribe of Issachar (1 Kings 15:27).
5. Son of Jerahmeel of Judah (1 Chronicles 2:25).
6. Related to Benjamin's tribe; mentioned in connection with Ehud's family (1 Chronicles 8:1, 7).
7. One of "the thirty" among David's warriors (2 Chronicles 11:36).
8. A Levite who maintained the treasury during David's reign (1 Chronicles 26:20).
9. A leader who took an oath to obey God (Nehemiah 10:1, 26).

Ahikam \Uh-*high*-kum\
Son of Shaphan; one of the officials King Josiah sent to ask the prophetess Huldah about the book of the Law (2 Kings 22:12).

Ahilud \A-*high*-lud\
Father of the recorder, Jehoshaphat, during the reign of David (2 Samuel 8:16).

Ahimaaz \Uh-*him*-ay-az\
1. Father of Saul's wife Ahinoam (1 Samuel 14:50).
2. High priest, son of Zadok (1 Chronicles 6:8).

Ahimelech \A-*him*-uh-leck\
1. A priest who innocently helped David and his men get away from Saul (1 Samuel 21) but who was slain as a traitor when Saul learned of it (1 Samuel 22:6-19).
2. A Hittite warrior who went with David to King Saul's camp (1 Samuel 26:6).
3. Son of Abiathar and grandson of Ahimelech (#1); served as priest during the reign of David (2 Samuel 8:17; 1 Chronicles 24:3, 6, 31).

Ahinoam \Uh-*hin*-o-am\
1. Wife of King Saul (1 Samuel 14:50).

2. Wife of King David and mother of David's first son, Amnon (2 Samuel 3:2; 1 Chronicles 3:1).

Ahisamach \A-*his*-a-mak\
Descended from the tribe of Dan; Aholiab's father (Exodus 31:6; 35:34; 38:23).

Ahithophel \A-*hith*-o-fel\
A respected advisor of King David who conspired with Absalom to take over the kingdom; his advice was not taken and Absalom's attempt was unsuccessful (2 Samuel 17:4-14).

Ahitub \A-*high*-tub\
1. Descendant of Ithamar and son of Phineas; father of Ahijah (1 Samuel 14:3) and of Ahimelech (1 Samuel 22:9). (Some suppose Ahijah and Ahimelech to be the same person; others, that they are brothers.)
2. Descendant of Aaron; Amariah's son and father of Zadok the priest (2 Samuel 8:17; 1 Chronicles 6:7, 8).

Aholiab \Uh-*ho*-lih-ab\
Descended from the tribe of Dan; equipped with divine skill to construct the tabernacle (Exodus 31:6).

Ahuzzath \Uh-*huz*-uth\
Abimelech's advisor; joined Abimelech on a trip to Beersheba to make a treaty with Isaac (Genesis 26:26).

Ai *Ay*-eye\ (Also spelled Hai.)
A town near Bethel, where Abraham pitched his tent (Genesis 12:8; 13:3). It was the second Canaanite town conquered by Joshua and the Israelites (Joshua 7, 8).

Aijalon *Ay*-juh-lon\ (Also spelled Ajalon.)
1. City in the tribe of Dan. It was in the valley of Aijalon that Israel fought when Joshua ordered the sun and moon to stand still (Joshua 10:12). It was also designated as a city of refuge (1 Chronicles 6:69).
2. A city in the tribe of Zebulun (Judges 12:12).

Ajalon *Aj*-uh-lon\
See AIJALON.

Akeldama (*Aramaic*) \Uh-*kel*-duh-muh\ (Also spelled Aceldama, Akel Dama, and Hakeldama.)
"Field of blood," the place where Judas Iscariot died (Acts 1:18, 19).

Akhisar \Ahk-iss-*ar*\
Modern name of the ancient city of Thyatira.

Akkub *Ak*-ub\
1. One of Elioenai's seven sons (1 Chronicles 3:24).
2. A Levite who was head of a family stationed at the King's Gate (1 Chronicles 9:17).

3. The head of a family of temple servants (Ezra 2:45).
4. A Levite who instructed the people in the Law (Nehemiah 8:7). Possibly the same as #2 or #3.

alabaster *al*-uh-*bas*-ter\ (strong accent on *al*).
A stone used to make vessels that held perfume or ointment (Matthew 26:7; Mark 14:3; Luke 7:37).

Alashehir *Al*-uh-shuh-*here*\ (strong accent on *here*)
Modern name of the city of Philadelphia, in Asia Minor (in modern Turkey), one of the churches mentioned in Revelation 3.

Alcmene \Alk-*mee*-nee\
Mother of Hercules in Greek mythology.

aleph (*Hebrew*) *ah*-leff\
The first letter in the Hebrew alphabet.

Alexander \Al-ex-*an*-der\
1. A son of Simon of Cyrene, the man who carried the cross of Jesus (Mark 15:21).
2. A relative of the high priest Annas. (Acts 4:6).
3. A Jew who was put in front of a noisy crowd in Ephesus to make a defense (Acts 19:33).
4. A metal worker who treated Paul and the gospel with contempt (2 Timothy 4:14). Paul handed him, along with Hymenaeus, over to Satan (1 Timothy 1:19, 20).

Alexandria \Al-iks-*an*-dree-uh\
A city in Egypt on the Mediterranean Sea founded by Alexander the Great in 322 bc. It was the hometown of Apollos (Acts 18:24).

almah (*Hebrew*) \al-*mah*\
Hebrew word for "young woman" or "virgin" (Isaiah 7:14).

alpha (*Greek*) *al*-fuh\
The first letter in the Greek alphabet. When *alpha* is used with *omega,* it refers to "the beginning and the end"; used to explain God (Revelation 1:8).

Alphaeus \Al-*fee*-us\ (Also spelled Alpheus.)
1. Father of Levi (i. e., Matthew) (Mark 2:14).
2. Father of James the Less (Matthew 10:3; Mark 3:18; Luke 6:15; Acts 1:13).
Some students have suggested that these two are the same person, but that is not likely.

Alpheus \Al-*fee*-us\
See ALPHAEUS.

altaschith (*Hebrew*) \al-*tas*-kith\
Found notated in the titles of Psalms 57, 58, 59 and 75. Means "do not destroy" in Hebrew.

Amalek *Am*-uh-lek\
1. Son of Eliphaz (Esau's oldest son) by his concubine Timna (Genesis 36:12; 1 Chronicles 1:36).
2. Country of the Amalekites (Exodus 17:8; Deuteronomy 25:17).

Amalekites *Am*-uh-leh-kites\ or \Uh-*mal*-ih-kites\
Descendants of Esau; kept the feud of Jacob and Esau going throughout history. Eventually were destroyed by Israel (Deuteronomy 25:17-19).

Amariah *Am*-uh-*rye*-uh\ (strong accent on *rye*)
1. Levite and relative of Ezra (1 Chronicles 6:7, 11, 52; Ezra 7:3).
2. A Levite in service during the reign of David (1 Chronicles 23:19; 24:23)
3. A chief priest that served during the reign of Jehoshaphat (2 Chronicles 19:11).
4. A Levite who served under King Hezekiah (2 Chronicles 31:15).
5. A descendant of Binnui who was guilty of marrying a foreign woman (Ezra 10:42).
6. Signed an agreement (Nehemiah 10:1, 3).
7. Returned with Zerubbabel from Babylon and signed Ezra's covenant (Nehemiah 12:2).
8. Son of Hezekiah and great-grandfather of Zephaniah (Zephaniah 1:1).

Amasa *Am*-uh-suh\
1. A nephew of David (2 Samuel 17:25); appointed commander of the army to replace Joab, but Joab killed him to retain the position (2 Samuel 19:13–20:12).
2. An Ephraimite leader in the time of Pekah, king of Israel; son of Hadlai (2 Chronicles 28:12).

Amaziah \Am-uh-*zye*-uh\
1. Eighth king of Judah (1 Chronicles 3:12). See Kings of Israel and Judah Chart.
2. A priest under Jeroboam I; complained about the prophet Amos to Jeroboam. Amos prophesied the death of Amaziah and his family (Amos 7:10-17).
3. A Simeonite; father of Joash (1 Chronicles 4:34).
4. One of the Merarites that King David assigned to the house of the Lord (1 Chronicles 6:45, 48).

ambassage *am*-buh-sij\
The business entrusted to an ambassador; the message or mission of an ambassador (Luke 14:32, *KJV*; the same word is rendered "message" in Luke 19:14, *KJV*).

amethyst *am*-uh-thust\
A purple quartz used to make jewelry; one of the precious stones in the breastplate of the high priest (Exodus 28:19; 39:12) and in the foundation of the New Jerusalem (Revelation 21:20).

Amittai \Uh-*mit*-eye\
The prophet Jonah's father (2 Kings 14:25; Jonah 1:1).

Ammi *(Hebrew)* *Am*-my\
A symbolic name given to Israel meaning "you are my people" (Hosea 2:1, *KJV*). Promises God's restoration of Israel after the exile; Peter cites it as a blessing of the new covenant (1 Peter 2:9, 10).

Amminadab \Uh-*min*-uh-dab\
1. Aaron's father-in-law (Exodus 6:23).
2. Father of Nahshon chosen to be head of Judah's tribe to assist Moses (Numbers 1:7; 2:3; 7:12; 10:14; Ruth 4:19, 20; 1 Chronicles 2:10; Matthew 1:4).
3. A son of Levi descended from Kohath (1 Chronicles 6:22). Possibly the same as #1.
4. A Kohathite who helped King David bring the ark back to Jerusalem (1 Chronicles 15:10, 11).

Ammon *Am*-mun\
1. Son of Lot's younger daughter by Lot; he became the father of the Ammonites (Genesis 19:38).
2. Area east of the Jordan River and north of Moab and south of the wadi Jabbok

Ammonites *Am*-un-ites\
Descended from Ammon. Related to the Moabites (Genesis 19:38). Also related to Israel, but made several attacks against them (Judges 11:13; 1 Samuel 11:2).

Amnon *Am*-nun\
1. A son of David; he raped his half-sister Tamar and was later killed by her brother Absalom (2 Samuel 13:1-29).
2. A son of Shimon from the tribe of Judah (1 Chronicles 4:20).

Amon *Ay*-mun\
1. Fourteenth king of Judah, son of King Manasseh. He was removed from the throne by a palace coup, and his son, Josiah, became king at 8 years of age (2 Kings 21:19-26; 2 Chronicles 33:21-25). See Kings of Israel and Judah Chart.
2. Governor of Samaria during the rule of King Ahab in Israel (1 Kings 22:26; 2 Chronicles 18:25).
3. A servant of King Solomon (Nehemiah 7:57-59). Another name for him is Ami (Ezra 2:57).

Amorites *Am*-uh-rites\
A people that descended from Canaan (Genesis 10:16).

Amos *Ay*-mus\
1. A prophet who resided in Tekoa during the reign of Uzziah and Jeroboam (Amos 1:1).
2. The 30th book of the Old Testament, the third in the "minor prophets" section. See Books of the Bible Chart.

3. An ancestor of Jesus listed in Luke's genealogy (Luke 3:25).

Amoz *Ay*-mahz\\
The father of the prophet Isaiah (2 Kings 19:2, 20; Isaiah 1:1).

Amphipolis \\Am-*fip*-o-liss\\
A city in northeast Greece where Paul passed through during his second missionary journey (Acts 17:1).

Amram *Am*-ram\\ (Also spelled Hamran and Hemdan.)
1. A descendant of Levi and Kohath. His wife was Jochebed, and they were the parents of Moses, Aaron, and Miriam (Exodus 6:16-20; Numbers 26:58, 59).
2. A priest from Bani's family guilty of marrying a foreign woman (Ezra 10:34).
3. Dishon's son (1 Chronicles 1:41).

Anaiah \\Uh-*nye*-uh\\
A priest who gathered with Ezra to read the book of the Law of Moses (Nehemiah 8:4). He signed Ezra's covenant to God (Nehemiah 10:22).

Anak *Ay*-nak\\
A notable Canaanite mentioned in Joshua 15:13 and ancestor of the Anakites or Anakim (Numbers 13:22, 28, 33).

Anakim *An*-a-kim\\
Descendants of Anak. The 12 spies Moses sent out reported the Anakim as giants (Numbers 13:17-22, 31-33). (Sometimes spelled Anakims, but the Hebrew -*kim* is a plural ending and does not need the *s*.)

Anakims *An*-a-kimz\\
See ANAKIM.

Ananias \\An-uh-*nye*-us\\
1. Early Christian in Jerusalem who, with his wife Sapphira, tried to deceive the church by giving part of the profit from the sale of their property while claiming to give the entire amount (Acts 5:1-11).
2. The Christian in Damascus whom God sent to Saul of Tarsus after Jesus had appeared to Saul on the road (Acts 9:10-19).
3. The high priest who brought charges against Paul before Felix (Acts 24:1).

Anath *Ay*-nath\\
The father of Shamgar, the third judge of Israel (Judges 3:31; 5:6). See JUDGES OF ISRAEL CHART.

anathema \\uh-*nath*-uh-muh\\
Greek word meaning "cursed" or "devoted to destruction" (1 Corinthians 16:22).

Anathoth *An*-uh-thoth\\
1. A Levite city and a city of refuge in the tribe of Benjamin (Joshua 21:18). The hometown of the prophet Jeremiah (Jeremiah 1:1).
2. Beker's son, from the tribe of Benjamin (1 Chronicles 7:8).
3. A leader who sealed the covenant of faithfulness to the Law (Nehemiah 10:19).

Andrew *An*-drew\\
One of the 12 apostles of Jesus, brother of Simon Peter (John 1:35-40).

Andronicus *An*-dro-*nye*-kus\\ (strong accent on *nye*)
One of Paul's relatives who had been in prison with Paul (Romans 16:7).

Annas *An*-nus\\
High priest during the time of Jesus (Luke 3:2; Acts 4:6). Father-in-law to the high priest Caiaphas (John 18:13). The Romans removed Annas from the position of high priest and appointed his son-in-law Caiaphas to the post. Apparently Annas continued to exert considerable influence on the Sanhedrin, as Jesus' trials evidence.

Anti-Lebanon *An*-ty-*Leb*-uh-nun\\ (strong accent on *Leb*)
A mountainous region that extends 100 miles northeast along the Syrian coast.

Antioch *An*-tee-ock\\
1. Antioch of Syria. A city in Syria on the Orontes River. The disciples were first called Christians in Antioch (Acts 11:26). Paul began his missionary career from Antioch (Acts 13:1-3).
2. Antioch of Pisidia. City in Asia Minor, near Phrygia. Paul and Barnabas preached in the synagogue here on their first missionary journey (Acts 13:14-50).

Antiochus \\An-*tie*-oh-kus\\
Several rulers of the Seleucid dynasty (including Asia Minor, Syria, and Judea) used the name *Antiochus* after the death of Alexander the Great. They ruled from 292–64 BC. Two are mentioned in the Bible.
1. Antiochus III (Antiochus the Great) was the king of the north in Daniel's prophecy (Daniel 11:13-19). He ruled from 223–187 BC, and was succeeded by his son Seleucus IV.
2. Antiochus IV (Antiochus Epiphanes) ruled from 175–167 BC. He was a son of Antiochus III and brother to Seleucus IV. His atrocities (prophesied in Daniel 11:21-32) involved him in the Maccabean War.

Antipas *An*-tih-pus\\
1. An early Christian martyr. Described as a faithful martyr or witness (Revelation 2:13).

2. A son of Herod the Great (the king who tried to kill the infant Jesus); he was tetrarch of Galilee and Perea during the ministry of Jesus (Luke 23:7). He beheaded John the Baptist (Matthew 14:1-12). *The New Living Translation* uses the name *Antipas* of Herod 10 times, but it does not translate an actual word in the Greek text. Rather, it is added for clarification. Most versions do not include this name.

Antipater \An-*tih*-puh-ter\
The father of Herod the Great. This name is not found in Scripture, but the city of Antipatris (see Acts 23:31) was named for him.

Antipatris \An-*tih*-puh-triss\
A city on the route between Jerusalem and Caesarea, built by Herod the Great and named in honor of his father, Antipater. Paul was brought here, where he spent the night, when he was being moved under Roman guard to the custody of Felix (Acts 23:31-35).

Antonia \An-*toe*-nee-uh\ or \An-*toe*-nyuh\
Name of the castle that Herod the Great built to connect with the temple at Jerusalem. It housed a Roman garrison. Paul was taken to this castle when he was arrested in Jerusalem (Acts 21:30-37).

Apharsathchites \A-*far*-sak-ites\ or \Af-ar-*sath*-kits\
People in Samaria who protested the rebuilding of the temple (Ezra 4:9, *KJV*). The Hebrew term translates as "Persians."

Aphek *Ay*-fek\
1. City in the Sharon Valley where the Philistines camped before the battle in which they captured the ark of the covenant (1 Samuel 4:1ff).
2. City in the Jezreel Valley where the Philistines camped before the battle on Mt. Gilboa, in which Saul and his sons were killed (1 Samuel 29:1ff).
3. City in territory of Asher from where the Canaanites were not driven out when the Israelites took possession of the land (Judges 1:31).

Aphiah \Uh-*fye*-uh\
An ancestor of King Saul (1 Samuel 9:1).

Aphrodite \Af-ruh-*dite*-ee\
Goddess of love in Greek mythology. Her temple in Corinth housed 1000 temple prostitutes.

apocalypse \uh-*pock*-uh-lips\
The term means "revelation" (Revelation 1:1), but it has come to designate a specific literary genre in which symbolic language is used to describe the conflict between good and evil. The book of Daniel and Revelation are apocalypses in the Bible. There were other apocalypses in antiquity, but they often display a pagan, dualistic view of good and evil.

Apocrypha \Uh-*pock*-ruh-fuh\
A number of non-canonical books written during the period between the writing of Malachi and the birth of Christ. These were written in Greek and were included in the Septuagint (Greek translation of the Old Testament) and also in the Latin Vulgate.

apocryphal \uh-*pock*-ruh-full\
Related to the Apocrypha. Sometimes used metaphorically of a story that is widely told but not true or not able to be verified as true. Used of a number of documents written early in the Christian era purporting to be written by apostles or other church leaders, but without any validity to the claims.

apokalupsis *(Greek)* \uh-pock-uh-*loop*-sis\
Greek for apocalypse, a term meaning "revelation" (Revelation 1:1).

Apollo \Uh-*pah*-low\
Greek god of music, poetry, prophecy, and medicine.

Apollonia \Ap-uh-*low*-nee-uh\
A city of Macedonia between Philippi and Thessalonica. Paul passed through on his second missionary journey (Acts 17:1).

Apollos \Uh-*pahl*-us\
A scholar from Alexandria who helped spread the gospel during the time of Paul. Originally he taught only John's baptism, but Aquila and Priscilla taught him in Corinth so that he then taught the whole gospel (Acts 18:24–19:1).

Apollyon \Uh-*pol*-yun\
Greek name for ABADDON. In Revelation 9:11 Apollyon is the angel of the bottomless pit or Abyss.

apostasy \uh-*pahs*-tuh-see\
Abandonment of belief in God.

apostatize \uh-*pahs*-tuh-tize\
To abandon one's faith.

apostolic \ap-uh-*stahl*-ick\
Related to the apostles. An *apostolic precedent* is a practice of the apostles held to be a pattern for believers ever since.

apotheosis \uh-*poth*-ee-*oh*-sus\ (strong accent on *oh*).
Projecting divine qualities onto a person.

Apphia *Af*-ee-uh\ or *Ap*-fee-uh\
A woman mentioned in Philemon 2. Some think she was Philemon's wife and the mother of Archippus.

Appii Forum *Ap*-pi-eye *For*-um\ (Also called the Forum of Appius.)
A city in Italy about 40 miles south of Rome. Paul passed through here on his way to Rome and was met there by a number of believers from Rome (Acts 28:15).

Appius *Ap*-pea-us\
See APPII FORUM.

Aqaba *Ock*-uh-buh\ (Gulf of Aqaba)
The eastern arm of the Red Sea. Solomon sent ships through the Gulf of Aqaba (2 Kings 9:26-28).

Aquila *Ack*-wih-luh\
Priscilla's husband; this couple worked with Paul and in his absence to spread the gospel and to assist the early church (Acts 18:2, 18, 26; 2 Timothy 4:19).

Arabia \Uh-*ray*-bee-uh\
A large peninsula surrounded by the Persian Gulf to the east, the Red Sea to the west, and the Fertile Crescent to the north. The site traditionally believed to be the biblical Mt. Sinai is in the southern tip of Arabia.

Arabians \Uh-*ray*-bee-unz\
The people of Arabia.

Aram *Air*-um\
1. A son of Shem (Genesis 10:22, 23; 1 Chronicles 1:17).
2. Kemuel's son; nephew of Abraham (Genesis 22:21).
3. Shomer's son from the tribe of Asher (1 Chronicles 7:34).
4. Another version of the name *Ram* (Matthew 1:3, 4; Luke 3:33).
5. Country to the north and east of Israel, roughly the same as Syria and part of Mesopotamia (Genesis 24:10; Numbers 23:7). Damascus was its capital.

Aramaic *Air*-uh-*may*-ik\ (strong accent on *may*)
An ancient language, similar to Hebrew, that became the spoken language of the people of Israel by the time of Christ. Some parts of the Bible were written in Aramaic, though most of it is written in Hebrew and Greek.

Arameans *Ar*-uh-*me*-uns\ (strong accent on *me*)
People of Aram.

Aratus *Air*-uh-tus\
A Greek poet that Paul quotes in Acts 17:28. The name does not appear in the Bible.

Araunah \Ah-*raw*-nuh\ or *Ar*-ah-nah\ (Also known as Ornan.)
The Jebusite who owned a threshing floor that David purchased to build an altar to give God thanks for the end of the pestilence (2 Samuel 24:17-25; 1 Chronicles 21:15-26). The site became the location for the temple that Solomon would build (1 Chronicles 21:27–22:1).

Archelaus \Are-kuh-*lay*-us\
Son of Herod the Great (the king who tried to kill the infant Jesus); he ruled Idumea, Samaria, and Judea (Matthew 2:22).

Archippus \Ar-*kip*-us\
A believer in Colosse whom Paul encourages to be strong in ministry (Colossians 4:17; Philemon 2).

Arcturus \Ark-*tour*-us\
The brightest star in the constellation Bootes; used in the *KJV* in Job 9:9; 38:32.

Areopagite \Air-ee-*op*-uh-gite\
A person who served on the court of Areopagus in Athens; Dionysius the Areopagite was named among Paul's converts in Athens (Acts 17:34).

Areopagus \Air-ee-*op*-uh-gus\ (Also called Mars Hill.)
1. Hill of Ares (Greek god of war) in Athens. Mars is another name for Ares.
2. The supreme court of Athens, named for the hill where it originally held its meetings. Paul was brought before this court (Acts 17:19) which by Paul's time had little judicial power except for matters of religion and morals.

Aretas *Air*-ih-tas\
A Nabatean king (9 BC–AD 40) who at some point took control of Damascus. While he held Damascus, he attempted to arrest Paul—possibly to curry favor with the Jewish leaders (2 Corinthians 11:32).

Arimathea *Air*-uh-muh-*thee*-uh\ (*th* as in *thin*; strong accent on *thee*)
Judean town and home of a man named Joseph, who provided the tomb in which the body of Jesus was buried (Matthew 27:57; Mark 15:43; Luke 23:51; John 19:38). Some have identified the city with Ramathaim, the birthplace of Samuel (1 Samuel 1:19), but that city is in Ephraim (Samaria), and not Judea.

Aristarchus *Air*-iss-*tar*-cuss\
A man of Thessalonica who traveled with Paul; he and Gaius were seized during the riot in Ephesus (Acts 19:29; 20:4; 27:2; Colossians 4:10; Philemon 24).

Aristophanes \A-ris-*tof*-uh-neez\
Greek playwright of the fifth century BC. who coined the Greek word *korinthiazesthai*—which means "to act like a Corinthian"—as a reference to sexually immoral behavior.

Armageddon \Ar-muh-*ged*-un\
Valley of Megiddo, where Josiah was killed in battle by Pharaoh Neco. It became synonymous with defeat, as "to meet one's Waterloo" is for us today. Thus it becomes an appropriate metaphor for the final defeat of Satan and his forces in Revelation 16:16.

Armenia \Ar-*me*-nee-uh\
The region around Mt. Ararat. The two sons of Sennacherib fled to Armenia (Ararat in some versions) after murdering their father (2 Kings 19:37; Isaiah 37:38).

Arnon *Ar*-non\
A wadi that empties into the eastern side of the Dead Sea. It was often used as a boundary line (Numbers 21:13-15; Deuteronomy 3:12, 16; Joshua 13:16).

Aroer \Uh-*row*-er\
1. A town located on a branch of the Jabbok brook in the tribe of Gad (Numbers 32:34).
2. A town located on the north bank of the Arnon River in the tribe of Reuben (Deuteronomy 2:36; Joshua 13:16).
3. A town in the southern part of Judah (1 Samuel 30:28).

Artaxerxes \Are-tuh-*zerk*-seez\
The name or title of three Persian kings. Artaxeres is noted in the Bible (Ezra 4:7, 8, 11, 23; 6:14; 7:1, 7, 11, 12, 21; 8:1; Nehemiah 2:1; 5:14; 13:6) as supportive of the work of Nehemiah and Ezra.

Artemis *Ar*-teh-miss\ (Also called Diana.)
The Greek goddess of the moon, hunting, and animals. She was worshiped in Ephesus at the Temple of Artemis (Acts 19:23-41).

Asa *Ay*-zuh\
1. Third king of Judah. He was a godly king even though his father and grandfather were idolatrous (1 Kings 15:9-24; 2 Chronicles 14-16). See KINGS OF ISRAEL AND JUDAH CHART.
2. A Levite who returned from the captivity (1 Chronicles 9:16).

Asahiah \As-uh-*hye*-uh\ (Also spelled Asaiah.)
1. A servant of Josiah (2 Kings 22:12-14).
2. A Simeonite clan leader (1 Chronicles 4:36).
3. A Levite of the Merari family during David's time (1 Chronicles 6:30). He helped bring the ark of the covenant to Jerusalem (1 Chronicles 15:6, 11).
4. A Shelonite; one of the first people to live in Jerusalem after the captivity (1 Chronicles 9:5).

Asaiah \As-uh-*eye*-uh\ (Also spelled Asahiah.)
See ASAHIAH.

Asaph *Ay*-saff\
1. A Levite who led praise for David and Solomon (1 Chronicles 16:5; 2 Chronicles 5:12). His name appears with Psalms 50 and 73 to 83.
2. Father to Joah, King Hezekiah's recorder (2 Kings 18:18, 37; Isaiah 36:3, 22).

ascension \uh-*sen(t)*-shun\
The term used for Jesus' return to Heaven. (See Luke 9:51, *NASB*.)

asceticism \uh-*set*-uh-sizz-um\
The concept of leading a lifestyle of strict self-denial for the pursuit of godliness. (See Colossians 2:18, 23, *ESV*.)

Asenath *As*-e-nath\
Daughter of Potiphera the priest of On in Egypt. Married Joseph and bore Ephraim and Manasseh (Genesis 41:45-50).

Aser *A*-ser\ (Alternate spelling of the name *Asher.*)
See ASHER.

Ashdod *Ash*-dod\ (Also known as Azotus.)
One of the five main Philistine cities inhabited by the Anakim (Joshua 13:3). Located on the Mediterranean coast between Joppa and Gaza.

Ashdodites *Ash*-duh-dites\
The Philistine people who inhabited Ashdod.

Asher *Ash*-er\ (Also spelled Aser.)
1. Eighth son of Jacob, born to Zilpah, Leah's handmaid (Genesis 30:12; 35:26). The tribe of Asher came from this ancestor.
2. The tribe descended from Asher (Joshua 19:24; 21:6).
3. The territory allotted to the tribe of Asher.

Asherah \Uh-*she*-ruh\ (Also called Ashtoreth or Astarte.)
1. A Canaanite goddess that the Israelites worshiped during their idolatry.
2. Images of this goddess were called Asherah poles (Exodus 34:13; 1 Kings 16:33).

Ashkelon *Ash*-ke-lon\ or *As*-ke-lon\
One of the five main Philistine cities; located on the coast of the Mediterranean south of Ashdod (Joshua 13:3; 1 Samuel 6:17).

Ashpenaz *Ash*-pih-naz\
Nebuchadnezzar's prince eunuch who gave Daniel and his companions their Babylonian names (Daniel 1:3, 7).

Ashtaroth *Ash*-tuh-rawth\\
1. The capital city of Bashan, where King Og lived and ruled. Given to the tribe of Manasseh by Moses (Joshua 9:10; 13:31).
2. Plural of Ashtoreth in some translations; see Judges 2:13; 10:6.

Ashtoreth *Ash*-toe-reth\\
Another name for the goddess Asherah (Judges 2:11-23). See Asherah.

Ashurbanipal *As*-shure-*bah*-nee-pahl\\ (strong accent on *bah*). (Alternate spelling of the name *Asnapper*.)
A famous Assyrian king who reigned from 668–626 BC. His library gives much of what is known of Babylonian and Assyrian literature (Ezra 4:10).

Asia *Ay*-zha\\
Refers to the province of Rome whose capital was Ephesus.

Asiarchs *Ay*-shih-arks\\
An honorary title given to the rulers of Asia (Acts 19:31).

Asnapper *Az*-nap-per\\
See Ashurbanipal.

Asshur *Ash*-er\\
1. Son of Shem (Genesis 10:22); possibly the founder of Assyria.
2. Another name for Assyria (Numbers 24:22, 24). Often the Hebrew word for Asshur is translated as "Assyria" in the English versions.

Assisi \\Uh-*see*-see\\
A town in Italy. Home of Francis (1182-1226), the founder of the Franciscan order.

Assyria \\Uh-*sear*-ee-uh\\
An empire along the Upper Tigris River north of Babylon. The capital was Nineveh. The Assyrians defeated the northern kingdom of Israel in 721/722 BC.

Assyrians \\Uh-*sear*-e-unz\\
The people of Assyria.

Astarte \\A-*star*-te\\ (first *a* as in *had*)
Another name for the goddess Asherah or Ashtoreth.

Athaliah \\Ath-uh-*lye*-uh\\
Mother of Ahaziah, sixth king of Judah (2 Kings 8:26). Upon the death of Ahaziah, she usurped the throne and ruled as queen for six years until the priest Jehoiada organized a coup and put Joash on the throne (2 Kings 11:1-20; 2 Chronicles 22:1—23:21; 24:7). See Kings of Israel and Judah Chart.

atheistic \\a-thee-*iss*-tick\\ (*th* as in *thin*)
Inclined to the belief that there is no God.

Athena \\Uh-*thee*-nuh\\
The Roman goddess of wisdom, skills, and warfare.

Athenians \\Uh-*thin*-e-unz\\
The people who lived in Athens.

Athens *Ath*-unz\\
A city in Greece, named for the goddess Athena; a leader in learning and culture. Paul visited this city on his second missionary journey (Acts 17:16-34).

Atsel *(Hebrew)* *Aht*-sell\\
Sluggard; lazy. The term is used 14 times in the book of Proverbs.

Attalia \\At-uh-*lye*-uh\\
Seaport in Pamphylia named for Attalus Philadelphus, king of Pergamum. Paul and Barnabas preached here on their first missionary journey (Acts 14:25).

Augustine *Aw*-gus-*teen*\\ (strong accent on *Aw*) or \\Aw-*gus*-tin\\
1. A Latin monk of Hippo, in northern Africa, known for the writing of *Confessions* and *De Civitate Die* (City of God). Much of what today is called Calvinism may be traced to Augustine.
2. A Roman monk who took Christianity to the English and became the first Archbishop of Canterbury.

Augustus \\Aw-*gus*-tus\\
Roman emperor Caesar Augustus (43 BC–AD 14). His great-uncle, Julius Caesar, named him as heir to the Roman throne. Jesus was born in Bethlehem during his reign (Luke 2:1).

aven *ay*-ven\\
Hebrew word for "wickedness." It was applied to several locations as condemnation of the evil that was practiced there.
1. Ezekiel used it for the city of On (Heliopolis). The people were involved in the worship of idols (Ezekiel 30:17).
2. Beth Aven (sometimes spelled as Bethaven) means "house of wickedness." It was near Bethel, which means "house of God" (Joshua 7:2; 18:12).
3. Sometimes used ironically to refer to Bethel (Hosea 10:8). Bethel (the "house of God") had become a center for idolatry (1 Kings 12:28, 29).
4. A valley in Syria that was a center for the Baal worship (Amos 1:5).

Azaliah *Az*-uh-*lye*-uh\\
A son of Meshullam and father of Shaphan the scribe (2 Kings 22:3).

Azariah \Az-uh-*rye*-uh\
  1. Judah's ninth king, son of Amaziah; also called Uzziah (2 Kings 14:21). See Kings of Israel and Judah Chart.
  2. The high priest who confronted King Uzziah about doing priestly duties (2 Chronicles 26:16-20).
  3. Son of Hoshaiah, who bitterly opposed Jeremiah (Jeremiah 43:2).
  4. A friend of Daniel whose name was changed to Abed-nego during captivity in Babylon (Daniel 1:7).
  (See also 1 Kings 4:2-5; 1 Chronicles 2:8, 38; 6:9-14; 2 Chronicles 15:1-8; 21:2; 23:1; 28:12; 29:12; Nehemiah 3:23; 8:7; 10:2; 12:32, 33.)

Azel *Aht*-sell\
  A man of Benjamin, descended from Jonathan (1 Chronicles 8:37, 38; 9:43, 44).

Azotus \Uh-*zo*-tus\ (Also known as Ashdod.)
  The New Testament form of Ashdod (Acts 8:40). A city on the Mediterranean coast between Joppa and Gaza.

Azriel *Az*-rih-el\
  A family head of Manasseh (1 Chronicles 5:24).

Azzah *Az*-uh\
  Another name for the Philistine city of Gaza (Deuteronomy 2:23; 1 Kings 4:24; Jeremiah 25:20).

Bb

Baal *Bay*-ul\
  1. The Canaanite gods were given the name *Baal*. The gods were primarily worshiped for fertility of plants, animals, and people. The people of Israel repeatedly indulged in Baal worship from the time of the conquest until the exile.
  2. Son of Reaiah from the tribe of Benjamin (1 Chronicles 5:5).
  3. One of the 10 sons born to Jeiel and Maacah (1 Chronicles 8:30; 9:36).
  4. A place located on the boundary line of Simeon (1 Chronicles 4:33); also known as Baalath-beer (Joshua 19:8).

Baalbek *Bay*-ul-bek\
  A city northwest of Damascus, the location of the temple of Baachus, which was used for the worship of Baal. The city was destroyed by an earthquake in AD 1749 and excavated by the Persians in 1902.

Baal-berith \Bay-ul-*bee*-rith\
  A god that Israel worshiped after the death of Gideon (Judges 8:33).

Baali *Bay*-ul-*ee*\ or *Bay*-ul-lye\
  Hebrew for "my lord" or "my master," but too similar to the name of the Canaanite god Baal for use in reference to the true God (Hosea 2:16, *KJV, NASB*).

Baal Gad *Bay*-ul-*gad*\ (strong emphasis on *gad*) (Also spelled Baalgad.)
  A city noted for Baal worship, located near Mt. Hermon (Joshua 11:17; 12:7; 13:5).

Baalim \Bay-uh-*leem*\
  Plural of *Baal.*

Baal-Peor \Bay-al-*pe*-or\ (Also spelled Baalpeor.)
  1. Also called Baal of Peor, the false god that the Israelites worshiped when they were seduced into Baal worship by the Moabites, and God punished their idolatry (Numbers 25:3-5; Psalm 106:28).
  2. Place where Israel was seduced into worshiping the Baal of Peor (Hosea 9:10).

Baal-Zebub *Bay*-ul-*zee*-bub\ (strong accent on *zee*) (Also spelled Baal-Zebul and Beelzebub.)
  A god of the Philistines in Ekron (2 Kings 1:2, 3, 6, 16). Baal-Zebub (Beelzebub) was called the prince of demons in Jesus' day (Matthew 10:25; 12:24; Mark 3:22; Luke 11:15, 18, 20).

Baal-Zebul *Bay*-ul-*zee*-bul\ (strong accent on *zee*)
  See Baal-Zebub.

Baasha *Bay*-uh-shuh\
  The third king of the northern kingdom (Israel); he ruled for 24 years. He captured the throne by killing King Nadab and waged war against Judah throughout his reign (1 Kings 15:33—16:7). See Kings of Israel and Judah Chart.

Babel *Bay*-bul\
  The city in the plain of Shinar where the people tried to build a huge tower but were thwarted when God confused the languages (Genesis 11:1-9).

Babylon *Bab*-uh-lun\
  The most important and influential city in Babylonia, located on the Euphrates River in Mesopotamia. The term is also used for the kingdom.

Babylonia \Bab-ih-*low*-nee-uh\
  The kingdom of which Babylon was the capital. It became a world power when it defeated the armies of Egypt and Assyria at Carchemish in 605 BC.

Babylonians \Bab-ih-*low*-nee-unz\
The people who lived in Babylon or Babylonia.

Baca *Bay*-ka\
A term used in Psalm 84:6 that means "valley of weeping." Possibly refers to a place or a figure of speech to describe sadness turned to joy.

Bacchanalia \Bah-keh-*nail*-yuh\
Ancient Roman celebration of Bacchus, Greek and Roman god of wine and revelry. This was the kind of "fleshly lusts" that Peter warned about (1 Peter 2:11, 12), though it is not identified by name in Scripture.

Balaam *Bay*-lum\
Son of Beor; a diviner whom Balak, king of Moab, hired to curse the Israelites. God used him to pronounce blessings instead (Numbers 22:21—24:25; 31:8, 16).

Balak *Bay*-lack\
A Moabite king who hired Balaam to curse Israel. (See Balaam.)

ballo (Greek) *bah*-low\
Greek word for "throw." The word *parable* comes from the Greek *para* (alongside) and *ballo* (throw).

Bani *Bay*-nye\
1. Man of the tribe of Gad, a member of "the thirty" (2 Samuel 23:36).
2. Father of a Levite who served in the tabernacle during the reign of David (1 Chronicles 6:46).
3. A descendant of Judah who lived in Jerusalem after captivity in Babylon (1 Chronicles 9:4).
4. The name of one or more of the Levites who returned to Judah from the exile (Nehemiah 3:17; 9:4; 10:13, 14; 11:22; Ezra 2:10).

baptism *bap*-tiz'm\
A ceremonial washing in which a person was immersed in water (see baptizo). Used metaphorically, as in "baptism of suffering," to describe a total involvement (an immersion) in something.
1. John the Baptist's baptism: John's baptism initiated repentant people into a new way of life, anticipating the Messiah (Matthew 3:1-12; Luke 3:2-18). John's baptism was not an acceptable alternative for Christian baptism Acts 19:1-5).
2. Christian baptism: Jesus commanded baptism to be practiced (Matthew 28:18-20; Mark 16:15, 16), and Peter introduced it on Pentecost (Acts 2:38). It was a common feature in conversions (2:41; 8:12, 13, 36-38; 9:18; 10:47, 48; 16:15, 33; 18:8; 19:5; 22:16).
3. Holy Spirit baptism: John prophesied that Jesus would baptize with the Holy Spirit (Matthew 3:11), and Jesus repeated the promise (Acts 1:5). Twice in the book of

Acts is recorded the fulfillment of that promise: on Pentecost (Acts 2:16-18) and in the house of Cornelius (Acts 11:16).
4. Baptism of fire: John also predicted a baptism of fire (Matthew 3:11, 12). This is a reference to the judgment of the wicked (the "chaff").
5. Baptism of suffering: Jesus warned James and John that they would have to be "baptized" with a baptism like His own (Mark 10:35-40). He was referring to His upcoming suffering (Note the "cup" metaphor in the same passage and Jesus' use of it in Gethsemane, Mark 14:36). The apostles did, indeed, share in Jesus' suffering, with James being the first to die for his faith (Acts 12:1, 2).

baptizo (Greek) \bap-*tid*-zo\
Greek word for "baptize," meaning "to dip, plunge, immerse."

Barabbas \Buh-*rab*-us\
The criminal chosen to be released by a mob in Jerusalem rather than Jesus (Matthew 27:15-26; Mark 15:6-15; Luke 23:18-25; John 18:39, 40).

Barachel *Bar*-uh-kel\ (Also spelled Barakel.)
The father of Elihu (Job 32:2, 6).

Barachias \Bear-uh-*kye*-us\ (Also spelled Barachiah, Berachiah, Berechiah, and Berakiah.)
Greek form of "Berekiah" (Matthew 23:35). See Berekiah.

Barak *Bair*-uk\
Son of Abinoam of Kedeshnaphtali (Kedesh in Naphtali); led Israel against the Canaanites during the judgeship of Deborah (Judges 4:1-24; Hebrews 11:32).

barbarians \bar-*bare*-ee-unz\
Originally referred to people who didn't speak Greek (Romans 1:14; Colossians 3:11). Later referred to people who spoke a foreign language (1 Corinthians 14:11; Acts 28:2, 4).

Barjona \Bar-*jo*-nuh\ (Also spelled Bar-jona.)
Aramaic name meaning "son of Jonah" or "son of John"; used of Simon Peter (Matthew 16:17).

Barnabas *Bar*-nuh-bus\
Aramaic name meaning "son of encouragement"; used of Joseph from Cyprus, an early believer who worked with Paul (Acts 13:2—14:7).

Barsabas *Bar*-sa-bus\ (also spelled Barsabbas.)
1. A surname of Joseph who was chosen to be an apostle in place of Judas (Acts 1:23).
2. A surname of a prophet named Judas, who was sent with Silas to Antioch with the letter of the Jerusalem Council (Acts 15:22).

Bb

Bb

Bar-Tholami \Bar-*Thahl*-uh-me\
Suggested spelling of Bartholomew; the name means "son of Tholami"; this may explain why he is known as Nathanael in John 1:45-48 and Bartholomew in Matthew, Mark, and Luke: he was "Nathanael, son of Tholami." This spelling is not found in the Bible.

Bartholomew \Bar-*thahl*-uh-mew\
One of the 12 apostles (Matthew 10:3; Mark 3:18; Luke 6:14; Acts 1:13). Also known as Nathanael (John 1:45-48). (See also Bar-Tholami.)

Bartimaeus *Bar*-tih-*me*-us\ (strong accent on *me*) (Also spelled Bartimeus.)
Son of Timaeus; healed of blindness by Jesus when He was near Jericho (Mark 10:46-52).

Bartimeus *Bar*-tih-*me*-us\
See Bartimaeus.

Baruch *Bare*-uk\ or *Bay*-ruk\
1. Son of Neriah; he assisted Jeremiah, especially acting as a scribe (Jeremiah 36:4; 45:1-5).
2. Zabbai's son who rebuilt the walls of Jerusalem during the time of Nehemiah and signed Ezra's agreement of faithfulness to God (Nehemiah 3:20; 10:6).
3. Maaseiah's father; a descendant of Judah (Nehemiah 11:5).
4. A book of the Apocrypha between Lamentations and Jeremiah.

Bashan *Bay*-shan\
A fertile region northeast of the Sea of Galilee, part of the land held by the tribe of Manasseh.

Bathsheba \Bath-*she*-buh\ (Also spelled Bath-sheba.)
Uriah's wife; King David committed adultery with her and had her husband Uriah killed. After Uriah's death she became David's wife (2 Samuel 11) and the mother of Solomon (2 Samuel 12:24).

bdellium *deh*-lee-um\
An aromatic gum resin, similar to myrrh (Genesis 2:12; Numbers 11:7).

Bechorath \Be-*ko*-rath\ (Also spelled Becorath.)
Son of Aphiah, an ancestor of Saul from Benjamin's tribe (1 Samuel 9:1).

Becorath \Be-*ko*-rath\
See Bechorath.

Bedouins *Bed*-uh-wunz\
Nomadic desert dwellers; usually Arab.

Beelzebub \Bih-*el*-zih-bub\
A corruption of the name *Baal-Zebub;* literally it means "lord of the flies" or "lord of the manure pile"; usually refers to Satan. Jesus' enemies used this name against Him (Matthew 10:25; 12:24; Luke 11:15).

Beelzebul \Bih-*el*-zih-bul\
Alternate spelling of Beelzebub.

Beeri \Be-*ee*-rye\
1. A Hittite; father of Judith, a wife of Esau (Genesis 26:34).
2. Prophet Hosea's father (Hosea 1:1).

Beer Lahai Roi \Beer-lah-*high*-roy\ (Also spelled Beerlahairoi and also called the well Lahairoi.)
The well where Hagar met the Lord (Genesis 16:7-14; Genesis 24:62; 25:11.)

Beersheba \Beer-*she*-buh\
1. A well dug by Abraham (Genesis 21:30, 31).
2. The location of the well became a major city of the Negev basin. It became the southern boundary of Judah—"from Dan to Beersheba" was a common designation for the whole of Israel (2 Samuel 24:2).

behemoth *bee*-heh-moth\ or \beh-*hee*-moth\
Hebrew word often translated "beasts" or "cattle" (Deuteronomy 28:2, 6; 32:24; Psalm 50:10; Isaiah 18:6; Habakkuk 2:17). The reference in Job 40:15-24 seems to refer to a specific animal, with suggested interpretations running from a water ox to a hippopotamus or elephant to a dinosaur. Of these, only the dinosaur, specifically the apatosaurus, has a "tail like a cedar" (Job 40:17).

Belial *Bee*-li-ul\
The Hebrew word describes a person who is worthless or lawless (Deuteronomy 13:13). Used once in the New Testament as a term for Satan (2 Corinthians 6:15).

Belshazzar \Bel-*shazz*-er\
Son of Nabonidus, last king of the Babylonian Empire. Belshazzar was serving as regent in his father's stead when he saw the hand of God writing on the wall of the palace. Daniel interpreted the writing as a warning of the fall of the empire (Daniel 5).

Belteshazzar \Bel-tih-*shazz*-er\
Daniel's Babylonian name (Daniel 1:7).

Benaiah \Be-*nay*-uh\
1. Son of Jehoiada (2 Samuel 23:20); captain of David's foreign bodyguard (2 Samuel 8:18; 20:23). After Solomon became king (1 Kings 1), Benaiah executed Adonijah, Joab, and Shimei at Solomon's command (1 Kings 2:25, 29-46), and replaced Joab as commander-in-chief (1 Kings 2:35).

2. One of "the thirty" (2 Samuel 23:30; 1 Chronicles 11:31), a second level of David's bodyguards.

3. A leader of his family who chased the Amalekites from pastureland (1 Chronicles 4:39, 40).

4. A Levite who played the lyre at the return of the ark to Jerusalem (1 Chronicles 15:20).

5. A priest who played the trumpet at the return of the ark to Jerusalem (1 Chronicles 15:24).

6. Grandfather of the prophet Jehaziel, who prophesied during the reign of King Jehoshaphat (2 Chronicles 20:14).

7. An official over the temple offering during King Hezekiah's reign (2 Chronicles 31:13).

8. Pelatiah's father; Pelatiah died for teaching falsely in the days of Ezekiel (Ezekiel 11:13).

9. The name of four men who were guilty of marrying foreign women (Ezra 10:25, 30, 35, 43).

Benedictus *(Latin)* *Ben*-eh-*dik*-tus\ (strong accent on *dik*)
Short hymn of praise that Zechariah (Zacharias) gave to God at the birth of John the Baptist (Luke 1:68-79).

Ben-Hadad \Ben-*hay*-dad\ (Also spelled Benhadad or Ben Hadad.)
"Son of Hadad," a title given to the rulers of Syria (Aram) after Hadad, the god of storm and thunder. Three are mentioned in the Old Testament: Ben-Hadad I (1 Kings 15:18); Ben-Hadad II (2 Kings 8:7-15); Ben-Hadad III (2 Kings 13:3, 4).

Benhail \Ben-*hay*-il\
An official that King Jehoshaphat sent out to teach the Law of the Lord in Judah (2 Chronicles 17:7).

Benjamin *Ben*-juh-mun\
1. The youngest son of Jacob; his mother was Rachel (Genesis 35:16-18, 24).

2. A great-grandson of Benjamin, son of Jacob (1 Chronicles 7:10).

3. A man guilty of marrying a foreign woman (Ezra 10:32).

4. One of the 12 tribes of Israel; named for Jacob's youngest son.

5. Territory allotted to the tribe of Benjamin after the conquest.

Benoni \Buh-*no*-nee\
The name Rachel gave her son Benjamin as she was dying (Genesis 35:18). It means "son of my sorrow." Jacob named him Benjamin, "son of my right hand."

Beor *Be*-or\ (Sometimes called Bosor.)
1. A king of Edom (Genesis 36:31, 32).

2. Balaam's father (Numbers 22:5; 2 Peter 2:15).

Berea \Buh-*ree*-uh\
A Macedonian city visited by Paul; its citizens who heard Paul were commended for examining the Scriptures to be sure he was telling the truth (Acts 17:10, 13). The home of Sopater (Acts 20:4).

Berekiah \Bair-uh-*kye*-uh\ (Also spelled Barachiah, Barachias, Berachiah, Berechiah, and Berakiah.)
1. A son of Zerubbabel (1 Chronicles 3:19, 20).

2. Father of Asaph, a temple singer during David's reign (1 Chronicles 6:39).

3. A Levite, son of Asa, who lived in Jerusalem after the exile (1 Chronicles 9:16).

4. A doorkeeper for the ark (1 Chronicles 15:23).

5. An Ephraimite who protested the sale of Hebrews to their countrymen (2 Chronicles 28:12-15).

6. Father of a builder named Meshullam (Nehemiah 3:4, 30; 6:18).

7. Prophet Zechariah's father (Zechariah 1:1, 7).

bereshith *(Hebrew)* \beh-reh-*sheet*\
"In the beginning." This is the first word of Genesis in the Hebrew Bible.

Bergama \Burr-*gah*-muh\
A town in western Turkey that was once ancient Pergamum.

Bernice \Ber-*nye*-see\
Oldest daughter of Herod Agrippa I. She heard Paul's defense before her brother, Agrippa II (Acts 25:13, 23).

beryl *ber*-ul\
A yellow jasper, possibly Spanish gold topaz, used in the high priest's breastplate (Exodus 28:20 except *NIV;* 28:17 *NIV,* where other versions have "emerald" or "carbuncle") and in the foundation of the New Jerusalem (Revelation 21:20).

beth *(Hebrew)* \bayth\ or \bait\
1. The second letter of the Hebrew alphabet and the Hebrew word for the number two.

2. Common word for "house" in the Old Testament.

Bethabara *Beth-ab*-uh-ruh\ (strong accent on *ab*)
A place on the east side of the Jordan where John used to baptize (John 1:28, *KJV;* other versions have Bethany here). Possibly the same as Bethbarah (Judges 7:24).

Bethany *Beth*-uh-nee\
1. A village two miles from Bethlehem (John 11:18). The town where Mary, Martha, and Lazarus lived (John 11:1).

2. A place on the east side of the Jordan where John used to baptize (John 1:28—called "Bethabara" in *KJV).*

Bb

Bethaven \Beth-*ay*-ven\ (strong accent on *ay*)
Hebrew for "house of wickedness." Hosea describes the city of Bethel as "Bethaven for its idolatry" (Hosea 4:15; 10:5, 8).

Bethbarah \Beth-*bar*-ruh\ (Also spelled Beth Barah.)
A place on the Jordan secured by the Israelites under Gideon to capture Oreb and Zeeb (Judges 7:24).

Beth–car *Beth*-kar\ or \Beth-*kar*\ (Also spelled Beth Car.)
A city somewhere between Mizpah and Philistine territory (1 Samuel 7:11).

Bethel *Beth*-ul\
A city 11 miles north of Jerusalem; it means "house of God." It was the site of an altar built by Abraham (Genesis 12:8), and the place where Jacob saw the vision of angels on a ladder ascending to Heaven and descending to earth (Genesis 28:10-21). Jeroboam I put idols here to prevent the people of Israel from returning to Jerusalem to worship (1 Kings 12:28, 29).

Bether *Be*-ther\
A mountainous area mentioned in Song of Solomon 2:17. Not necessarily a proper name.

Bethesda \Buh-*thez*-duh\
A spring-fed pool in Jerusalem where Jesus healed a man born blind (John 5).

Beth Horan \Bayth (or Bait) *Hoe*-ron\
Also Beth–Horon. Twin towns (Lower Beth Horon and Upper Beth Horon) in the hill country of Ephraim found along a main route of the time (Joshua 16:3, 5; 1 Chronicles 7:24; 2 Chronicles 8:5).

Bethlehem *Beth*-lih-hem\
1. A town five miles southwest of Jerusalem in the Judean hill country; Jesus' birthplace (Luke 2).
2. A town in Zebulun seven miles northwest of Nazareth (Joshua 19:15).

Bethpeor \Beth-*pea*-or\
A valley in the land of the tribe of Reuben; the burial ground of Moses (Joshua 13:20; Deuteronomy 34:6).

Bethphage \Beth-*fuh*-jee\
A village on the Mount of Olives mentioned twice in the New Testament (Mark 11:1; Luke 19:29).

Bethsaida \Beth-*say*-uh-duh\
"House of fish." City located west of the Sea of Galilee. The hometown of the disciples Philip, Andrew, and Peter (John 1:44; 12:21).

Bethsaida Julias \Beth-*say*-uh-duh *Joo*-lee-ahs\
A town located on the east of the Sea of Galilee (Luke 9:10); named after Julia, the daughter of Emperor Augustus.

Bethshan \Beth-*shan*\ (Also spelled Beth Shan, Beth-shan, Bethshean, Beth Shean, or Beth-shean.)
A city allotted to Manasseh but inhabited by the Canaanites (Joshua 17:11, 16; 1 Samuel 31:10, 12).

Bethshean \Beth-*she*-un\
See BETHSHAN.

Beth-shemesh \Beth-*she*-mesh\
1. City northwest of Judah (Joshua 15:10; 1 Samuel 6:12); given by Judah to the Levites (Joshua 21:16).
2. A city of Issachar (Joshua 19:22).
3. A city of Naphtali (Joshua 19:38; Judges 1:33).
4. An idolatrous Egyptian city (Jeremiah 43:13). Other names for the city are On and Heliopolis.

Bethuel \Beh-*thu*-ul\
1. Father of Rebekah and nephew of Abraham (Genesis 22:22, 23; 24:15).
2. A city mentioned in 1 Chronicles 4:30.

Bezaleel \Bih-*zal*-ih-el\ (Also spelled Bezalel.)
1. Son of Uri from the tribe of Judah; given artistic skills by God to build the tabernacle (Exodus 31:1-5; 35:30-33).
2. One of the Israelites who returned from the exile; he married a foreign woman (Ezra 10:30).

Bible *By*-bul\
Collection of inspired books (2 Timothy 3:16, 17), consisting of the Old Testament and the New Testament, through which God has revealed himself as creator and sustainer of the universe and the redeemer and ruler of people. See BOOKS OF THE BIBLE CHART on next page.

Bigthan *Big*-thun\ (Also spelled Bigthana.)
One of the eunuchs who guarded the court of Ahasuerus (or Xerxes) but conspired against the king's life. Mordecai detected the conspiracy, and Bigthan and his co-conspirator, Teresh, were executed (Esther 2:21-23).

Bigthana *Big*-thun-uh\
See BIGTHAN.

Bildad *Bill*-dad\
One of Job's three friends (Job 2:11-13; 42:7-10).

Bilhah *Bill*-ha\
1. Rachel's maidservant given to Jacob to bear children on Rachel's behalf; mother of Dan and Naphtali (Genesis 29:29; 30:1-8).
2. City in the tribe of Simeon (1 Chronicles 4:29); also called Baalah (Joshua 15:29) or Balah (Joshua 19:3).

BOOKS OF THE BIBLE

OLD TESTAMENT

Book	Section/Type	Author
Genesis	Law	Moses
Exodus	Law	Moses
Leviticus	Law	Moses
Numbers	Law	Moses
Deuteronomy	Law	Moses
Joshua	History	Joshua
Judges	History	Samuel
Ruth	History	Samuel
1 Samuel	History	Samuel & Nathan (?)
2 Samuel	History	Nathan (?)
1 Kings	History	Jeremiah
2 Kings	History	Jeremiah
1 Chronicles	History	Samuel
2 Chronicles	History	Ezra
Ezra	History	Ezra
Nehemiah	History	Nehemiah
Esther	History	Mordecai (?)
Job	Poetry	Moses
Psalms	Poetry	David and others
Proverbs	Poetry	Solomon
Ecclesiastes	Poetry	Solomon
Song of Solomon	Poetry	Solomon
Isaiah	Major Prophets	Isaiah
Jeremiah	Major Prophets	Jeremiah
Lamentations	Major Prophets	Jeremiah
Ezekiel	Major Prophets	Ezekiel
Daniel	Major Prophets	Daniel
Hosea	Minor Prophets	Hosea
Joel	Minor Prophets	Joel
Amos	Minor Prophets	Amos
Obadiah	Minor Prophets	Obadiah
Jonah	Minor Prophets	Jonah
Micah	Minor Prophets	Micah
Nahum	Minor Prophets	Nahum
Habakkuk	Minor Prophets	Habakkuk
Zephaniah	Minor Prophets	Zephaniah
Haggai	Minor Prophets	Haggai
Zechariah	Minor Prophets	Zechariah
Malachi	Minor Prophets	Malachi

NEW TESTAMENT

Book	Section/Type	Author
Matthew	Gospels	Apostle Matthew
Mark	Gospels	John Mark
Luke	Gospels	Luke
John	Gospels	Apostle John
Acts	History	Luke
Romans	Letter to Church	Apostle Paul
1 Corinthians	Letter to Church	Apostle Paul
2 Corinthians	Letter to Church	Apostle Paul
Galatians	Letter to Churches	Apostle Paul
Ephesians	Prison Epistle	Apostle Paul
Philippians	Prison Epistle	Apostle Paul
Colossians	Prison Epistle	Apostle Paul
1 Thessalonians	Letter to Church	Apostle Paul
2 Thessalonians	Letter to Church	Apostle Paul
1 Timothy	Pastoral Epistle	Apostle Paul
2 Timothy	Pastoral Epistle	Apostle Paul
Titus	Pastoral Epistle	Apostle Paul
Philemon	Prison Epistle	Apostle Paul
Hebrews	General Epistle	Apostle Paul (?)
James	General Epistle	James, bro. of Jesus
1 Peter	General Epistle	Apostle Peter
2 Peter	General Epistle	Apostle Peter
1 John	General Epistle	Apostle John
2 John	General Epistle	Apostle John
3 John	General Epistle	Apostle John
Jude	General Epistle	Judas, bro. of Jesus
Revelation	Apocalypse	Apostle John

journey (Acts 16:7) but is mentioned by Peter as one of the provinces where many Jewish Christians lived (1 Peter 1:1).

blasphemer *blas*-feem-er\\
A person guilty of blasphemy.

blasphemous *blas*-fuh-mus\\
Pertaining to blasphemy.

blasphemy *blas*-fuh-me\\
Insulting or mocking anything that has to do with God. Claiming to be divine or to have the abilities or rights of God is also blasphemy.

Bithynia \\Bih-*thin*-ee-uh\\
A Roman province along the south coast of the Black Sea. It was bypassed by Paul and Silas on the second missionary

Boanerges *Bo*-uh-*nur*-geez\\ (strong accent on *nur*)
A name given to James and John meaning "sons of thunder" (Mark 3:17).

Bb

Cc

Boaz *Bo*-az\
Kinsman of Elimelech who married Ruth (Ruth 2–4).

Boscath \Boz-kath\
See BOZKATH.

Bosor *Bo*-sore\
Alternate spelling of *Beor* (2 Peter 2:15, *KJV*). See BEOR.

Bozkath *Boz*-kath\ (Also spelled Boscath.)
A city in Judah (2 Kings 22:1).

Bozrah *Boz*-ruh\
A city in north Edom (Genesis 36:33; 1 Chronicles 1:44).

Buddha *Boo*-duh\
Indian philosopher of the fifth/sixth century BC; founder of Buddhism.

Bul \Bool\
The eighth month of the Jewish calendar (1 Kings 6:38); known as Marchesvan after the exile, but that name is not found in Scripture. See CALENDAR CHART.

Buzi *Bew*-zye\
Ezekiel's father (Ezekiel 1:3).

Cc

Caesar *See*-zur\
The name applied to Roman emperors from the time of Julius Caesar; origin of such titles as *czar* and *kaiser*.

Caesar Augustus *See*-zer Aw-*gus*-tus\
Roman emperor at the time Jesus was born (Luke 2:1). His great-uncle, Julius Caesar, named him heir to the Roman throne.

Caesarea \Sess-uh-*ree*-uh\
Major seaport city on the Mediterranean coast of Israel. Built by Herod the Great and named to honor Caesar Augustus. The place where Peter converted the first Gentile (Acts 10) and where Paul stood trial before Felix (Acts 24) and Festus (Acts 25). Sometimes called Caesarea Maritime to distinguish it from Caesarea Philippi.

Caesarea Philippi \Fih-*lip*-pie\ or *Fil*-ih-pie\
City at the foot of Mt. Hermon. Philip the tetrarch named it to honor Tiberius Caesar and himself. In this region Peter made what has come to be called the Good Confession (Matthew 16:13-20; Mark 8:27-30).

Caiaphas *Kay*-uh-fus\ or *Kye*-uh-fus\
High priest when Israel was under Roman rule; involved in Jesus' trial (John 18:24).

Cairo *Kie*-row\
The capital city of modern Egypt.

Calah *Kay*-luh\
A city built by Nimrod, Noah's great-grandson; a place where many Assyrian kings built their palaces (Genesis 10:6-12).

Caleb *Kay*-leb\
Son of Jephunneh; one of the 12 spies that Moses sent to give a report on the promised land. Only he and Joshua believed God would give the land to Israel (Numbers 13:6).

Calendar
See CALENDAR CHART on next page.

Calneh *Kal*-neh\
One of the four cities founded by Nimrod, Noah's son, after the flood (Genesis 10:10).

Calvary *Cal*-vuh-ree\
Place outside Jerusalem where Jesus was crucified (Luke 23:33, *KJV*), usually called Golgotha (Matthew 27:33). It comes from the Latin word for skull.

Cambyses \Kam-*bye*-seez\
Son of Cyrus the Great; last Median king of Persia.

Cana *Kay*-nuh\
A city of Galilee; the location of Jesus' first miracle (John 2:1-11).

Canaan *Kay*-nun\
1. An old name for the territory that the nation of Israel inhabited after the exodus.
2. Ham's son; his descendants occupied the land of Canaan (Genesis 9:18; 10:6).

Canaanites *Kay*-nun-ites\
A general term for the people of various tribes who occupied the land of Canaan.

Candace *Can*-duh-see\
The queen of Ethiopia at the time when Philip converted the Ethiopian eunuch (Acts 8:27).

Canticles *Kan*-tih-culz\
See SONG OF SOLOMON.

Capernaum \Kuh-*per*-nay-um\
A city by the Sea of Galilee that became the headquarters for Jesus and His ministry (Matthew 4:13).

CALENDAR

The Hebrew calendar had 12 lunar months, with some kind of periodic adjustment to account for the difference between a lunar year and a solar year. The Jews seem to have adopted different names for the months during or after the exile, though only a few of the pre-exilic names are known. The table below lists the months with their modern equivalents. (Names in parentheses are pre-exilic names.)

1.	Nisan (Abib)	March–April
2.	Iyyar (Ziv)	April–May
3.	Sivan	May–June
4.	Tammuz	June–July
5.	Ab	July–August
6.	Elul	August–September
7.	Tishri (Ethanim)	September–October
8.	Marchesvan (Bul)	October–November
9.	Chisleu	November–December
10.	Tebeth	December–January
11.	Shebat	January–February
12.	Adar	February–March

Caphtor *Kaf*-tor\\
Ancient name for Crete, an island in the Mediterranean (Amos 9:7; Jeremiah 47:4).

Cappadocia \\Kap-uh-*doe*-shuh\\
Located in Asia Minor. Jews from Cappadocia were among those present on Pentecost (Acts 2:9).

carbuncle *car*-bunk-ul\\
A red gemstone; in some versions it is listed as one in the high priest's breastplate (Exodus 28:17 *KJV, ASV, ESV*). In some places where this term is used, other versions have "ruby," "emerald," "beryl," or "garnet."

Carchemish *Kar*-keh-mish\\
Major Hittite city on the west bank of the Euphrates River. Nebuchadnezzar's defeat of Egypt and Assyria here in 605 BC signaled the rise of Babylon as the dominant world power.

Careah \\Ka-*ree*-uh\\ (Also spelled Kareah.)
Father of Jonathan and Johanan; Johanan warned Gedaliah of a plan for his assassination (Jeremiah 40).

Carmel *Car*-mul\\
1. A fertile, mountainous region in the tribe of Asher by the Mediterranean. It was here that Elijah had his showdown with the prophets of Baal (1 Kings 18:20-40).

2. A town in the tribe of Judah, seven miles south of Hebron; David's wife Abigail was from Carmel (1 Samuel 25:2, 3, 42).

Carmelite *Car*-mul-ite\\
A person from Carmel (1 Samuel 27:3; 1 Chronicles 11:37).

carnelian \\car-*neel*-yun\\
A red gemstone, a type of chalcedony (Revelation 21:20 *NIV, NLT*). Some versions (including *NLT*, Exodus 28:17) include it among the stones in the high priest's breastplate, but other versions usually render the term "sardius" or "ruby." *The King James Version* does not use this term.

Carpus *Car*-pus\\
A Christian from Troas with whom Paul stayed and left his cloak and some scrolls (2 Timothy 4:13).

Catholicism \\Cath-*thawl*-ih-*siz*-um\\ (strong accent on *thawl*)
The beliefs and rituals of the Catholic church.

Cauda *Caw*-duh\\
See CLAUDA.

Cedron *See*-drun\\ (Another name for Kidron.)
A ravine between Jerusalem and the Mt. of Olives (John 18:1, *KJV*).

Cenchrea *Sen*-kree-uh\\ (Also spelled Cenchreae.)
Seaport city near Corinth (Acts 18:18; Romans 16:1).

centurion \\sen-*ture*-ee-un\\
A Roman commander in charge of 100 soldiers.
1. A centurion asked Jesus to heal his servant and was commended by the Lord for his great faith (Matthew 8:5-13; Luke 7:2-10).
2. A centurion was at the cross; his statement about Jesus is reported with some variation by the synoptic Gospel writers (Matthew 27:54; Mark 15:39; Luke 23:47).
3. Cornelius, the first Gentile Christian, was a centurion (Acts 10:1).
4. Paul asked a centurion whether it was legal to scourge a Roman; the centurion went to the commander and Paul was not scourged (Acts 22:25-29).
5. A centurion escorted Paul's nephew to the commander in Jerusalem to expose a plot to kill Paul (Acts 23:16-18).
6. Felix put Paul under the guard of a centurion when Paul was transferred from Jerusalem to Caesarea (Acts 24:23).
7. A centurion named Julius had charge of Paul on the voyage to Rome (Acts 27:1).

Cephas *See*-fus\\
Aramaic for "rock"; the name Jesus gave to Simon Peter (John 1:42). Peter *(petros)* is Greek for "rock."

Cerinthians \Suh-*rin*-thee-unz\
Followers of Cerinthus.

Cerinthus \Suh-*rin*-thus\
A false Christian teacher of the late first century who denied that Jesus came in the flesh. Possibly an early Gnostic.

Chalcedon *Kal*-suh-don\
Located in the province of Bithynia and Pontus.

chalcedony \kal-*sed*-uh-nee\
A precious stone of translucent quartz; mentioned in the foundation of the New Jerusalem (Revelation 21:19). The *New Living Translation* calls it "agate."

Chaldea \Kal-*dee*-uh\
Ancient name for Babylonia.

Chaldeans *Kal*-dee-unz\
The people of Chaldea.

Chaldees *Kal*-deez\
Chaldea.

charakter *(Greek)* \kar-ahk-*tare*\
An engraving tool, dye, or stamp; also the impression made by stamping; the term used in Hebrews 1:3 for "express image" *(KJV)* or "exact representation" *(NIV)*.

charis *(Greek)* *kar*-us\
The Greek word for "grace."

charisma *(Greek)* \kah-*riss*-mah\
The Greek word for "gift"; from *charis,* "grace."

Charran *Kar*-an\
Another name for the town of Haran (Acts 7:4). See Haran.

chastisement \chas-*tize*-munt\ or *chas*-tuz-munt\
A discipline or punishment.

Chebar *Kee*-bar\ (Also spelled Kebar.)
A river or canal in Babylon where Ezekiel saw many visions (Ezekiel 1:1; 3:23; 10:15, 20, 22; 43:3).

Chedorlaomer \Ked-or-lay-*oh*-mer\ or \Ked-or-*lay*-oh-mer\ (Also spelled Kedorlaomer.)
King of Elam; one of four kings that rallied together to attack five cities near the Dead Sea, including Sodom. Lot was captured in the raid (Genesis 14).

Chemosh *Kee*-mosh\
False god worshiped by the Moabites (Numbers 21:29).

Chenaanah \Kih-*nay*-uh-nah\ (Also spelled Kenaanah.)
  1. The father of the false prophet Zedekiah, who rebuked Micaiah's prophecy (1 Kings 22:11, 24).
  2. Son of Bilham from the tribe of Benjamin (1 Chronicles 7:10).

Cherethites *Ker*-uh-thites\ (Also spelled Kerethites.)
A unit of King David's bodyguards (2 Samuel 8:18; 15:18; 20:7, 23; 1 Kings 1:38, 44; 1 Chronicles 18:17).

Cherith *Key*-rith\ (Also spelled Kerith.)
A brook where Elijah was protected from Ahab and famine (1 Kings 17:2-6).

cherubim *chair*-uh-bim\
Plural of cherub; winged angelic beings that God has used in different roles; images of two cherubim overlooked the ark of the covenant (Exodus 25:22; Ezekiel 10; Genesis 3:24).

Chesil *Kess*-ill\ (Also spelled Kesil.)
  1. A town in southern Judah (Joshua 15:30).
  2. *(Hebrew)* Fool or foolish (Psalm 49:10; 92:6; 94:8).

Chileab *Kil*-e-ab\ (Also spelled Kileab.)
First son of King David and Abigail (2 Samuel 3:3). Called Daniel in 1 Chronicles 3:1.

Chilion *Kil*-ee-on\ (Also spelled Kilion.)
One of Elimelech and Naomi's two sons; married a Moabite named Orpah (Ruth 1:2, 5; 4:9, 10).

Chinnereth *Kin*-eh-reth\ or *Chin*-neh-reth\ (Also spelled Chinneroth and Kinnereth.)
  1. A fortified town of Naphtali conquered by King Ben-Hadad of Syria (Joshua 19:35; 1 Kings 15:20).
  2. An early name for the Sea of Galilee (Numbers 34:11; Deuteronomy 3:17; Joshua 13:27).

Chinneroth *Kin*-eh-roth\ or *Chin*-neh-roth\
See Chinnereth.

Chisleu *Kiss*-loo\
The ninth month of the Hebrew calendar, roughly equivalent to November–December (Nehemiah 1:1; Zechariah 7:1). See Calendar Chart.

chiton *(Greek)* \key-*tone*\
Greek for "coat" or "garment." It is used of Jesus' seamless garment (John 19:23) and of Peter's coat (John 21:7; Acts 9:39).

Chittim *Kit*-tim\ (Also spelled Kittim.)
Descendants of Javan (Genesis 10:4; 1 Chronicles 1:7).

Chloe *Klo*-ee\\
A woman who informed Paul of arguments in the church at Corinth (1 Corinthians 1:11).

Chorazin \\Ko-*ray*-zin\\
A Palestinian city that Jesus denounced for unbelief (Matthew 11:21; Luke 10:13).

chrestos *(Greek)* *Crest*-awss\\
Greek adjective meaning "good or kind"; also a common proper name of the first century.

Chrestus *Crest*-us\\
Suetonius says the Jews were expelled from Rome (Acts 18:2) because of turmoil over the influence of one by this name; many believe the writer was mistaken and that he was actually referring to Christus (Christ).

Christ \\Krist\\ (*i* as in *ice*)
Title for Jesus in the New Testament (Matthew 1:1; 16:16; Mark 1:1; 8:29). Equivalent to the Hebrew Messiah, it comes from the Greek word for "anointed."

Chronicles (1 and 2) *Kron*-ih-culz\\
Thirteenth and fourteenth books of the Old Testament, the eighth and ninth in the "history" section. They tell the history of Israel and Judah from the reign of David (after a brief introduction that includes genealogies from the time of Adam) to the proclamation of Cyrus to end the Exile. See Books of the Bible Chart.

chrysalis *kris*-uh-liss\\
A pupa of a butterfly; cocoon, protecting covering, a sheltered state or stage.

chrysolite *kris*-uh-lite\\
The ancient term for yellow topaz or yellow quartz; one of the precious stones in the foundation of the New Jerusalem (Revelation 21:20).

chrysoprase *krih*-suh-*praise*\\ (strong accent on *krih*) (Also spelled chrysoprasus.)
One of the precious stones in the foundation of the New Jerusalem (Revelation 21:20), possibly a gold-tinted variety of a stone like chalcedony.

chrysoprasus \\krih-*sop*-ruh-sus\\
See chrysoprase.

Chrysostom *Kris*-us-tum\\ or *Krih*-*sahss*-tum\\
Syrian preacher, writer, and martyr John Chrysostom (AD 347–407).

Chuza *Koo*-za\\ (Also spelled Cuza.)
Manager of Herod Antipas's household; his wife Joanna supported Jesus during His travels (Luke 8:3).

cieled \\seeld\\
Paneled (2 Chronicles 3:5; Jeremiah 22:14; Ezekiel 41:16; Haggai 1:4; all *KJV*).

Cilicia \\Sih-*lish*-ih-uh\\
A country in southeast Asia Minor; capital was Tarsus, the birthplace of Paul (Acts 21:39; 22:3; 23:34).

Clauda *Claw*-duh\\ (Also spelled Cauda.)
An island off Crete where Paul and his companions almost shipwrecked during the journey to Rome (Acts 27:16).

Claudius *Claw*-dee-us\\
1. Claudius Caesar, the fourth Roman emperor (AD 41–54). Ordered all Jews to leave Rome (Acts 18:2).
2. Claudius Lysias, a Roman commander who rescued Paul from a Jewish mob and later sent him to Caesarea, writing a letter to Felix on behalf of Paul (Acts 21:31-34; 23:23-33).

Cleanthes *Clee*-an-theez\\ (th as in thin)
Head of the Stoic school of philosophy in Athens. Paul quotes a line of his poem, *Phaenomena*, in Acts 17:28.

Cleopas *Clee*-uh-pass\\
One of the two disciples who saw Jesus on the way to Emmaus after the resurrection (Luke 24:18).

Cleopatra *Clee*-oh-*pat*-ruh\\
Name of two Egyptian queens (51–49 BC; 48–30 BC).

Cleophas *Klee*-o-fus\\ (Also spelled Clopas.)
The husband of Mary, the sister of Jesus' mother (John 19:25).

Clopas *Klo*-pus\\
See Cleophas.

Colossae \\Ko-*lahss*-ee\\
See Colosse.

Colosse \\Ko-*lahss*-ee\\ (Also spelled Colossae.)
A city of Phrygia located on an important trade route from Ephesus to the Euphrates. Paul wrote an epistle to this church. The city lost importance when the roads were rerouted.

Colosseum \\Kah-luh-*see*-um\\
An amphitheater in Rome that was built by Vespasian in AD 75. This became the site of the martyrdom of many early Christians.

Colossians \\Kuh-*losh*-unz\\
1. Residents of Colosse.
2. The 12th book of the New Testament, third of the prison epistles; a letter from Paul to the church in Colosse. See Books of the Bible Chart.

Coniah \Ko-*nye*-uh\

Alternate name for Jehoiachin, king of Judah (Jeremiah 22:24, 28; 37:1). See Jehoiachin.

coral \kor-ul\

As used in the Bible, it is a red gem made from the hard skeleton of the marine coral (Job 28:18; Ezekiel 27:16).

Corban *Kor*-bun\

An offering dedicated to God (Leviticus 1:2, 3). Some of the Pharisees used the Corban laws to avoid supporting their parents (Mark 7:11).

Corinth *Kor*-inth\

Prominent Greek city, the capital of Achaia, and home of the temple of Aphrodite. Also the city where Paul met Aquila and Priscilla (Acts 18:2).

Corinthians \Ko-*rin*-thee-unz\ (*th* as in *thin*)

1. People who lived in Corinth.
2. The seventh and eighth books of the New Testament (1 and 2 Corinthians), letters from Paul to address problems in the church of Corinth. See Books of the Bible Chart.

Cornelius \Cor-*neel*-yus\

A centurion of the Italian Regiment; the first Gentile disciple (Acts 10).

Crescens *Kress*-enz\

A fellow worker with Paul who departed for Galatia (2 Timothy 4:10).

Crete \Creet\

A Greek island in the Mediterranean. Cretans were present on the day of Pentecost (Acts 2:11).

Crispus *Kris*-pus\

A synagogue leader in Corinth who was baptized by Paul (Acts 18:8; 1 Corinthians 1:14).

Croeses *Kree*-sus\

King of Lydia, in Asia Minor, in the sixth century bc and builder of a temple to Artemis in Sardis. Croeses was captured by Cyrus in 546 bc.

Cush \Koosh\

1. One of the sons of Ham (Genesis 10:6-8).
2. A country in Africa, up the Nile river from Egypt, possibly Ethiopia (Isaiah 11:11). Except for Isaiah 11:11, the *King James Version* always (22 times) translates the word for Cush (as a place) as "Ethiopia."
3. A land encompassed by the Gihon River before the Noahic flood (Genesis 2:13). It may be the same as #2,

but since the flood would have caused many geographic changes, it is impossible to identify with any certainty pre-flood sites with those after the flood.
4. A Benjamite mentioned in the title to Psalm 7.

Cushi *Koosh*-ee\

1. The father of the prophet Zephaniah (Zephaniah 1:1).
2. An ancestor of Jehudi, who was sent to summon Baruch to read from Jeremiah's scroll (Jeremiah 36:14).
3. In the *King James Version*, this is the name of the herald sent to tell David of his force's victory over Absalom (2 Samuel 18:21-23, 31). Other versions have "the Cushite."

Cushite *Koosh*-ite\

A person from, or inhabitant of, Cush. The term does not appear in the *King James Version*, but the *New International Version* has it 21 times (e.g. Numbers 12:1).

Cuza *Koo*-za\

See Chuza.

Cyprian *Sip*-ree-un\

Bishop of Carthage who was martyred in AD 258. His followers eventually formed the Donatist church (AD 311), which they claimed to be a "pure church," as opposed to the Roman Catholic church.

Cyprus *Sigh*-prus\

The third largest island in the Mediterranean. Barnabas, who traveled with Paul on his first missionary journey, was from Cyprus (Acts 4:36).

Cyrene *Sigh*-*ree*-nee\

A city in north Africa. Simon, who carried Jesus' cross, was from Cyrene (Matthew 27:32; Mark 15:21; Luke 23:26).

Cyrenian \Sigh-*ree*-nee-un\

A native of Cyrene, originally a Greek colony.

Cyrenius \Sigh-*ree*-nee-us\ (Also known as Quirinius.)

The governor of Syria at the time of the birth of Christ (Luke 2:2).

Cyrus *Sigh*-russ\

The Persian king who established the Persian Empire. He allowed the Jews to return to their homeland and rebuild the temple. God ordered Cyrus's power for His purpose (Isaiah 45:1).

Dd

Dagon *Day*-gon\\
A false god of the Philistines. Saul's head was put into a temple of Dagon (1 Chronicles 10:10).

Dalaiah \\Duh-*lay*-yuh\\
See DELAIAH.

Dalmanutha \\Dal-muh-*new*-thuh\\
Region on the western side of the Sea of Galilee; Jesus and His disciples crossed the lake to Dalmanutha after the feeding of the 4000 (Mark 8:10-12).

Dalmatia \\Dal-*may*-shuh\\
A Roman province inhabited by Greeks. Dalmatia was located across the Adriatic Sea from Italy. Titus visited this area (2 Timothy 4:10).

Damaris *Dam*-uh-ris\\
A woman from Athens whom Paul converted (Acts 17:34).

Damascus \\Duh-*mass*-kus\\
Capital city of Syria (Aram), significant in both the Old and New Testaments. Saul of Tarsus (Paul) met the risen Jesus on the way to this city (Acts 9:1-19) and later escaped the city by going over the wall in a basket (Acts 9:23-25; 2 Corinthians 11:32, 33).

Dan \\Dan\\
1. The fifth son of Jacob, born to Bilhah, a maidservant of Rachel (Genesis 30:1-6; 35:25).
2. Descendants of Dan, one of the 12 tribes of Israel.
3. The land that was the inheritance of the tribe of Dan.
4. City in the far north of Israel, formerly called Laish (Judges 18:29) or Leshem (Joshua 19:47) taken by the Danites when their own tribal inheritance seemed too small for them. In this city Jeroboam set up one of the golden calves that were a snare to Israel (1 Kings 12:26-30).
5. City to which Abraham pursued the five kings of Mespotamia to rescue Lot (Genesis 14:14).

Daniel *Dan*-yul\\
1. Prophet and author of the book of Daniel. He was taken from Jerusalem to Babylon by Nebuchadnezzar and trained for service in the king's court, eventually becoming a leader among the wise men. He interpreted the handwriting on the wall for King Belshazzar (Daniel 5). He was put into a den of lions for praying to the Lord God, and the Lord rescued him from the lions (Daniel 6).
2. A son of David and Abigail (1 Chronicles 3:1).
3. One of the men who returned to Jerusalem with Ezra (Ezra 8:2) and later signed the covenant (Nehemiah 10:1-6).
4. The 27th book of the Old Testament, fifth in the "major prophets" section. It gives much information about the history of Babylon and Persia and contains apocalyptic prophesy of the end times. See BOOKS OF THE BIBLE CHART.

daric *dair*-ik\\
A Persian gold coin (1 Chronicles 29:7; Ezra 8:27).

Darius \\Duh-*rye*-us\\
The name of three emperors in the Persian Empire.
1. Darius the Mede, the king who put Daniel in the lions' den (Daniel 6).
2. Darius I, son of Hystaspes, the king who allowed the Jews to rebuild the temple at Jerusalem with Jeshua and Zerubbabel (Ezra 4:5; 6:1-15; Haggai 1:1; Zechariah 1:1).
3. Darius the Persian (Nehemiah 12:22).

darnel *darn*-ul\\
A variety of grass that yields a small black grain that is not fit for consumption. It looks like wheat in the early stages of growth; it is likely the "tares" or "weeds" sown by the enemy in Jesus' parable (Matthew 13:24-30).

Davidic \\Duh-*vid*-ick\\
Related to King David.

Deborah *Deb*-uh-ruh\\
1. A prophetess and judge of Israel, the only woman to serve as judge (Judges 4, 5). See JUDGES OF ISRAEL CHART.
2. Rebekah's nurse (Genesis 35:8).

Decalogue \\dek-uh-log\\
The Ten Commandments.

Decapolis \\Dee-*cap*-uh-lis\\
A region of 10 Gentile cities located east of Jordan. In one city, Jesus cast the demons from a man into a herd of pigs (Mark 5:1-20).

Decius *Dee*-shus\\ or *Dee*-she-us\\
Roman emperor (AD 249–251) who persecuted Christians.

Delaiah \\Dee-*lay*-yuh\\ (Also spelled Dalaiah.)
1. A descendant of David (1 Chronicles 3:1, 24).
2. Priest during the time of David (1 Chronicles 24:18).
3. Official who tried to urge King Jehoiakim not to burn Jeremiah's scroll (Jeremiah 36:12, 25).
4. Head of a tribe that returned from captivity (Ezra 2:60; Nehemiah 7:62).

Dd

5. Father of Shemaiah who tried to trick Nehemiah (Nehemiah 6:10). Possibly the same as #4.

Delilah \Dih-*lye*-luh\
A Philistine woman who seduced Samson into telling the secret of his strength (Judges 16:4-20).

Delphi *Del*-fi\
A city in ancient Greece.

Demas *Dee*-mus\
Paul's one-time fellow worker who eventually deserted the ministry (Colossians 4:14; Philemon 24; 2 Timothy 4:10).

Demetrius \De-*mee*-tree-us\
1. A silversmith who rallied a mob against Paul when he preached against the goddess Artemis/Diana (Acts 19:23-27).
2. A Christian leader praised by John in 3 John 12.

demoniac \duh-*moe*-nee-ak\
A person who is under the influence of a demon (Luke 8:2, 30).

demoniacal \dee-muh-*nye*-uh-kul\
Demonical.

demonical \dih-*mahn*-ih-kul\
Under the influence of, or behaving like, a demon.

denarii \dih-*nair*-ee\ or \dih-*nair*-eye\
Plural of denarius.

denarius \dih-*nair*-ee-us\
A Roman coin worth a day's wages (Matthew 20:2, 10).

Derbe *Der*-be\
A city in Lycaonia visited by Paul on his first and second missionary journeys (Acts 14:6, 20; 16:1); Gaius's hometown (Acts 20:4).

Deuel *Doo*-el\
Father of Eliasaph, a leader of Gad during the wilderness wandering (Numbers 2:14, *NIV* and others; *KJV* and others have "Reuel").

Deuteronomy \Due-ter-*ahn*-uh-me\
The fifth book of the Old Testament, and fifth in the "law" section. Written by Moses, it relates the Law of God to the Israelites. See BOOKS OF THE BIBLE CHART.

diadema *(Greek)* \dye-uh-*dee*-muh\
Greek for "crown," a symbol of absolute power (Revelation 12:3; 13:1, 2; 19:12), as opposed to *stephanos,* a crown that may be earned or given (1 Corinthians 9:25; Revelation 2:10).

Diana \Dye-*ann*-uh\
See ARTEMIS.

diakoneo *(Greek)* \dih-ah-ko-*neh*-o\ (strong accent on *neh*).
Greek verb for "serve" or "to wait tables."

diakonia *(Greek)* \dih-ah-ko-*nee*-uh\ (strong accent on *nee*).
Greek word for "service" or "ministry."

diakonos *(Greek)* \dee-*ah*-ko-nawss\
Greek verb for "servant" or "deacon."

dialectos *(Greek)* \dee-*ah*-lek-tos\
Greek for "language," the origin of the English word *dialect.*

diamond *dye*-mund\
A precious gem of crystalline carbon. The term translates two Hebrew words in the *King James Version* and others. One always refers to a gem (Exodus 28:18; 39:11; Ezekiel 28:13). *The New International Version* renders it "emerald" in these passages. In Jeremiah 17:1 it translates a different word, which other versions render "flint" or simply "hard."

Diblaim \Dib-*lay*-im\
The prophet Hosea's father-in-law (Hosea 1:3).

Didymus *Did*-uh-mus\
"Twin"; a name for Thomas (John 11:16; 20:24; 21:2).

dikaios *(Greek)* *dik*-eye-oss\
Greek for "just" or "righteous" (Romans 1:17; 3:10).

Diognetus \Dye-ahg-*nee*-tus\
The *Epistle to Diognetus* is a second-century apology for Christianity.

Dionysius \Die-oh-*nish*-ih-us\
A member of the Areopagus in Athens; became a Christian through Paul (Acts 17:34).

Diogenes \Die-*ah*-jin-eez\
A Greek Cynic philosopher.

Diotrephes \Die-*ot*-rih-feez\
A church leader who opposed the apostle John and other true teachers (3 John 9).

disputations \dis-pyoo-*tay*-shunz\
The strong must receive the weak, welcoming them without creating "doubtful disputations" (Romans 14:1, *KJV*). These are matters of opinion that should not be allowed to cause tensions or rifts in the body of Christ.

dissimulation \dis-sim-you-*lay*-shun\
Paul states that love must be "without dissimulation" (Romans 12:9, *KJV*). This means that love must be genuine, without hypocrisy.

Dives *Dye*-veez\
A name given to the rich man in Jesus' Parable of the Rich Man and Lazarus (Luke 16:19-31). The name was not given in the parable, but was accepted in the church in the third century.

Docetic \Doe-*set*-ik\
Related to Docetism.

Docetism \Doe-*set*-iz-um\
A first-century heresy that, among other errors, denied that Jesus was a flesh-and-blood human or that He died.

Docetists \Doe-*set*-ists\
Believers in Docetism.

Domitian \Duh-*mish*-un\
Roman Emperor (AD 81–96) who persecuted Christians and Jews. It is believed that he was the emperor who sent John to the Island of Patmos (Revelation 1:9).

Donatus *Don*-uh-tuss\
Head of the Donatist church, following the teachings of Cyprian.

Dothan *Doe*-thun\ (*th* as in *thin*)
A city located about 13 miles north of Shechem. Here is where Joseph's brothers first put him in a pit and then sold him to Midianite (or Ishmaelite) traders (Genesis 37:17-28).

doulos *(Greek)* *doo*-lahss\
Greek for "slave."

Drusilla \Drew-*sil*-lah\
Youngest daughter of Herod Agrippa I who became the wife of Felix, procurator of Judea (Acts 24:24, 25).

dunamis *(Greek)* *doo*-nuh-mis\
Greek for "power."

Dura *Dur*-uh\
A plain in Babylon (Daniel 3:1).

Ee

Ebal *Ee*-bull\
1. A mountain in the land of Samaria where Joshua built an altar and read the curses and blessings of the Law (Joshua 8:30, 34). See also GERIZIM.
2. Son of Shobal (Genesis 36:23; 1 Chronicles 1:40).

Ebed-Melech \E-bed-*mee*-lek\ (Also spelled Ebedmelech.)
An Ethiopian (Cushite) who served in the court of the king of Judah; he secured the king's permission to rescue Jeremiah out of a cistern (Jeremiah 38:7-13).

Ebenezer *Eb*-en-*ee*-zer\
1. A place near Aphek where Israel lost two battles to the Philistines, the second of which saw the capture of the ark of the covenant by the Philistines (1 Samuel 4:1-11; 5:1).
2. "Stone of help," a stone that Samuel set up between Mizpeh and Shen to commemorate the Lord's help in giving Israel victory over the Philistines (1 Samuel 7:12).

Ecbatana \Ek-buh-*tahn*-uh\ (Also known as Achmetha.)
The capital of Media, where King Darius signed a decree that gave the Jews permission to rebuild the temple (Ezra 6:1, 2). See ACHMETHA.

Ecclesiastes \Ik-*leez*-ee-*as*-teez\ (strong accent on *as*)
The 21st book of the Old Testament, fourth in the "poetry" section. Written by Solomon, it contrasts the vanity of life "under the sun" with living in the fear of the Lord. See BOOKS OF THE BIBLE CHART.

Eden *Ee*-den\
1. Location of the garden in which Adam and Eve lived (Genesis 2:8).
2. Son of Joah, a Levite who assisted in the reforms of Hezekiah (2 Chronicles 29:12).
3. Place known for trade in embroidered fabric and ornamental rugs (Ezekiel 27:23; 2 Kings 19:12; Isaiah 37:12).

Edenic \E-*den*-ik\
Related to Eden or to the Garden of Eden; paradise-like.

Edom *Ee*-dum\
1. Another name for Esau. It means "red," after Esau's exchange of red stew for his birthright (Genesis 25:30; 36:18, 19).
2. The land south and east of the Dead Sea where Esau's descendants lived (Genesis 32:3).

Dd
Ee

Edomites *Ee*-dum-ites\\
Descendants of Esau, who inhabited the land of Edom.

Egypt *Ee*-jipt\\
A country in northeast Africa that played a major role in biblical history from the time of Abraham (Genesis 12:10) to the birth of Christ (Matthew 2:13-15).

Egyptians \\Ee-*jip*-shunz\\
The people who inhabited the land of Egypt.

Ehud *Ee*-hud\\
1. A judge of Israel who killed the king of Moab and brought peace to Israel for 80 years (Judges 3:15-30). See Judges of Israel Chart.
2. A descendant of the tribe of Benjamin (1 Chronicles 7:10; 8:6).

Ehyeh *(Hebrew)* \\Eh-*yeh*\\
Hebrew for "I am" (Exodus 3:14).

eirene *(Greek)* \\eye-*ray*-nay\\
Greek for "peace."

eis *(Greek)* \\ice\\
Greek preposition for "into" or "for."

ekklesia *(Greek)* \\ek-lay-*see*-uh\\
Greek for "church" or "assembly." Its literal meaning is "called out ones."

Ekron *Ek*-run\\
The city located the farthest north among the chief cities of the Philistines (1 Samuel 6:17).

ekteino *(Greek)* \\ek-*tye*-no\\ or \\ek-*tay*-no\\
Greek for "stretch forth" or "stretch out" (Matthew 12:13; Acts 4:30).

Elah *Ee*-lah\\
1. A tribal chief of Edom (Genesis 36:41).
2. A son of Caleb, son of Jephunneh (1 Chronicles 4:15).
3. The valley where David killed Goliath (1 Samuel 17:2, 19; 21:9).
4. Fourth king of the northern kingdom of Israel after Baasha (1 Kings 16:6). He was murdered by Zimri, who succeeded him but reigned just seven days (1 Kings 16:8-10, 15-20). See Kings of Israel and Judah Chart.
5. Father of Hoshea, the last king of the northern kingdom of Israel (2 Kings 15:30; 17:1; 18:1, 9).
6. A Benjamite who returned to Jerusalem from Babylon (1 Chronicles 9:8).

Elam *E*-lum\\
1. A son of Shem (Genesis 10:22; 1 Chronicles 1:17).
2. A country east of the Tigris River near Assyria and Babylon. Chedorlaomer was its king in the days of Abraham (Genesis 14).
3. A town in Judah (Ezra 2:31).
4. The name of one or more men who returned to Judah after the exile (Ezra 2:7, 31; 8:7; 10:2, 26; Nehemiah 7:12, 34; 10:14; 12:42).

Elamites *Ee*-luh-mites\\
Inhabitants of Elam (Ezra 4:9; Acts 2:9).

Elasah *El*-ah-sah\\
1. Son of Shaphan; one of the messengers sent by Jeremiah with a letter to the exiles in Babylon (Jeremiah 29:3).
2. One of the returned exiles guilty of marrying foreign women (Ezra 10:22).

Elath *Ee*-lath\\ (Also spelled Eloth.)
An Edomite port city located on the Gulf of Aqaba (Deuteronomy 2:8; 1 Kings 9:26).

El-bethel \\El-*beth*-ul\\
A name Jacob gave a place in Bethel (Luz) where he built an altar to God while he was returning from Mesopotamia, where he had fled to avoid the wrath of his brother Esau (Genesis 35:6, 7).

Eleazar \\El-ih-*ay*-zar\\ or \\Ee-lih-*ay*-zar\\
1. The third son of Aaron (Exodus 6:23) who became high priest (Numbers 3:32).
2. Abinadab's son who was assigned to guard the ark of the covenant (1 Samuel 7:1).
3. Dodai's son; known as one of the three mighty men in battle against the Philistines (2 Samuel 23:9, 10).
4. A Merarite who bore only daughters (1 Chronicles 23:21, 22; 24:28).
5. Son of Phinehas; appointed by Ezra to the temple treasury (Ezra 8:32-34).
6. A priest at the dedication of the rebuilt walls of Jerusalem (Nehemiah 12:42).
7. Ancestor of Joseph, the husband of Mary (Matthew 1:15).

Eli *Ee*-lye\\
1. High priest and judge over Israel; he reared Samuel after Hannah presented Samuel to him at the tabernacle in Shiloh (1 Samuel 1-4; 14:3).
2. Alternate spelling of *Eloi* (Matthew 27:45, *KJV, ASV, NLT*; compare with Mark 15:34 in those versions).

Eliab *Ee*-*lye*-ab\\
1. Son of Helon; leader of the tribe of Zebulun (Numbers 1:9; 2:7; 7:24, 29; 10:16).

2. Son of Pallu (Phallu); father of Dathan and Abiram, two men who rebelled against Moses in the wilderness (Numbers 16:1, 12; 26:8, 9; Deuteronomy 11:6).

3. Oldest brother of King David (1 Samuel 16:6; 1 Chronicles 2:13).

4. A Levite who was a temple porter and musician in David's time (1 Chronicles 15:18, 20; 16:5).

5. A Gadite warrior who hid with David in the wilderness (1 Chronicles 12:1, 8, 9).

6. Great-grandfather of Samuel the prophet (1 Chronicles 6:27).

Eliah \E-*lye*-ah\

Another spelling of the name *Elijah* (1 Chronicles 8:27; Ezra 10:26). See ELIJAH.

Eliakim \Ee-*lye*-uh-kim\

1. Seventeenth king of Judah; his name was changed to Jehoiakim (2 Kings 23:34; 2 Chronicles 36:4).

2. A son of Hilkiah; steward of King Hezekiah's household and court (2 Kings 18:18, 26, 37).

3. A priest during the dedication of the rebuilt wall in Jerusalem (Nehemiah 12:41).

4. Son of Abiud listed in Matthew's genealogy of Jesus (Matthew 1:13).

5. Son of Melea listed in Luke's genealogy of Jesus (Luke 3:30, 31).

Eliam \Ih-*lye*-am\

1. Bathsheba's father (2 Samuel 11:3). Called Ammiel in 1 Chronicles 3:5.

2. One of David's mighty men, son of Ahithophel (2 Samuel 23:34).

Elias \Ee-*lye*-us\

Greek form of the name *Elijah* (Matthew 11:14; Mark 9:4, 5; Romans 11:2 *KJV*). See ELIJAH.

Eliashib \E-*lye*-uh-shib\

1. A priest in David's time, from whom the 11th priestly course took its name (1 Chronicles 24:12).

2. Elioenai's son from the royal line (1 Chronicles 3:24).

3. High priest during the rebuilding of the wall (Ezra 10:6; Nehemiah 3:1, 20, 21; 12:10, 22, 23; 13:4, 7, 28).

4. Ezra 10 lists three by this name among those guilty of marrying foreign women (Ezra 10:24, 36).

Eliel *El*-lee-el\

See ELIHU, #2.

Eliezer \El-ih-*ee*-zer\

1. Eliezer of Damascus, Abraham's chief servant (Genesis 15:2).

2. Moses and Zipporah's second son (Exodus 18:4; 1 Chronicles 23:15, 17; 26:25).

3. Beker's son and Benjamin's grandson (1 Chronicles 7:8).

4. A trumpeter who helped return the ark of the covenant to Jerusalem (1 Chronicles 15:24).

5. A son of Zicri; an officer of the tribe of Reuben (1 Chronicles 27:16).

6. Prophet who prophesied against Jehoshaphat and predicted the destruction of his fleet because he had made an alliance with Ahaziah (2 Chronicles 20:37).

7. One or more of the men who returned to Judah from the exile (Ezra 8:16; 10:18, 23, 31).

8. An ancestor of Jesus (Luke 3:29).

Elihu \Ih-*lye*-hew\

1. One of Job's counselors; he does not speak until the other three "friends" have had their say (Job 32:2-6; 34:1; 35:1; 36:1).

2. Great-grandfather of Samuel the prophet (1 Samuel 1:1). Also spelled Eliel (1 Chronicles 5:24) and Eliab (1 Chronicles 6:27).

3. Oldest brother of David (1 Chronicles 27:18); also spelled Eliab (1 Samuel 16:6; 17:13).

4. A man who joined David in Ziklag (1 Chronicles 12:20).

5. A gatekeeper from the line of Korah during the reign of David (1 Chronicles 26:7).

Elijah \Ee-*lye*-juh\ (Also spelled Eliah and Elias.)

1. A prophet during the days of Ahab. He challenged the people of Israel to choose between God and Baal in a powerful demonstration on Mt. Carmel (1 Kings 18).

2. A son of Jeroham in Benjamin's tribe (1 Chronicles 8:27).

3. A descendant of Harim, one of the priests who were guilty of marrying foreign wives (Ezra 10:21).

4. A descendant of Elam, another of the men who were guilty of marrying foreign wives (Ezra 10:26).

Elim *Ee*-lim\

The second place the Israelites stopped after crossing the Red Sea (Exodus 15:27; 16:1; Numbers 33:9, 10).

Elimelech \Ee-*lim*-eh-leck\

An Israelite who relocated his family to Moab because of a famine. His daughter-in-law Ruth remained faithful to his widow Naomi (Ruth 1:2, 3; 4:9, 10).

Eliphaz *El*-ih-faz\

1. One of Esau's sons (Genesis 36:10-12; 1 Chronicles 1:35, 36).

2. A friend of Job; a Temanite, who were known for their wisdom (Job 2:11; Jeremiah 49:7).

Elisabeth \Ih-*lih*-suh-beth\

See ELIZABETH.

Elisha \E-*lye*-shuh\

Prophet of Israel in the time of the divided kingdom; he succeeded Elijah (1 Kings 19:16-21; 2 Kings 2—9).

Ee

Elishama \Ee-*lish*-uh-muh\
1. Leader of Ephraim's tribe at the start of the wilderness journey (Numbers 1:10; 2:18; 7:48, 53); grandfather of Joshua (1 Chronicles 7:26, 27).
2. Jekamiah's son, a descendant of Judah (1 Chronicles 2:41).
3. Alternate spelling of Elishua, a son of David (2 Samuel 5:15; 1 Chronicles 3:6).
4. Another of David's sons, born in Jerusalem (2 Samuel 5:16; 1 Chronicles 3:8).
5. Jehoiakim's scribe (Jeremiah 36:12, 20, 21).
6. A priest sent by Jehoshaphat to teach the people of Judah the Law of God (2 Chronicles 17:8).

Elizabeth \Ih-*lih*-zuh-beth\ (Also spelled Elisabeth.)
The mother of John the Baptist and a relative of Mary (Luke 1:5-60).

Elkanah *El*-kuh-nuh\ or *El*-*kay*-nuh\
1. Father of the prophet Samuel (1 Samuel 1:1–2:21).
2. A son of Korah (Exodus 6:23, 24).
3. A close adviser of King Ahaz of Judah (2 Chronicles 28:7).
4. One of the men who joined David at Ziklag (1 Chronicles 12:6).
5. The name of several Levites (1 Chronicles 6:22-28; 33-38; 9:16).

Elnathan \El-*nay*-thun\ (*th* as in *thin*)
1. King Jehoiachin's grandfather (2 Kings 24:8).
2. Son of Achbor; sent by King Jehoiakim to bring the prophet Uriah from Egypt to Judah for execution (Jeremiah 26:22; 36:12, 25).
3. The name of one of the men Ezra sent to Babylonia to get temple servants (Ezra 8:16).

Elohim *(Hebrew)* \El-o-*heem*\
Hebrew for "God" or "gods"; the earliest name for God in the Old Testament.

Eloi *(Aramaic)* \Ee-*lo*-eye\ (Also spelled Eli.)
Aramaic for "God" or "my God" (Mark 15:34).

Eloi, Eloi, lama sabachthani *(Aramaic)* \Ee-*lo*-eye, Ee-*lo*-eye, *lah*-mah suh-*back*-thuh-nee\
One of the cries of Jesus from the cross: "My God, My God, why have you forsaken me?" (Mark 15:34). It is a quotation of Psalm 22:1. (Also in Matthew 27:46, with some variations in spelling in some translations.)

Eloth *Ee*-loth\
See ELATH.

El-Shaddai *(Hebrew)* \El-*Shad*-eye\
Hebrew for "God Almighty" (Psalm 68:14).

Elul *Ee*-lull\ or \Eh-*loo*\
Sixth month on the Hebrew calendar, roughly equivalent to mid-August to mid-September (Nehemiah 6:15). See CALENDAR CHART.

Elymas *El*-ih-mass\
Another name for the Jewish sorcerer Bar-Jesus (Acts 13:4-13).

embrimaomai *(Greek)* \em-brih-*mah*-oh-my\
Greek word that is translated as a variety of very emotional utterances (Matthew 9:30; Mark 1:43; 14:5; John 11:33, 38).

emerald *em*-rahld\
A gemstone of green beryl. In the Bible, most versions agree when this gem is intended in New Testament passages (Revelation 4:3; 21:19), but there is less agreement in the Old Testament. Of the twelve gems of the high priest's breastpiece, at least three different stones are identified as the emerald in different translations (Exodus 28:17-20; Exodus 39:10-13).

Emmanuel *(Hebrew)* \E-*man*-you-el\
Alternate spelling of Immanuel (Matthew 1:23 *KJV, NRSV*). See IMMANUEL.

Emmaus \Em-*may*-us\
A town located seven miles from Jerusalem; Jesus joined two disciples on their way to Emmaus after His resurrection (Luke 24:13).

Endor *En*-dor\
An ancient Canaanite city; Saul visited a witch here before going into the battle in which he was killed (1 Samuel 28:7).

En Gedi \En-*gee*-dye\ or \En-*geh*-dee\ (Also spelled Engedi and En-Gedi.)
An oasis in Judah by the Dead Sea (Joshua 15:62); one of David's hiding places (1 Samuel 23:29; 24).

enmity *en*-mut-ee\
Hostility (Genesis 3:15; Luke 23:12; Romans 8:7; Ephesians 2:15, 16; James 4:4).

Enoch *E*-nock\
1. Son of Cain (Genesis 4:17, 18).
2. Son of Jared and father of Methuselah (Genesis 5:18-24; 1 Chronicles 1:3). Walked with God and never experienced death (Genesis 5:22).
3. Apocryphal book cited in Jude 14.
4. City named after Cain's son (Genesis 4:17).

Enos *Ee*-nuss\ (Also spelled Enosh.)
Seth's son and Adam's grandson; Lived to be 905 years of age (Genesis 4:26; 5:6-11; Luke 3:38).

Enosh *Ee*-nush\\
See ENOS.

Enrogel \\En-*roe*-gel\\ (*g* as in *get*)
A spring in Judah just south of Jerusalem (Joshua 15:7; 18:16).

Epaenetus \\E-*pee*-ne-tus\\
See EPENETUS

Epaphras *Ep*-uh-frass\\
A worker with Paul; Paul refers to him as a servant and faithful minister of Christ (Colossians 1:7; 4:12).

Epaphroditus \\Ee-*paf*-ro-*dye*-tus\\ (strong accent on *dye*)
The messenger and helper of Paul from the church of Philippi (Philippians 2:25-30; 4:18).

epekteino (*Greek*) \\ep-ek-*tie*-no\\ or \\ep-ek-*tay*-no\\
To stretch toward something (Philippians 3:13).

Epenetus \\E-*pee*-ne-tus\\ (Also spelled Epaenetus.)
The first believer in Asia and "dear friend" to Paul (Romans 16:5).

ephah *ee*-fah\\
Unit of measure; about a half bushel (Exodus 16:36).

Ephah *Ee*-fah\\
1. A son of Midian, one of the sons of Abraham by Keturah (Genesis 25:1-4).
2. A concubine of Caleb (1 Chronicles 2:46).
3. Midianite tribe descended from #1 (Isaiah 60:6).

Ephesians \\Ee-*fee*-zhunz\\
1. Residents of Ephesus.
2. The 10th book of the New Testament, first of the prison epistles; a letter from Paul to the church in Ephesus. See BOOKS OF THE BIBLE CHART.

Ephesus *Ef*-uh-sus\\
The most important city of Asia Minor; located by the Aegean Sea. Paul stopped briefly here on his second missionary journey, leaving Aquila and Priscilla (Acts 18:18-21); he returned on the third journey and stayed more than two years (Acts 19:1-12). Here the silversmiths who made shrines for Artemis/Diana instigated a riot (Acts 19:23-41).

ephod *ee*-fod\\
A garment worn by the high priest (Exodus 28:31).

ephphatha (*Aramaic*) *ef*-uh-thuh\\
Aramaic for "be opened." Spoken by Jesus when healing the deaf man (Mark 7:34).

Ephraim *Ee*-fray-im\\
1. Joseph and Asenath's younger son (Genesis 41:52). Jacob adopted Ephraim and his brother Manasseh and imparted a blessing to them as tribes of Israel (Genesis 48:1-22).
2. The territory given to the tribe of Ephraim as an inheritance (Joshua 16:5-8; 17:7-11).

Ephraimites *Ee*-fray-im-ites\\
Members of Ephraim's tribe (Joshua 16:10; Judges 12).

Ephrain *Ee*-fray-in\\
Alternate spelling of Ephron in 2 Chronicles 13:19, *KJV.* See EPHRON.

Ephrathah *Ef*-rah-tah\\ (Also spelled Ephrath and Ephratah.)
1. Part of Caleb's inheritance in the tribe of Judah that includes the area around Bethlehem (Micah 5:2).
2. Alternate spelling for Ephrath, the second wife of Caleb and mother of Hur (1 Chronicles 2:19, 50; 4:4).

Ephrath *Ef*-rath\\
1. An area near Bethlehem where Benjamin was born and Rachel died (Genesis 35:16, 19; 48:7). Probably the same as Ephrathah (see above).
2. The second wife of Caleb and mother of Hur (1 Chronicles 2:19, 50; 4:4).

Ephrathite *Ef*-ruh-thite\\
One who lived in Ephrath or Ephrathah (1 Samuel 17:12).

Ephron *Ee*-fron\\ (Also spelled Ephrain and possibly Ophrah.)
1. A Hittite who sold the field of Machpelah to Abraham for Sarah's burial (Genesis 23:8, 9).
2. A mountainous region of the northwest border of Jerusalem (Joshua 15:9).
3. A city near Bethel that Abijah captured from King Jeroboam (2 Chronicles 13:19); perhaps the Ophrah in Joshua 18:23.

Epicureanism *Ep*-ih-kyu-*ree*-uh-niz-uhm\\ (strong accent on *ree*) or *Ep*-ih-*kyur*-ee-uh-niz-uhm\\ (strong accent on *kyur*)
A philosophy by Epicurus that taught the pursuit of happiness was the avoidance of pain.

Epicureans *Ep*-ih-kew-*ree*-unz\\ or *Ep*-ih-*cure*-ee-unz\\
Followers of the Greek philosopher, Epicurus, who lived from 341–270 BC. Paul encountered people with these beliefs in Athens (Acts 17:16-33).

Epicurus *Ep*-ih-*cure*-us\\
A Greek philosopher of Athens (341–270 BC). He founded a school and developed a following that spanned over three centuries after his death.

Ee

Epimenides \Ep-ih-*men*-ih-deez\
Pagan poet quoted by Paul in his sermon on Mars Hill (Acts 17:28).

Epiphanes \Ih-*piff*-a-neez\
Title given to Antiochus IV of Syria, who defiled the temple in 167 BC. The title means "illustrious."

Ee

epistles \ee-*pis*-uls\
New Testament letters to individuals or churches.

Erastus \E-*rass*-tus\
1. One of Paul's helpers; he and Timothy went to Macedonia while Paul concluded his ministry in Ephesus (Acts 19:22). Probably the same helper who was left at Corinth when Paul had gone to Rome (2 Timothy 4:20).
2. A disciple and city official at Corinth (Romans 16:23). Possibly the same as #1.

eros *(Greek)* *air*-oce\
1. Greek for "sexual love"; root of the word *erotic*.
2. The god of sexual love in Greek mythology; also known as Cupid.

Esaias \E-*zay*-us\
Greek version of the name *Isaiah* (Matthew 3:3; 4:14; Mark 7:6; Luke 3:4; John 12:38-42; Acts 8:28-30).

Esarhaddon \Ee-sar-*had*-un\
Sennacherib's son; heir to the Assyrian throne after his brothers murdered their father. King of Assyria (681–669 BC) at the peak of its dominance (2 Kings 19:36, 37; Ezra 4:2; Isaiah 37:37, 38).

Esau *Ee*-saw\
Firstborn twin of Isaac and Rebekah. Traded his birthright to his brother, Jacob, for pottage (Genesis 25:24-34). Also called Edom (Genesis 25:30; 36:1, 8).

eschatology \ess-kuh-*tah*-luh-jee\
The study of the theology of the last things, such as death, resurrection, the second coming, and Judgment. Study of the end times.

eschatos *(Greek)* \es-kuh-tos\
Greek for "last." Root of the word *eschatology,* the study of last things (i.e., end times).

escheweth \ess-*shoe*-ith\
Shuns or avoids; hates (Job 1:8; 2:3, *KJV*).

Esdraelon \Es-druh-*ee*-lon\ (strong accent on *ee*).
The Greek name for the fertile Jezreel Valley in the hills of Galilee and Samaria.

Esdras *Ez*-druss\
An apocryphal book.

Esek *Ee*-sek\
A well dug by Isaac's servants in Gerar but claimed by local herdsmen (Genesis 26:19, 20). The name means "dispute."

Eshbaal *Esh*-bay-ul\ (Also spelled Esh-baal.)
See Ishbosheth.

Eshtaol *Esh*-tuh-oll\
A town on the border of Judah and Dan near where Samson was buried (Joshua 15:33; 19:41; Judges 16:31).

Essenes \Eh-*seenz*\
A sect of Jews in Palestine during the time of Christ and later; they seem to have had a center at Qumran and may have been responsible for collecting and preserving the Dead Sea Scrolls.

Esther *Ess*-ter\
1. Jewish woman, originally called Hadassah, who became queen of Persia and providentially saved the Jewish people from a murderous plot by Haman.
2. The 17th book of the Old Testament, the 12th in the "history" section. It recounts the events of Esther's service as queen and how she thwarted the plot of Haman. See Books of the Bible Chart.

Etham *E*-thum\
A place where the Israelites who left Egypt camped after leaving Succoth (Exodus 13:20).

Ethanim *Eth*-uh-nim\
The seventh month on the Jewish calendar, roughly equivalent to mid-September to mid-October (1 Kings 8:2). Name was changed to Tishri after the exile. See Calendar Chart.

Ethbaal \Eth-*bay*-ul\
King of Sidon and father of Jezebel, who married Ahab, king of Israel (1 Kings 16:31).

Ethiopia \E-thee-*o*-pee-uh\ (*th* as in *thin*)
A land south of Egypt, called Cush in the Old Testament (Isaiah 11:11).

Ethiopians \E-thee-*o*-pee-unz\ (*th* as in *thin*)
Residents of Ethiopia.

eucharistia *(Greek)* *you*-kar-iss-*tee*-uh\ (strong accent on *tee*)
Greek word for "thanksgiving." Transliterated, it becomes "Eucharist," a name for the Lord's Supper.

Eunice \U-*nye*-see\ or \U-*nis*\
Mother of Timothy (2 Timothy 1:5).

eunuch *you*-nick\
A sometimes castrated man who would serve as an officer in courts, households, or harems (2 Kings 20:18; Isaiah 56:3; Jeremiah 29:2; Acts 8:27).

Euodias \You-*o*-dee-us\ (Also spelled Euodia.)
A Christian woman of Philippi whom Paul urged to be reconciled to Syntyche (Philippians 4:2, 3).

Euphrates \You-*fray*-teez\
1. The largest river in western Asia; it flows 1800 miles to the Persian Gulf.
2. One of the four rivers running from the Garden of Eden (Genesis 2:8-14). It may or may not have been at or near the same location as the modern Euphrates as the flood doubtless altered world geography.

Eusebius \You-*see*-be-us\
Church historian of the fourth century (c. 260–c. 340), from Caesarea.

Eve \Eev\
The wife of Adam; the first woman (Genesis 2:21-25; 3:20).

Evil-Merodach *Eh*-vil *Mare*-oh-dack\
Son and successor of Nebuchadnezzar, king of Babylon; he released Jehoiachin from prison (2 Kings 25:27; Jeremiah 52:31). He was assassinated after he had reigned just two years.

exhortation \eks-or-*tay*-shun\
Teaching, preaching, or urging. In the New Testament it often translates a Greek word meaning a "calling someone alongside for help"; also translated "encouragement" or "comfort" (Romans 12:8; 1 Timothy 4:13; Hebrews 13:22).

Exodus *Ex*-uh-dus\
The second book of the Old Testament, and second in the "law" section. Written by Moses, it tells of the deliverance of the Israelites from Egyptian bondage. See Books of the Bible Chart.

Ezekiel \Ee-*zeek*-ee-ul\ or \Ee-*zeek*-yul\
1. Son of Buzi; author of the Old Testament book of Ezekiel (Ezekiel 1:3). He was taken captive and deported to Babylon in 597 BC, ten years before Jerusalem fell. The deportation is described, though Ezekiel is not named, in 2 Kings 24:10-16.
2. The 26th book of the Old Testament, fourth in the "major prophets" section. Using vivid imagery, it warns

Judah of coming calamity, calling for repentance, and then—presumably in prophecies written after the fall of Jerusalem—offers hope to the exiles that God will deliver them. See Books of the Bible Chart.

Ezion Geber *Ee*-zih-on-*ge*-ber\ (strong accent on *ge*; *g* as in *get*) (Also spelled Eziongaber.)
A city on the north end of the Gulf of Aqaba. A place where the Israelites camped in the wilderness (Numbers 33:35, 36).

Ezra *Ez*-ruh\
1. A man of Judah's tribe (1 Chronicles 4:17).
2. A priest who returned from Babylon with Zerubbabel (Nehemiah 12:1); author of the book of Ezra.
3. The 15th book of the Old Testament, the tenth in the "history" section. It tells of the people who returned to Judah after the Babylonian Exile. See Books of the Bible Chart.

Ff

Felix *Fee*-licks\
Roman governor in Caesarea. Paul was brought before Felix after Paul's arrest in Jerusalem and subsequent transfer to Caesarea when a plot against him was discovered. He kept Paul in prison for two years without making any decision on his case because he was hoping for a bribe (Acts 23:24–24:27).

Festus *Fes*-tus\
Succeeded Felix as the Roman governor in Caesarea. Paul made his appeal to Caesar in Festus's court (Acts 25:1-12).

firkin *fir*-kun\
Unit of liquid measure, about 10 gallons (John 2:6, *KJV*).

fornication \for-neh-*kay*-shun\
Usually this term is applied to sexual immorality involving a person who is not married—*adultery* being the term used of such behavior by a married person. It translates the Greek word *porneia,* which is a general term for immorality.

frankincense *frank*-in-sense\
A costly incense made from the resin of the balsam tree (Exodus 30:34; Matthew 2:11; Revelation 18:13).

Gg

Gaash *Gay*-ash\
A region near Mt. Ephraim and close to the burial site of Joshua (Judges 2:8, 9).

Gabbatha *(Hebrew)* *Gab*-buh-thuh\
A place in or near the governor's palace in Jerusalem; it contained the judgment seat used by Pilate as he sentenced Jesus (John 19:13).

Gabriel *Gay*-bree-ul\
The angel who appeared to Daniel, Zechariah (Zacharias), and Mary—and perhaps others—to deliver divine messages (Daniel 8:16; 9:21; Luke 1:19, 26).

Gad \Gad\ (Short *a* as in *bad*)
1. Seventh son of Jacob, born to Zilpah, Leah's handmaid (Genesis 30:9-11; 46:16).
2. A tribe of Israel (Numbers 2:14).
3. Territory given to the tribe of Gad as an inheritance.
4. One of David's prophets (1 Chronicles 29:29).

Gadara *Gad*-uh-ruh\ (Also known as Gerasa.)
City to the southeast of the Sea of Galilee, near where Jesus cast demons from a man known as Legion because so many demons possessed him (Mark 5:1-20; Luke 8:26-39). Matthew's account reveals there were two men (Matthew 8:28-34). The country of the Gadarenes is also known as the country of the Gerasenes or Gergesenes.

Gadarenes *Gad*-uh-reens\
The people who lived near Gadara. See GERASENES.

Gadites *Gad*-ites\
Inhabitants of the tribe of Gad; descendants of Gad, son of Jacob (Deuteronomy 3:12, 16).

Gaius *Gay*-us\
1. A man from Derbe who traveled with Paul (Acts 20:4). He, along with Aristarchus, was seized during the riot in Ephesus (Acts 19:29, where mention of Macedonia either refers only to Aristarchus or to the fact that they had most recently accompanied Paul from Macedonia).
2. A Corinthian believer who hosted a church in Corinth and also was host to Paul; he sent greetings to the church at Rome (1 Corinthians 1:14; Romans 16:23).
3. John addressed him in his third letter (3 John 1ff.).

Galatia \Guh-*lay*-shuh\
A Roman province that Paul visited on all three missionary journeys (Acts 16:6; 18:23).

Galatians \Guh-*lay*-shunz\
1. People who live in Galatia.
2. The ninth book of the New Testament, a letter from Paul to the churches of Galatia. See BOOKS OF THE BIBLE CHART.

Galeed *Gal*-e-ed\
A Hebrew word meaning "a heap of witness." A monument of friendship between Jacob and Laban (Genesis 31:47, 48).

Galilaeans \Gal-uh-*lee*-unz\
See GALILEANS.

Galileans \Gal-uh-*lee*-unz\ (Also spelled Galilaeans.)
Natives or inhabitants of Galilee (John 4:45).

Galilee *Gal*-uh-lee\
1. A province in northern Israel that includes such cities as Cana (John 2:1), Nazareth (Luke 2:39), and Capernaum (Matthew 4:12, 13). Much of Jesus' ministry was conducted in Galilee.
2. A lake in northern Israel that feeds the Jordan River. This is the lake where Peter, Andrew, James, and John fished before Jesus called them to follow (Matthew 4:18-22). It is also the lake on which Jesus walked on water (Matthew 14:22-33). Also known as the Sea of Chinnereth (Chinneroth, Kinnereth; see CHINNERETH), or Sea of Tiberias (see TIBERIAS), or Lake of Gennesaret (see GENNESARET).

Gallio *Gal*-ee-o\
Roman governor of Achaia during Paul's ministry (Acts 18:12-17).

Gamaliel \Guh-*may*-lih-ul\ or \Guh-*may*-lee-al\
1. Famous Jewish rabbi, a Pharisee who was a member of the Sanhedrin. He counseled caution in dealing with the apostles (Acts 5:34–40). Paul was instructed by him (Acts 22:3).
2. Pedahzur's son, a leader in the tribe of Manasseh (Numbers 1:10; 2:20; 7:54, 59; 10:23).

Gath \Gath\ (*a* as in *bath*)
One of the five chief cities of the Philistines (Joshua 13:3; 1 Samuel 6:17).

Gath Hepher \Gath-*he*-fer\ (Also spelled Gittahhepher.)
A town on the border of Zebulun (Joshua 19:13); Jonah's place of residence (2 Kings 14:25).

Gaulanitis \Gall-on-*eye*-tis\
The province east of the Sea of Galilee; Herod's son, Philip, made its capital Bethsaida Julias.

Gauls \Gawlz\
People of the Celtic tribe of Gaul (modern France and Belgium) famed for warcraft and shrewdness. They also are believed to have inhabited Galatia.

Gaza *Gay*-zuh\ or *Gah*-zuh\
One of the five chief Philistine cities (Joshua 13:3).

Geba *Gee*-buh\ (*g* as in *get*) (Also spelled Gaba.)
A town in Benjamin's territory (Joshua 18:24).

Gedaliah *Ged*-uh-*lye*-uh\ (*g* as in *get*; strong accent on *lye*)
1. Son of Jeduthun, a temple musician at the time of David (1 Chronicles 25:1-3).
2. Grandfather of the prophet Zephaniah (Zephaniah 1:1).
3. One of the conspirators against Jeremiah who persuaded King Zedekiah to allow them to imprison Jeremiah in an empty cistern (Jeremiah 38:1-6).
4. Governor of Judah, appointed by Nebuchadnezzar at the time of the exile (586 bc; assassinated by Ishmael, a son of Nethaniah, and 10 men. (2 Kings 25:22-25).

Gehenna *(Hebrew)* \Geh-*hen*-uh\ (*g* as in *get*)
Valley of Ben Hinnom; the place had been used for idolatrous practices (Jeremiah 7:31, 32); later it became a city dump with fires smoldering continuously. As such it became an illustration of the fires of Hell (Matthew 5:22).

Gemariah \Gem-uh-*rye*-uh\ (*g* as in *get*)
1. Son of Shaphan; he and Elnathan and Delaiah tried to keep King Jehoiakim from burning Jeremiah's scroll (Jeremiah 36:10-25).
2. Son of Hilkiah, he was King Zedekiah's ambassador to Nebuchadnezzar (Jeremiah 29:3).

Genesis *Jen*-eh-sis\
The first book of the Old Testament, and first in the "law" section. Written by Moses, it gives history from creation to the time of Joseph. See Books of the Bible Chart.

Gennesaret \Geh-*ness*-uh-ret\ (*g* as in *get*)
1. A town on the Sea of Galilee's northwest shore to which Jesus and the disciples took a boat after the feeding of the 5,000 (Matthew 14:34).
2. Another name for the Sea of Galilee (Luke 5:1).

Gentiles *Jen*-tiles\
Refers to people who are not Jewish.

Gerar *Gear*-rar\ (*g* as in *get*)
A Philistine city and/or region south of Gaza (Genesis 26:1). See Abimelech.

Gerasa *Gur*-uh-suh\ (Also known as Gadara.)
A city of Perea between the Sea of Galilee and the Dead Sea. Not mentioned in Scripture except as the region or country of the Gerasenes. (See below.)

Gerasenes *Gur*-uh-seenz\ (Also spelled Gadarenes and Gergesenes.)
Inhabitants of Geresa; Jesus healed a Gerasene demoniac and cast the demons into a herd of pigs. The *KJV* gives "country of the Gergesenes" in Matthew's account (Matthew 8:28), but has Gadarenes in Mark and Luke (Mark 5:1; Luke 8:26, 37). The *NIV* and others have "Gadarenes" in Matthew and "Gerasenes" in Mark and Luke.

Gergesenes *Gur*-guh-seenz\ (See Gerasenes.)
See Gerasenes.

Gerizim *Gair*-ih-zeem\ or \Guh-*rye*-zim\
A mountain in Samaria. The blessings for keeping the Law were read from this mountain. See also Ebal (Deuteronomy 11:29; 27:4-26). Herod the Great, who made vast improvements on the Jewish temple in Jerusalem, also rebuilt an ancient Samaritan temple on this mountain, and it is "this mountain" to which the woman of Samaria referred as a site of Samaritan worship (John 4:20).

Gershom *Gur*-shom\
1. Moses and Zipporah's first son (Exodus 2:22).
2. A descendant of Phineas who returned from Babylon with Ezra (Ezra 8:2).
3. Father of Jonathan, the priest for Dan (Judges 18:30) when Micah's idol was stolen and the Danites conquered Laish and renamed it Dan (Judges 18).

Gershon *Gur*-shahn\ (Also spelled Gershom.)
The oldest son of Levi (1 Chronicles 6:1, 16, 17, 20, 43; 23:6, 7).

Geshem *Gee*-shem\ (*g* as in *get*)
An Arab leader who opposed Nehemiah in rebuilding the wall of Jerusalem (Nehemiah 2:19).

Geshur *Gee*-shur\ (*g* as in *get*)
A kingdom in Syria whose king, Talmai, was the father of one of David's wives, the mother of Absalom (2 Samuel 3:2, 3). Absalom fled to Geshur after he murdered Amnon (2 Samuel 13:37).

Gethsemane \Geth-*sem*-uh-nee\ (*g* as in *get*)
Garden, or olive grove, on the Mt. of Olives, where Jesus and the disciples prayed before the betrayal and arrest of Jesus (Matthew 26:36-56).

Gezer *Gee*-zer\ (*g* as in *get*)
A fortified city located northwest of Jerusalem; Joshua conquered the king of Gezer (Joshua 10:33; 12:12).

Gg

Gibbethon *Gib*-eh-thon\ (*g* as in *get*)
A city in the tribe of Dan (Joshua 19:44; 21:23) where Baasha killed Nadab to become the third king of the northern kingdom, Israel (1 Kings 15:27).

Gibea *Gib*-ee-uh\ (*g* as in *get*)
Caleb's grandson (1 Chronicles 2:49).

Gibeah *Gib*-ee-uh\ (*g* as in *get*)
1. A city in the tribe of Judah (Joshua 15:57).
2. A city in the tribe of Benjamin (Joshua 18:28) where a Levite's concubine was raped and murdered, which nearly led to the extermination of the tribe of Benjamin (Judges 19, 20). It was also the birthplace of King Saul (1 Samuel 10:26).

Gg

Gibeon *Gib*-e-un\ (*g* as in *get*)
The city from which ambassadors came to Joshua and claimed to be from a distant country and tricked him into making a treaty with them (Joshua 9). Joshua prayed that the sun stand still as he defended Gibeon from the Canaanites (Joshua 10:1-14).

Gideon *Gid*-e-un\ (*g* as in *get*)
A judge of Israel who defeated the Midianites with 300 men (Judges 7; Hebrews 11:32). He is also called Jerub-Baal (Judges 6:32; 7:1). See JUDGES OF ISRAEL CHART.

Gihon *Gye*-hahn\
1. One of the four rivers running from the Garden of Eden (Genesis 2:8-14).
2. A spring that supplied water to Jerusalem (2 Chronicles 32:27-30).
3. A place in or near Jerusalem that was the site of Solomon's coronation (1 Kings 1:33-40). The spring (#2) is probably named for this place.

Gilboa \Gil-*bo*-uh\ (*g* as in *get*)
A mountain in the territory of Manasseh, west of the Jordan, where Saul and three of his sons died in battle (1 Samuel 31:1, 8).

Gilead *Gil*-ee-ud\ (*g* as in *get*)
1. Mountainous area east of the Jordan where Reuben, Gad, and half of Manasseh took their inheritance (Numbers 32:1-40). The region was known for its spices and aromatic gums, which were exported widely as a healing balm (Jeremiah 8:22).
2. Father of Jephthah, who was a judge of Israel (Judges 11:1, 2).
3. Son of Michael, from the tribe of Gad (1 Chronicles 5:14).

Gilgal *Gil*-gal\ (*g* as in *get*)
Site of the Israelites' first camp after crossing the Jordan into the promised land (Joshua 4:19, 20).

Giloh *Gy*-lo\ (*g* as in *get*)
City in the hill country of Judah (Joshua 15:51), the hometown of David's counselor Ahithophel, who joined in Absalom's rebellion (2 Samuel 15:12).

Gilonite *Gy*-lo-nite\ (*g* as in *get*)
Resident of Giloh, as Ahithophel the Gilonite (2 Samuel 15:12).

Ginath *Guy*-nath\
Father of Tibni. Tibni attempted to become king of Israel but was killed by the forces of Omri (1 Kings 16:21, 22).

Girgashites *Gur*-guh-shites\
A tribe of Canaan (Genesis 10:16; 1 Chronicles 1:14).

Gittahhepher *Git*-ah-*he*-fer\ (strong accent on *he*; *g* as in *get*)
Another version of the town of Gath Hepher (Joshua 19:13 *KJV*). See GATH HEPHER.

Gittite *Git*-ite\ (*g* as in *get*)
People of Gath. Obed-Edom, who housed the ark of the covenant, was a Gittite (2 Samuel 6:10). Some of David's valiant men were Gittites (2 Samuel 15:18, 19).

Gnostic *Nahss*-tick\
1. One who believes in Gnosticism.
2. Related to Gnosticism, as the Gnostic heresy.

Gnosticism *Nahss*-tih-sizz-um\ (strong accent on *Nahss*)
An ancient heresy that taught a secret knowledge and a dualistic view of God. It arose in the second century, but some scholars believe there is evidence of its roots in what Paul and other writers refute in the prison epistles, the pastoral epistles, and the general epistles.

God \God\
1. The creator and ruler of the universe (Genesis 1:1). The one true and living God is known by several names, such as Elohim, Yahweh, and others.
2. The term *god* (no capital *g*) is also used for imaginary deities worshiped by pagans.

Golgotha *Gahl*-guh-thuh\
The place outside the gates of Jerusalem where Jesus was crucified (Matthew 27:33).

Goliath \Go-*lye*-uth\
The Philistine giant that David killed (1 Samuel 17).

Gomorrah \Guh-*more*-uh\
A town by the Dead Sea that was destroyed by God (Genesis 19:24, 25).

Goshen *Go*-shen\\
1. A fertile region located in the land of Egypt where Jacob and his sons and their flocks came to live at Joseph's request (Genesis 46, 47).
2. The territory between Gaza and Gibeon in south Palestine (Joshua 10:41).
3. A town in Judah (Joshua 15:51).

Gozan *Go*-zan\\
1. One of the lands conquered by the Assyrians before the fall of Samaria (2 Kings 19:12).
2. A river that runs through the land of Gozan (2 Kings 17:6; 18:11; 1 Chronicles 5:26).

Graeco *Greck*-owe\\
Related to Greece or Greek culture, as in the Graeco-Roman world.

Grecians *Gree*-shunz\\
Greek or Greek-speaking peoples (Acts 6:1).

gune *(Greek)* \\goo-*nay*\\
Greek for "woman." It is also the word for "wife," leaving some confusion among Bible students as to whether 1 Timothy 3:11 speaks of wives of deacons or women servants who filled a role similar to deacons.

Hh

Habakkuk \\Huh-*back*-kuk\\
1. Prophet to Judah and author the Old Testament book of Habakkuk.
2. The 35th book of the Old Testament, the eighth in the "minor prophets" section. See Books of the Bible Chart.

Habaziniah \\Hab-uh-zi-*nye*-uh\\ (Also spelled Habazziniah.)
An ancestor of the Rechabites (or Recabites) in Jeremiah's time (Jeremiah 35:3).

habergeon *hab*-er-jun\\ (Also spelled habergeons.)
Used five times in the *King James Version* to translate two different Hebrew words. One refers to a soldier's armor (2 Chronicles 26:14; Nehemiah 4:16) or possibly a weapon (Job 41:26). The other refers to part of a priest's garments (Exodus 28:32; 39:23).

Habor *Hay*-bor\\
A city or region near the river Gozan to which the Assyrians deported the Israelites (2 Kings 17:6; 18:11; 1 Chronicles 5:26).

Hachaliah \\Hack-uh-*lye*-uh\\
The father of Nehemiah (Nehemiah 1:1).

Hachilah \\Hah-*kye*-lah\\ (Also spelled Hakilah.)
One of David's hideouts in southern Judah when he was hiding from Saul (1 Samuel 23:19; 26:1).

Hadad *Hay*-dad\\ (Also spelled Hadar.)
1. A son of Ishmael and grandson of Abraham (Genesis 25:15, *NIV, NASB*; 1 Chronicles 1:30).
2. King of Edom, son of Bedad, who defeated the Midianites (Genesis 36:35; 1 Chronicles 1:46).
3. King of Edom, successor to Baalhanan (Genesis 36:39, *NIV, NLT*; 1 Chronicles 1:50.)
4. An Edomite prince whose father David defeated; he became an adversary to Solomon (1 Kings 11:14-25).

Hadar *Hay*-dar\\ (Another version of the name Hadad.)
1. A son of Ishmael and grandson of Abraham (Genesis 25:15, *KJV, NKJV*).
2. King of Edom, successor to Baalhanan (Genesis 36:39, *KJV, NASB*).

Hadassah \\Huh-*das*-suh\\
The Hebrew name of Queen Esther (Esther 2:7).

Hades *Hay*-deez\\
A Greek translation of the Hebrew word *Sheol* meaning "death," "the grave," or "Hell" (Matthew 11:23; 16:18; Luke 16:23; Revelation 1:18).

Hadoram \\Huh-*doe*-rum\\
1. Son of Tou, king of Hamath, who was sent to congratulate David on his victory over Hadadezer of Zobah (1 Chronicles 18:10). See also Joram, #3.
2. A prominent overseer of labor during the reigns of David, Solomon, and Rehoboam (2 Chronicles 10:18). See Adoniram.

Hagar *Hay*-gar\\
An Egyptian handmaid of Sarah; mother of Ishmael (Genesis 16:1-16; 21:9-21).

Haggai *Hag*-eye\\ or *Hag*-ay-eye\\
1. Prophet and author of the Old Testament book of Haggai; he encouraged the former Jewish exiles to return to the task of rebuilding of the temple.
2. The 37th book of the Old Testament, the tenth in the "minor prophets" section. See Books of the Bible Chart.

Hai *Hay*-eye\\
Alternate spelling of Ai. See Ai.

Gg
Hh

Halah *Hay*-luh\\

A city or region near the river Gozan to which the Assyrians deported the Israelites (2 Kings 17:6; 18:11; 1 Chronicles 5:26).

Halak *Hay*-lak\\

Mountain in western Arabah marking the boundary of Joshua's conquered territory (Joshua 11:17; 12:7).

Haman *Hay*-mun\\

The official in the Persian court of Xerxes (Ahasuerus) who attempted to exterminate the Jews (Esther 3:4-15).

Hh

Hamath *Hay*-muth\\

A city in Syria by the Orontes River; its king sent greetings to David when David had defeated its long-time enemy Hadadezer (2 Samuel 8:9, 10).

Hammedatha \\Ham-med-*day*-thuh\\

Father of Haman the Agagite in the book of Esther (Esther 3:1).

Hammelech *Ham*-uh-lek\\

Father of Jerahmeel (Jeremiah 36:26). Some take it to be a common noun meaning "the king."

Hammurabi *Ham*-muh-*rah*-bee\\ (strong accent on *rah*)

A Babylonian king who devised the Law of Hammurabi for his kingdom.

Hamram *Ham*-ram\\

See AMRAM.

Hamutal \\Ha-*mu*-tal\\

A wife of King Josiah; mother of Jehoahaz and Zedekiah (2 Kings 23:31; 24:18; Jeremiah 52:1).

Hanameel *Han*-uh-meel\\ (Also spelled Hanamel.)

Owned a field in Anathoth that Jeremiah purchased to encourage Jews to believe that God would restore them to their land after the Babylonian exile (Jeremiah 32:7-12).

Hanan *Hay*-nuhn\\

1. Son of Azel from the tribe of Benjamin (1 Chronicles 8:38; 9:44).
2. Son of Maacah and one of David's mighty men (1 Chronicles 11:43).
3. A temple worker who returned to Judah with Zerubbabel (Ezra 2:46; Nehemiah 7:49; 8:7).
4. Name of three of those who sealed the covenant with Nehemiah (Nehemiah 10:10, 22, 26).
5. Jeremiah met with the Rechabites in the chamber of the sons of Hanan in the temple (Jeremiah 35:4).

Hanani \\Huh-*nay*-nye\\

1. Heman's son and musician in the temple during David's time (1 Chronicles 25:4, 25).
2. A prophet who was imprisoned for rebuking King Asa for making a foreign alliance instead of trusting the Lord (2 Chronicles 16:7-10).
3. A priest guilty of marrying a foreign woman (Ezra 10:20).
4. Brother of Nehemiah who informed Nehemiah of the condition of post-exilic Jerusalem; he was given a post of leadership in Nehemiah's administration (Nehemiah 1:2; 7:2).
5. A priestly musician during the dedication of the temple (Nehemiah 12:36).

Hananiah \\Han-uh-*nye*-uh\\

1. Heman's son and leader of a division of temple musicians (1 Chronicles 25:4, 23).
2. A commander in King Uzziah's army (2 Chronicles 26:11).
3. Father of Zedekiah, who was an official to King Jehoiakim (Jeremiah 36:12).
4. Grandfather of Irijah, who arrested Jeremiah (Jeremiah 37:13).
5. A false prophet in the days of Zedekiah (Jeremiah 28).
6. Father of a house of Benjamin in Jerusalem (1 Chronicles 8:24).
7. The Hebrew name of Shadrach; a companion of Daniel in Babylon (Daniel 1:6, 7).
8. One of Zerubbabel's sons (1 Chronicles 3:19, 21).
9. A priest guilty of marrying a foreign woman (Ezra 10:28).
10. A perfume maker who helped repair the wall of Jerusalem during Nehemiah's time (Nehemiah 3:8).
11. Another repairer of the wall of Jerusalem (Nehemiah 3:30).
12. A godly man in Jerusalem whom Nehemiah put in a position of leadership (Nehemiah 7:2).
13. A leader who sealed the agreement of Ezra (Nehemiah 10:23).
14. A head of a priestly family in the days of Jehoiakim (Nehemiah 12:12, 41).

Hannah *Han*-uh\\

Mother of Samuel (1 Samuel 1:1–2:21).

Hanukkah *Hahn*-uh-kuh\\

A Jewish festival that celebrates the rededication of the temple by Judas Maccabeus.

Haran *Hair*-un\\

1. Abraham's youngest brother and the father of Lot (Genesis 11:27, 28).
2. Caleb's son by his concubine, Ephah (1 Chronicles 2:46).

3. A Levite of the Gershonites, son of Shimei (1 Chronicles 23:9).

4. A city in Mesopotamia where Abraham lived until God called him out (Genesis 12:1-4). (Also spelled Charran.)

Harhas *Har*-haz\\
The grandfather-in-law of Huldah the prophetess (2 Kings 22:14; spelled Hasrah in 2 Chronicles 34:22).

Harod *Hay*-rod\\
A spring southeast of Jezreel near Mt. Gilboa where Gideon and his army camped before their defeat of the Midianites (Judges 7:1).

Harosheth \\Huh-*roe*-sheth\\
A place where Jabin's army of Canaan was defeated by Deborah and Barak's army (Judges 4:2, 13, 16).

Hashbadana \\Hash-*bad*-uh-nuh\\ (Also spelled Hashbaddanah.)
One of the Levites who stood at Ezra's left as he read the Law (Nehemiah 8:4).

Hashum *Hay*-shum\\
1. A family who returned with Zerubbabel from exile (Ezra 2:19; 10:33; Nehemiah 7:22).

2. One of the Levites who stood at Ezra's left as he read the Law (Nehemiah 8:4).

Hasidim \\Haz-sid-*theem*\\ (*th* as in *the*)
A Hebrew word meaning "the pious ones," it refers to a group of Jews who arose in the time of the Maccabees to resist the Greeks and to preserve strict adherence to the heritage of Judaism. Probably this group became the Pharisees.

Hatach *Hay*-tak\\ (Also spelled Hathach.)
A eunuch appointed to Esther who brought warning to her of Haman's plot (Esther 4:5-10).

Havilah *Hav*-ih-law\\
1. Pre-Noahic region through which the Pishon River, one of the four rivers of Eden, flowed. It may or may not be the same as the later Havilah, as the flood doubtless altered world geography.

2. Son of Cush and grandson of Ham (Genesis 10:7).

3. Son of Joktan, descendant of Shem (Genesis 10:29).

4. A region in Arabia, near Egypt (Genesis 25:18; 1 Samuel 15:7).

Havothjair *Hav*-oth-*jay*-ir\\ (strong accent on *jay*)
See HAVVOTH JAIR (Numbers 32:41; Judges 10:4, *KJV*).

Havvoth Jair *Hav*-oth *Jay*-ir\\ (strong accent on *Jay*)
(Also spelled Havothjair or Havvoth-jair.)
Literally, settlements of Jair, a group of cities or towns

under the control of Jair (Numbers 32:41; Judges 10:4; 1 Chronicles 2:22, 23). See JAIR.

Hazael *Haz*-zay-el\\
Became king of Syria (or Aram) by murdering Ben-Hadad (2 Kings 8:7-15).

Hazor *Hay*-zor\\
1. An important Palestinian town in the days of Joshua (Joshua 11:1, 10).

2. A town of southern Judah mentioned only in Joshua 15:23.

3. Another town in southern Judah named Hazor Hadattah meaning "New Hazor" (Joshua 15:25).

4. A city in northern Judah inhabited by Benjamites (Nehemiah 11:33).

5. A town in the Arabian Desert that Jeremiah prophesied against (Jeremiah 49:28-33).

heathen *He*-thun\\ (*th* as in *this*)
Pagan. The word is used nearly 150 times in the *King James Version,* but rarely in other translations. It refers to the Gentiles, usually with particular emphasis on their idolatry. The one use in the *New International Version* is 1 Thessalonians 4:5, where the emphasis is on their not knowing God. *The New Living Translation* uses the term only in Acts 7:51, where other translations have *uncircumcised.*

Heber *Hee*-ber\\
1. Jacob's great-grandson through Asher and Beriah (Genesis 46:17).

2. Husband of Jael, the woman who killed Sisera (Judges 4:11-21).

3. A son of Ezra of the tribe of Judah (1 Chronicles 4:18).

4. A son of Elpaal, from the tribe of Benjamin (1 Chronicles 8:17).

5. The head of a family in Gad (1 Chronicles 5:13).

Hebrew *Hee*-brew\\
1. A descendant of Eber, specifically of Abraham (Genesis 11.)

2. The Hebrew language; the language of the Old Testament other than some passages found in Ezra and Daniel and a verse in Jeremiah 10:11.

3. The language commonly spoken by Hebrew or Jewish people. In the New Testament, this may refer to what we today call Aramaic instead of Hebrew (John 5:2; 19:13, 17, 20; Acts 21:40; 22:2).

Hebrews *Hee*-brews\\
1. Descendants of Eber, particularly of Abraham, Isaac, and Jacob; Jews.

2. The 19th book of the New Testament, first of the general epistles; a letter written to Christian Jews. Traditionally ascribed to Paul. See BOOKS OF THE BIBLE CHART.

Hh

Hebron \Hee-brun\ or \Heb-run\
1. City in the hill country of Judah near where Abraham buried his wife Sarah (Genesis 23:17-20). It was David's first headquarters when Judah made him king after the death of Saul (2 Samuel 5:5).
2. Son of Kohath and uncle of Moses, Aaron, and Miriam (Exodus 6:18).
3. A town in Asher (Joshua 19:28, *KJV*).
4. A relative of Caleb, son of Hezron (1 Chronicles 2:42, 43).

Hemdan \Hem-dan\
See AMRAM.

henotheism \heh-nuh-thee-ih-zum\ (*th* as in *thin*)
The belief in many gods but worship of only one.

Hephzibah \Hef-zih-bah\
1. Mother of Manasseh and wife of King Hezekiah (2 Kings 21:1).
2. A symbolic name for the restored city of Zion (Isaiah 62:4).

Herculaneum \Her-cue-lay-nee-um\
A city in southern Italy that was destroyed by the eruption of Mt. Vesuvius in AD 79.

Hercules \Her-cue-leez\
Heroic warrior of Greek mythology, supposedly the son of the god Zeus and the mortal Alcmene.

heresy \hair-uh-see\
False doctrine; a deliberate perversion of truth.

Hermes \Her-meez\ (Also called Mercury.)
1. The messenger god of Greek mythology. The people of Lystra thought Paul was this god in human form (Acts 14:11, 12; Mercurius, *KJV*).
2. A man to whom Paul sent greeting (Romans 16:14).

Hermon \Her-mun\
Mountain in northern Israel (Deuteronomy 3:8), probably the "high mountain" on which the transfiguration took place (Mark 9:2).

Hermonites \Her-mun-ites\
A reference to the peaks of Mt. Hermon (Psalm 42:6, *KJV*).

Herod \Hair-ud\
1. Herod the Great, the king who ordered the deaths of the babies in Bethlehem (Matthew 2).
2. Herod Archelaus, son of Herod the Great who ruled in Judea after Herod's death (Matthew 2:22).
3. Herod Antipas, or Herod the tetrarch, another son of Herod the Great; the king who beheaded John the Baptist (Matthew 14:1-12).

4. Herod Phillip, another son of Herod the Great; his wife Herodias married Herod Antipas (Matthew 14:3, 4).
5. Herod Agrippa I, grandson of Herod the Great; the king who had James executed (Acts 12:1).
6. Herod Agrippa II, son of Agrippa I; he heard Paul's case in Caesarea (Acts 25:13–26:32).

Herodians \Heh-roe-dee-unz\
Jews who supported the Herodian dynasty under Roman occupation (Matthew 22:16; Mark 3:6; 12:13).

Herodias \Heh-roe-dee-us\
Wife of Herod Philip and then of Herod Antipas; she had John the Baptist killed (Mark 6:14-29).

Herodotus \Heh-rod-uh-tus\
Greek historian (485–425 BC).

hesed *(Hebrew)* \hess-ed\
Hebrew for "kindness" or "lovingkindness."

Hezekiah \Hez-ih-kye-uh\
Twelfth king of Judah, son of Ahaz (2 Kings 18:1–20:21). Hezekiah was a righteous king, but his son Manasseh was very wicked. Hezekiah was king of Judah when Samaria (Israel) fell to Assyria. See KINGS OF ISRAEL AND JUDAH CHART.

Hezron \Hezz-ron\
1. One of Judah's grandsons through Perez (or Pharez) (Genesis 46:12).
2. A son of Reuben (Genesis 46:9).
3. A place on Judah's southern border (Joshua 15:3).

Hiddekel \Hid-eh-kell\
Ancient name for the Tigris River.
1. One of the four rivers that flowed through Eden (Genesis 2:14 *KJV, ASV, NKJV*). It may or may not have been at or near the same location as the modern Tigris as the flood doubtless altered world geography.
2. River in Mesopotamia (Daniel 10:4 *KJV, ASV*); the same as the modern Tigris.

Hierapolis \Hi-er-ap-o-lis\
A city of Asia Minor, 12 miles north of Colosse (Colossians 4:12, 13).

high place \hye plase\
A site with an altar for making sacrifices. Pagan high places abounded in Canaan, and the Israelites were told to destroy them (Numbers 33:52). Still the practice of worshiping at these places continued, with sacrifices made to pagan gods and to the true God at these sites (1 Kings 3:2-4; 11:7; 12:31, 32).

Hilkiah \Hill-*kye*-uh\
1. Father of Eliakim, who managed Hezekiah's household (2 Kings 18:18).
2. A Merarite Levite (1 Chronicles 6:45).
3. A gatekeeper under David (1 Chronicles 26:11).
4. A high priest who found the book of the Law during Josiah's repair of the temple (2 Kings 22; 2 Chronicles 34).
5. A priest who returned with Zerubbabel to Jerusalem (Nehemiah 12:7).
6. Prophet Jeremiah's father (Jeremiah 1:1).

Hillel *Hill*-el\
The father of the judge Abdon (Judges 12:13, 15).

Hinnom *Hin*-um\
A deep valley south of Jerusalem (Joshua 15:8; 18:16). See Gehenna.

Hiram *High*-rum\ (Also spelled Huram or Huram-Abi.)
1. The king of Tyre who was friends with King David and Solomon; he provided materials and labor for building David's house and the temple (2 Samuel 5:11; 1 Kings 5:10-18; 2 Chronicles 2:3, 11, 12).
2. A brass worker who helped build the temple (1 Kings 7:13, 14; 2 Chronicles 2:13, 14.)

Hittites *Hit*-ites\ or *Hit*-tites\
Canaanite tribe (Genesis 15:20); one of the nations conquered by Joshua (Joshua 24:11). The seller of the field and cave Abraham bought as a burial site was a Hittite (Genesis 23:3-18).

Hivites *Hi*-vites\
A Canaanite tribe; one of the nations conquered by Joshua (Joshua 24:11).

Hobab *Hoe*-bab\
1. Son of Reuel, Moses' father-in-law, whom Moses asked to be as guide to the Israelites in the wilderness (Numbers 10:29-31). As son of Reuel, he would have been Moses' brother-in-law.
2. Judges 4:11 in most versions gives this name as another name for Moses' father-in-law (otherwise called Reuel or Jethro). But the *New International Version* and the *New Living Translation* use the term *brother-in-law* in this passage, identifying him as the same Hobab as #1.

Hodijah \Ho-*dye*-juh\ (Also spelled Hodiah.)
1. A member of the tribe of Judah (1 Chronicles 4:19).
2. A Levite who taught the Israelites as Ezra read the Law (Nehemiah 8:7; 9:5).
3. Three by this name are mentioned in the list of leaders of the former exiles in Nehemiah's day (Nehemiah 10:10, 13, 18).

Holy Ghost *Hoe*-lee Goast\
See Holy Spirit.

Holy of Holies *Hoe*-lee uv *Hoe*-leez\
See Most Holy Place.

Holy Place *Hoe*-lee Plase\
A room in the tabernacle/temple in which were the altar of incense, the lampstand, and the table of showbread (Exodus 26:33, 34; Hebrews 9:2).

Holy Spirit *Hoe*-lee *Spear*-ut\
A manifestation of God, equal with God the Father and God the Son. Sometimes called simply "the Spirit," He empowered the apostles and others to do miracles (Acts 1:8) and indwells each believer (Acts 2:38). Characteristics such as love, joy, and peace are the fruit of the Spirit (Galatians 5:22, 23).

Hophni *Hoff*-nye\
One of the two wicked sons of Eli the high priest (1 Samuel 1:3; 2:34; 4:4, 17).

Horeb *Ho*-reb\
Another name for Mt. Sinai (Exodus 3:1; 17:6; 33:6).

Horonaim \Hor-oh-*nay*-im\ (strong accent on *nay*)
A place in Moab south of the Arnon River (Isaiah 15:5; Jeremiah 48:3, 5, 34).

Horonite \Hor-oh-*night*\
A native or resident of Horonaim or of Beth-horon. Sanballat, who opposed Nehemiah, was a Horonite (Nehemiah 2:10, 19; 13:28).

Hosea \Ho-*zay*-uh\
1. A prophet of the northern kingdom of Israel who wrote the book of Hosea.
2. The 28th book of the Old Testament, first in the "minor prophets" section. See Books of the Bible Chart.

Hoshea \Ho-*shay*-uh\
1. Son of Elah, he murdered King Pekah to become the nineteenth king of Israel (2 Kings 15:30). He would be the last: when the Assyrians learned he was plotting with the Egyptians, they invaded Israel and arrested Hoshea, besieged and captured Samaria, and deported the Israelites (2 Kings 17:1-6; 18:9, 10). See Kings of Israel and Judah Chart.
2. The original name of Joshua before Moses renamed him (Numbers 13:8, 16; *KJV* has "Oshea"). This slight spelling change has an enormous change in meaning. *Hoshea* simply means "salvation," but *Joshua* means "Yahweh is salvation."

Hh

3. Son of Azaziah and an officer of the Ephraimites (1 Chronicles 27:20).

4. A leader who worked with Nehemiah (Nehemiah 10:23).

Huldah *Hul*-duh\\

A prophetess who verified the authenticity of the book of the Law when it was found in the temple cleanup during the reign of Josiah (2 Kings 22:14-20; 2 Chronicles 34:22-28).

Huram *Hoo*-rum\\

See HIRAM.

Hushai *Hoo*-shy\\

A trusted adviser of King David; when Absalom tried to take the throne, David sent Hushai back to Jerusalem to pretend to support Absalom while working instead to frustrate the usurper's plans (2 Samuel 15:32, 37; 16:16—17:16).

Hymenaeus \\Hi-meh-*nee*-us\\

A false teacher whom Paul had to excommunicate (1 Timothy 1:19, 20; 2 Timothy 2:16-18).

hyssop *hiss*-up\\

A reed plant that could be used as a brush (Exodus 12:22; Leviticus 14:4; Hebrews 9:19). It apparently could have a stem some three feet or so in length, as it was used to lift a sponge to Jesus' mouth when He was on the cross (John 19:29).

Hystaspes \\Hiss-*tas*-pus\\

Surname for a king, meaning "the Great." The King Darius of Haggai 1:1 was Darius Hystaspes (522–486 BC).

Ii

Ichabod *Ik*-uh-bod\\ or *Ike*-uh-bod\\

Son of Phinehas; Phinehas's wife named their son *Ichabod*, meaning "no glory," when her husband died in the battle in which the Philistines took the ark of the covenant (1 Samuel 4:19-22).

Iconium \\Eye-*ko*-nee-um\\

A Roman city that was along two trade routes to Ephesus and Rome. Paul and Barnabas visited the city on their first missionary journey (Acts 13:51).

Iddo *Id*-do\\

1. Father of Ahinadab, one of Solomon's 12 governors of Israel (1 Kings 4:14).

2. A Gershonite of the tribe of Levi (1 Chronicles 6:21).

3. A son of Zechariah and a leader of the tribe Manasseh (1 Chronicles 27:21).

4. A prophet who recorded details of Solomon's reign in a book of visions concerning Jeroboam (2 Chronicles 9:29).

5. Grandfather of the prophet Zechariah (Zechariah 1:7). "Son" is used in a more general sense of "descendant" in Ezra 5:1; 6:14. (Or some believe the prophet was raised by his grandfather.)

6. An official in Babylon who granted Ezra's request for temple servants in Jerusalem (Ezra 8:17).

Idumaea \\Id-you-*me*-uh\\ (Also Idumea.)

Another name for the country of Edom (Mark 3:8).

Idumean \\Id-you-*me*-un\\

A native or resident of Idumea (or Idumaea); Herod the Great was an Idumean.

Igdaliah \\Ig-duh-*lye*-uh\\

The prophet Hanan's father (Jeremiah 35:4). See HANAN, #5.

Ignatius \\Ig-*nay*-shus\\

Second-century church father, bishop of Antioch. He died a martyr's death in the Roman Coliseum.

Illyricum \\Il-*lear*-i-kum\\

Country to the north and west of Macedonia, on the eastern shores of the Adriatic Sea; modern Albania (Romans 15:19).

Imlah *Im*-luh\\

Father of the prophet Micaiah (1 Kings 22:8, 9; 2 Chronicles 18:8, *KJV* "Imla").

Immanuel *(Hebrew)* \\Ih-*man*-you-el\\ (Also spelled Emmanuel.)

A Hebrew name meaning "God with us" (Isaiah 7:14; 8:8; Matthew 1:23).

iniquities \\in-*ik*-wu-teez\\

Sins (Isaiah 53:5; 59:2; Psalm 79:8).

Irenaeus *I*-ree-*nee*-us\\ (strong accent on *nee*)

Second-century church father, bishop of Lyons in southern France, author of *Against Heresies*.

Irijah \\I-*rye*-juh\\

A guard who arrested the prophet Jeremiah (Jeremiah 37:13, 14).

Isaac *Eye*-zuk\\

Only son of Abraham and Sarah; one of 3 forefathers of Israel along with Abraham and Jacob (Genesis 21).

Isaiah \Eye-*zay*-uh\ (Sometimes spelled Esaias.)
  1. Son of Amoz; this prophet wrote the Old Testament book that bears his name.
  2. The 23rd book of the Old Testament, first in the "major prophets" section. It foretells the coming of Jesus and is quoted more times in the New Testament than all other prophetic books combined. See Books of the Bible Chart.

Iscah *Is*-ka\
  Abraham's niece, daughter of Haran and sister of Milcah and Lot (Genesis 11:29, 31).

Iscariot \Iss-*care*-e-ut\
  Surname of Judas, the disciple who betrayed Jesus to the Jewish leaders (Matthew 10:4). See Kerioth.

ish *(Hebrew)* \ish\
  "Man" in the generic sense, as in mankind (Genesis 2:23).

Ishbosheth \Ish-*bo*-sheth\ (Also spelled Ish-Bosheth.)
  Saul's son who rivaled David to become king of Israel (2 Samuel 2–4). Called Eshbaal, or Esh-Baal, in 1 Chronicles 8:33; 9:39.

Ishi \Ish-*eye*\ or *Ish*-eye\
  1. "My husband," the name God promised the Israelites would call Him when He restored them (Hosea 2:16, *KJV*). Used in contrast to *Baali* ("my lord"), which is too much like the pagan name *Baal.*
  2. The term appears as the name of four different men in 1 Chronicles 2:31; 4:20, 42; 5:24. Nothing is known of them except what is in these immediate contexts.

Ishmael *Ish*-may-el\
  1. Abraham's son by Sarah's handmaid, Hagar (Genesis 16:15, 16).
  2. A son of Azel; a descendant of Saul (1 Chronicles 8:38; 9:44).
  3. Father of Zebediah, a man of Judah who served in the court of King Jehoshaphat (2 Chronicles 19:11).
  4. A son of Jehohanan; he teamed with the high priest Jehoiada to oust Athaliah and put Joash on the throne of Judah (2 Chronicles 23:1).
  5. A man from the royal line who assassinated Gedaliah, whom Nebuchadnezzar had appointed governor of Judah (2 Kings 25:25; Jeremiah 40:7–41:18).
  6. Son of Pashhur; he had married a foreign wife, whom Ezra forced him to put away (Ezra 10:22).

Ishmaelites *Ish*-may-el-ites\ (Also spelled Ishmeelites.)
  Descendants of Ishmael, son of Abraham and Hagar; a band of Ishmaelites bought Joseph from his brothers and sold him in Egypt (Genesis 37:25-28; 39:1). The term seems synonymous with Midianites (Genesis 37:28).

ishshah *(Hebrew)* \ish-*shaw*\
  "Woman," the generic name of all the female members of humanity (Genesis 2:23). The feminine suffix added to the word for man, *ish,* results in *ishshah,* "woman."

Ishtar *Ish*-tar\
  Babylonian goddess of love and fertility. Biblical references to the "queen of Heaven" are probably references to this goddess (Jeremiah 7:18; 44:17-19, 25).

Ishvi *Ish*-vye\ (Also spelled Ishui, Isui, Ishuai, and Jesui. Ishvi is never found in the *King James Version*, but each of the others spellings is.)
  1. Son of Asher (Genesis 46:17; Numbers 26:44; 1 Chronicles 7:30).
  2. A son of King Saul, apparently the same as Abinadab (compare 1 Samuel 14:49 with 31:2).

Isis *Eye*-sis\
  Nature goddess of Egyptian mythology.

Israel *Iz*-ray-el\
  A name given to Jacob and to the nation his descendants became (Genesis 32:28, 32). Also the name given to the northern tribes after the nation was divided into two kingdoms (1 Kings 12:19-21).

Israelites *Iz*-ray-el-ites\
  Descendants of Jacob, also known as Israel; citizens of the nation of Israel.

Issachar *Izz*-uh-kar\
  1. The ninth son of Jacob; the fifth by Leah (Genesis 30:17, 18; 35:23).
  2. One of the 12 tribes of Israel.
  3. Territory allotted to the tribe of Issachar.
  4. A Korahite doorkeeper during David's reign (1 Chronicles 26:5).

Ithamar *Ith*-uh-mar\
  The fourth son of Aaron (Exodus 28:1) and ancestor of Eli (1 Chronicles 24:4-6; Ezra 8:2).

Iturea \It-you-*ree*-uh\
  The territory northeast of Palestine that was named for Jetur, Ishmael's son. (Genesis 25:15). It was a part of the tetrarchy of Philip (Luke 3:1).

Iyyar \Ee-*yar*\ (Also spelled Iyar.)
  Second month on the Jewish calendar, roughly equivalent to April–May. Called Ziv before the exile. See Calendar Chart.

Izmir *Izz*-meer\
  Modern city at the site of the ancient city of Smyrna.

Ii

Jj

Jaazaniah \Jay-ah-zuh-*nye*-uh\ (Also spelled Jezaniah.)
1. An officer of the army of Judah who supported Gedaliah (2 Kings 25:23, Jeremiah 40:8).
2. A Rechabite who would not drink wine offered by Jeremiah (Jeremiah 35:1-11).
3. A son of Shaphan; Ezekiel saw a vision of Jaazaniah worshiping idols in the temple among Israel's idols (Ezekiel 8:10-12).
4. Son of Azzur; an evil leader in Israel (Ezekiel 11:1, 2).

Jabbok *Jab*-uck\
A river that flows from Gilead into the Jordan; it was the boundary between the tribe of Gad and the land of Ammon and the site where Israel defeated Og of Bashan (Numbers 21:24; Deuteronomy 3:16; Joshua 12). Peniel, the site where Jacob wrestled with the angel, is near this river (Genesis 32:22-32).

Jabesh *Jay*-besh\
1. Father of Shallum, who killed Zechariah (or Zachariah) and ruled Israel for a month (2 Kings 15:8-13).
2. Short for Jabesh Gilead (1 Chronicles 10:12).

Jabesh Gilead *Jay*-besh-*gil*-ee-ud\ (strong accent on *gil*; *g* as in *get*) (Also spelled Jabeshgilead.)
A town in Gilead that Saul rescued from an Ammonite attack (1 Samuel 11); the people of this town gave Saul and his sons a proper burial (1 Samuel 31:11-13; 1 Chronicles 10:11, 12).

Jabez *Jay*-bez\
1. City where some clans of scribes of the tribe of Judah lived (1 Chronicles 2:55).
2. A man of the tribe of Judah who was more honorable than his brothers (1 Chronicles 4:9, 10).

Jabin \Jay-bin\
1. King of Hazor, who led an attack against Joshua but was defeated (Joshua 11:1-10).
2. A Canaanite king who joined Sisera in making war against Israel but was defeated (Judges 4).

jacinth *jay*-sinth\
A precious stone of the same color as the hyacinth; it is found in the high priest's breastplate (Exodus 28:19; ligure, *KJV*) and in the foundation of the New Jerusalem (Revelation 21:20).

Jacob *Jay*-kub\
Son of Isaac and Rebekah, younger brother of twin Esau (Genesis 25:19-28). He later became known as Israel (Genesis 32:22-32), and the nation of Israel is named for him.

Jael *Jay*-ul\
The Kenite woman who killed Sisera (Judges 4:17-22).

Jahaziel \Juh-*hay*-zih-el\
1. A Levite, son of Zechariah, who prophesied success for Jehoshaphat in the battle with the Moabites and Ammonites (2 Chronicles 20:14-17).
2. One of the Benjamite warriors who joined David at Ziklag (1 Chronicles 12:1-4)
3. A priest charged with blowing the trumpet before the ark of the covenant after David had brought it into Jerusalem (1 Chronicles 16:6).
4. Son of Hebron; one of the Kohathite Levites in service at the sanctuary at the time David passed the kingdom to Solomon (1 Chronicles 23:1-6, 19; 24:23).
5. Father of Shecaniah, a leader among those who returned to Jerusalem from the exile (Ezra 8:5).

Jair *Jay*-er\
1. A son of Segub, of the tribe of Judah (1 Chronicles 2:22, 23) but reckoned a descendant of Manasseh (Numbers 32:41) through his mother. He and his sons controlled several towns or cities in Gilead, which came to be known as Havvoth Jair, or the settlements of Jair (Deuteronomy 3:14; Joshua 13:30). See Havvoth Jair.
2. A Gileadite, and possibly a descendant of the Jair named above, who became a judge of Israel after Tola (Judges 10:3-5). He also controlled several towns, which he put under the rule of his sons, that were called Havvoth Jair. See Judges of Israel Chart.
3. Father of the warrior Elhanan (1 Chronicles 20:5).
4. Father of Mordecai (Esther 2:5).

Jairus *Jye*-rus\ or *Jay*-ih-rus\
A synagogue ruler whose daughter Jesus raised from the dead (Mark 5:22-43; Luke 8:41-56).

Jakeh *Jay*-keh\
Father of Agur, author of Proverbs 30 (Proverbs 30:1).

James \Jaymz\
1. Son of Zebedee and brother of John; one of the first of Jesus' disciples called to follow Jesus (Matthew 4:21; 10:2). He was the first of the apostles to be killed (Acts 12:1, 2).
2. Son of Alpheus; another of Jesus' 12 disciples (Matthew 10:3). Also called James the Less or James the Younger (Mark 15:40).
3. A half-brother of Jesus (son of Joseph and Mary) who became a leader of the Jerusalem church and wrote the book of James (Matthew 13:55; Mark 6:3; Acts 12:17; 15:13; Galatians 2:9; James 1:1).
4. Father (or brother) of Judas (not Judas Iscariot), one of Jesus apostles (Luke 6:16; Acts 1:13).

5. The 20th book of the New Testament, second of the general epistles; written by James the brother of Jesus. See BOOKS OF THE BIBLE CHART.

Jamin *Jay*-min\\
1. A son of Simeon (Genesis 46:10; 1 Chronicles 4:24).
2. A son of Ram, of the tribe of Judah (1 Chronicles 2:27).
3. One of the men who taught the Israelites as Ezra read the Law (Nehemiah 8:7).

Jannaeus \\Jan-*nee*-us\\
Alexander Jannaeus, one of the Maccabean rulers (103–76 BC).

Japheth *Jay*-feth\\
One of Noah's three sons (Genesis 5:32; 7:13; 9:18, 23, 27; 10:1-5; 1 Chronicles 1:4-6).

Jasher *Jay*-sher\\ (Also spelled Jashar.)
A book of Hebrew history and literature; mentioned in Joshua 10:13 and in 2 Samuel 1:18.

jasper *jass*-per\\
A quartz gemstone of any of several colors. It appears in the high priest's breastplate (Exodus 28:20; 39:13) and in the foundation of the New Jerusalem (Revelation 21:19).

Jebus *Jee*-bus\\
The name of the city of Jerusalem before David captured it from the Jebusites (Judges 19:10, 11; 1 Chronicles 11:4).

Jebusites *Jeb*-yuh-sites\\
Inhabitants of Jebus (i.e., Jerusalem) (2 Samuel 5:6-10).

Jecholiah \\Jek-o-*lye*-uh\\ (Also spelled Jecoliah.)
Mother of King Uzziah (2 Kings 15:2; 2 Chronicles 26:3).

Jeconiah *Jek*-o-*nye*-uh\\ (strong accent on *nye*)
Another name for King Jehoiachin of Judah (1 Chronicles 3:16, 17; Jeremiah 24:1). See JEHOIACHIN.

Jedidah \\Jee-*dye*-duh\\
Mother of King Josiah (2 Kings 22:1).

Jedidiah \\Jed-ih-*die*-uh\\
A name given to Solomon by God through the prophet Nathan at birth (2 Samuel 12:24, 25).

Jeduthun \\Jeh-*doo*-thun\\
Father of a family of priestly musicians during David's reign (1 Chronicles 16:41, 42; 25:1). His descendants were musicians in Nehemiah's time (Nehemiah 11:17).

Jehoaddan \\Jee-*ho*-ud-dan\\ (Also spelled Jehoaddin.)
King Joash's wife and mother of Amaziah (2 Chronicles 25:1).

Jehoahaz \\Jeh-*ho*-uh-haz\\
1. Son of Jehu; the eleventh king of Israel. He followed in the ways of Jeroboam (i.e., idolatry), but even so, when he asked the Lord for help, the nation was delivered from the oppression of Hazael (2 Kings 13:1-8). See KINGS OF ISRAEL AND JUDAH CHART.
2. Sixteenth king of Judah, son and successor to Josiah; he reigned but three months before Pharaoh Neco took him in chains to Egypt (2 Kings 23:30-35). See KINGS OF ISRAEL AND JUDAH CHART.
3. Another name for Ahaziah, son of Jehoram, sixth king of Judah (compare 2 Chronicles 21:17 with 22:1—except *NIV*, for which see footnote at 2 Chronicles 21:17). See AHAZIAH.

Jehoash \\Jeh-*hoe*-ash\\ (Also spelled Joash.)
1. Seventh king of Judah, son of Ahaziah; as an infant, he was saved from Athaliah's murder of the royal line (2 Kings 11–13; 2 Chronicles 24, 25). See KINGS OF ISRAEL AND JUDAH CHART.
2. Twelfth king of Israel, son of Jehoahaz; another of the kings who led the people in idolatry (2 Kings 13:10-13). See KINGS OF ISRAEL AND JUDAH CHART.

Jehoiachin \\Jeh-*hoy*-uh-kin\\ (Also known as Coniah and Jeconiah.)
Eighteenth king of Judah; he reigned for 3 months and 10 days and then was taken as a prisoner to Babylon (2 Chronicles 36:9).

Jehoiada \\Jee-*hoy*-uh-duh\\
1. Father of Benaiah, one of David's most trusted warriors (2 Samuel 20:23; 23:20; 1 Kings 1:38).
2. Son of Benaiah, a counselor to King David (1 Chronicles 27:34).
3. One of the men who joined David at Ziklag (1 Chronicles 12:27).
4. High priest who hid Joash from Athaliah and later restored the kingdom to Joash (2 Kings 11:4-21).

Jehoiakim \\Jeh-*hoy*-uh-kim\\
Seventeenth king of Judah and a son of Josiah, originally called Eliakim. He succeeded his brother Jehoahaz, who was deposed by Pharaoh Neco (2 Kings 23:31-34). (See KINGS OF ISRAEL AND JUDAH CHART.) A godless king, he burned Jeremiah's scroll of prophecies (Jeremiah 36).

Jehonadab \\Jeh-*hawn*-uh-dab\\
The son of Rechab; he helped Jehu rid Samaria of the practices of Baal worship (2 Kings 10:15, 16).

Jehoram \\Jeh-*ho*-rum\\ (Also spelled Joram.)
1. Fifth king of Judah, son of Jehoshaphat (2 Kings 8:16-24). See KINGS OF ISRAEL AND JUDAH CHART.
2. Ninth king of Israel, the son of Ahab and Jezebel (2 Kings 3:1). See KINGS OF ISRAEL AND JUDAH CHART.

3. One of the priests King Jehoshaphat sent to teach the law to the people of Judah (2 Chronicles 17:8).

Jehoshaphat \Jeh-*hosh*-uh-fat\
1. A priest who blew a trumpet as David brought the ark of the covenant to Jerusalem (1 Chronicles 15:24).
2. Son of Ahilud, a recorder during David's reign (2 Samuel 8:16; 20:24).
3. Paruah's son; an official in Solomon's court (1 Kings 4:17).
4. Fourth king of Judah, son of King Asa; he sent priests throughout Judah to teach the Law of the Lord (1 Kings 22:41, 42). See Kings of Israel and Judah Chart.
5. Father of Jehu (2 Kings 9:2, 14).

Jehosheba \Je-*hosh*-e-ba\
Daughter of Jehoram (of Judah) and wife of high priest Jehoiada, who hid Joash from Athaliah (2 Kings 11:2). The name is spelled Jehoshabeath in 2 Chronicles 22:11.

Jehoshua \Je-*hosh*-you-uh\
Alternate spelling of Joshua in Numbers 13:16 and 1 Chronicles 7:27 in the *King James Version.*

Jehovah \Jeh-*hoe*-vah\
See Yahweh.

Jehovahjireh \Jeh-*ho*-vuh-*jye*-ruh\ (Strong accent on *jye.*)
"The Lord will provide"; it's the name Abraham gave the place where God provided a ram in place of Isaac for a sacrifice (Genesis 22:14).

Jehozadak \Jeh-*hahss*-uh-dak\
See Josedech.

Jehu *Jay*-hew\
1. Tenth king of Israel after Jehoram, whom he killed in a bloody coup that wiped out the entire line of Ahab and even fatally wounded the king of Judah (2 Kings 9, 10). See Kings of Israel and Judah Chart.
2. Son of Obed of the tribe of Judah (1 Chronicles 2:38).
3. Son of Josibiah (or Joshibiah) of the tribe of Simeon (1 Chronicles 4:35).
4. A warrior from Anathoth who joined David at Ziklag (1 Chronicles 12:3).
5. Son of Hanani; a prophet of Judah who prophesied against Baasha of Israel (1 Kings 16:1-7). He also recorded the history of Jehoshaphat, king of Judah (2 Chronicles 20:34).

Jehudi \Je-*hew*-dye\
Son of Nethaniah, he read the prophecies of Jeremiah to King Jehoiakim (Jeremiah 36:14, 21).

Jephthae *Jef*-the\ (*th* as in *thin*).
Greek spelling of the name Jephthah (Hebrews 11:32, *KJV).*

Jephthah *Jef*-thuh\ (*th* as in *thin*)
A judge of Israel who defeated the Ammonites after vowing to offer in sacrifice the first thing to come out of his house when he returned. His daughter was first from the house to meet him, and scholars are divided over whether he offered her as a burnt offering or in some other way offered her to the Lord (Judges 11).

Jephunneh \Jih-*fun*-eh\
1. The father of Caleb, one of the spies sent out by Moses (Numbers 13:6).
2. A son of Jether from the tribe of Asher (1 Chronicles 7:38).

Jerahmeel \Je-*rah*-me-el\
1. A son of Hezron from the line of Judah; brother to Ram (or Aram) from whom David was descended (1 Chronicles 2:9-42).
2. Son of Kish; a Levite in David's time (1 Chronicles 24:29).
3. One of the officers King Jehoiakim sent to arrest Baruch and Jeremiah (Jeremiah 36:26).

Jeremiah \Jair-uh-*my*-uh\
1. A prophet of Judah and author of the Old Testament book of Jeremiah.
2. Three of the warriors who joined David in the wilderness had this name (1 Chronicles 12:4, 10, 13).
3. The maternal grandfather of King Jehoahaz of Judah (2 Kings 23:31).
4. The 24th book of the Old Testament, second in the "major prophets" section. It foretells the coming of the exile and its end, as well as the New Covenant to come in the messianic age. See Books of the Bible Chart.

Jeremias \Jair-uh-*my*-us\
Another spelling of the prophet Jeremiah's name in Matthew 16:14 *(KJV).*

Jeremy *Jair*-uh-me\
Another spelling of the prophet Jeremiah's name in Matthew 2:17; 27:9 *(KJV).*

Jericho *Jair*-ih-co\
A city located west of the Jordan River; the first city conquered by Israel (Joshua 6). It was the city where Jesus healed Bartimaeus (Mark 10:46-52) and where He met Zacchaeus (Luke 19:1, 2).

Jeroboam \Jair-uh-*boe*-um\
1. First king of the northern kingdom of Israel (1 Kings 12:20). See Kings of Israel and Judah Chart.
2. Jeroboam II, son of Jehoash, thirteenth king of Israel; he followed the idolatrous ways of Jeroboam I in a reign of 41 years (2 Kings 14:23-29). See Kings of Israel and Judah Chart.

Ji

Jeroham \Je-*ro*-ham\
1. Grandfather of Samuel (1 Samuel 1:1; 1 Chronicles 6:27, 34).
2. A priest's ancestor who lived in Jerusalem (1 Chronicles 9:12; Nehemiah 11:12).
3. A Benjamite whose two sons joined David at Ziklag (1 Chronicles 12:7).
4. The father of Azarel, a chief of Dan's tribe during David's reign (1 Chronicles 27:22).
5. Father of Azariah; a captain who helped put Joash on the throne of Judah and depose Athaliah (2 Chronicles 23:1).
6. See also 1 Chronicles 8:27; 9:8.

Jerub-Baal \Jair-uh-*bay*-ul\ (Also spelled Jerubbaal.)
"Let Baal contend," a name for Gideon after he destroyed an altar to Baal; his father defended him by saying that if Baal were a god, he himself could contend against the one who broke down his altar (Judges 6:32).

Jerusalem \Juh-*roo*-suh-lem\
The capital of Israel since David's reign.

Jeshua *Jesh*-you-uh\
1. A name used for Joshua, son of Nun (Nehemiah 8:17, *KJV*).
2. The head of one of the priestly courses (1 Chronicles 24:11).
3. A Levite who distributed the tithe during Hezekiah's reign (2 Chronicles 31:15).
4. The high priest who helped oversee the rebuilding of the temple (Ezra 2:2; 4:3; 5:2; Nehemiah 7:7). Also spelled Joshua in Haggai 1:1 and in Zechariah 3:1ff.).
5. Relative of Pahath-Moab who returned to Jerusalem with Zerubbabel (Ezra 2:6; Nehemiah 7:11).
6. A town in Judah settled by the Jews after the exile (Nehemiah 11:26).

Jesse *Jess*-ee\
An Ephrathite from Bethlehem in Judah, father of King David (1 Samuel 17:12-14); grandson of Boaz and Ruth (Ruth 4:18-22).

Jesus *Jee*-zuz\
1. Son of Mary, the Son of God (Luke 1:30-33). The four Gospels—Matthew, Mark, Luke, and John—tell the story of His life on earth.
2. A Jewish disciple, also called Justus, who sent greetings to the Colossian church (Colossians 4:11).
3. Greek spelling of Joshua in the *KJV* (Acts 7:45; Hebrews 4:8).

Jethro *Jeth*-ro\
Moses' father-in-law (Exodus 3:1; 18:1). He is also called Reuel (Exodus 2:16-18). See REUEL; HOBAB.

Jezaniah \Jez-uh-*nye*-uh\
See JAAZANIAH.

Jezebel *Jez*-uh-bel\
The wicked wife of Ahab, king of Israel; killed the Lord's prophets (1 Kings 18:4-13); she died in the coup of Jehu (2 Kings 9:30-37).

Jezreel *Jez*-ree-el\ or *Jez*-reel\
1. A town of Issachar (Joshua 19:18); Ahab made a second palace there, where he tried to buy the vineyard of Naboth (1 Kings 21:1, 2).
2. A town of Judah (Joshua 15:56); David's wife Ahinoam was from there (1 Samuel 25:43; 27:3).
3. A descendant of Judah (1 Chronicles 4:3).
4. Hosea's son, who was named by God as a prediction of the fall of Israel to avenge the bloody coup of Jehu in Jezreel (Hosea 1:4, 5).

Jezreelite *Jez*-ree-el-ite\
An inhabitant of Jezreel, as Naboth (1 Kings 21).

Jezreelitess *Jez*-ree-el-*ite*-ess\ (strong accent on *ite*).
A female inhabitant of Jezreel, as Ahinoam (1 Samuel 27:3).

Joab *Jo*-ab\
1. David's nephew from Zeruiah, his half-sister; commander of David's army (2 Samuel 8:16).
2. Son of Seraiah, of the tribe of Judah (1 Chronicles 4:14).
3. Ancestor of a family that returned from exile with Zerubbabel (Ezra 2:6; 8:9; Nehemiah 7:11).

Joah *Jo*-uh\
1. Son of Obed-Edom (1 Chronicles 26:4).
2. Son of Zimmah from the family of Gershon of the tribe of Levi (1 Chronicles 6:20, 21).
3. Asaph's son and King Hezekiah's recorder (2 Kings 18:18, 26).
4. Joahaz's son and King Josiah's recorder (2 Chronicles 34:8).

Joahaz *Jo*-ah-haz\
The father of Joah, the recorder for King Josiah (2 Chronicles 34:8).

Joanna \Joe-*an*-uh\
1. One of the women who supported Jesus in His ministry and to whom He appeared after His resurrection (Luke 8:3; 24:10).
2. Son of Rhesa in Jesus' genealogy (Luke 3:27, *KJV*).

Joash *Jo*-ash\ (Also spelled Jehoash.)
1. Father of Gideon (Judges 6:11).
2. Seventh king of Judah; as an infant, he was saved from Athaliah's murder of the royal line (2 Kings 11–13; 2 Chronicles 24, 25).

Jj

3. One of David's supply officers (1 Chronicles 27:28).

4. A descendant of Shelah, the youngest son of Judah (1 Chronicles 4:21, 22).

5. A son of Beker from the tribe of Benjamin (1 Chronicles 7:8).

6. One of the men who joined David at Ziklag (1 Chronicles 12:3).

7. Son of King Ahab who had custody of Micaiah, the prophet who challenged Ahab's plan to attack Ramoth (1 Kings 22:26).

Job \Jobe\

1. A man of the land of Uz who suffered great losses but refused to curse God for his trials. His story is told in the book of Job.

2. The 18th book of the Old Testament, the first in the "poetry" section. It recounts the events of Job's trials, his friends' counsel, and his own plea for answers. See Books of the Bible Chart.

Jochebed \Jock-eh-bed\

Mother of Moses, Aaron, and Miriam (Exodus 6:20; Numbers 26:59).

Joel \Joe-ul\

1. A prophet, son of Pethuel (Joel 1:1). Peter quoted his prophecy on Pentecost (Acts 2:16).

2. The 29th book of the Old Testament, the second in the "minor prophets" section. See Books of the Bible Chart.

3. A Kohathite Levite and ancestor of the prophet Samuel (1 Samuel 1:1; 1 Chronicles 6:36).

4. The first son of Samuel (1 Samuel 8:2; 1 Chronicles 6:28; called "Vashni" in second reference KJV).

5. A clan leader in the tribe of Simeon (1 Chronicles 4:35, 38).

6. The name of two descendants of Reuben (1 Chronicles 5:4, 8).

7. A descendant of Gad, named as a leader in the tribe (1 Chronicles 5:12).

8. A warrior of the tribe of Issachar in David's time (1 Chronicles 7:2, 3).

9. One of David's mighty men (1 Chronicles 11:38).

10. One of the Levites involved in bringing the ark of the covenant into Jerusalem (1 Chronicles 15:7). He was among those who later had charge of the temple treasuries (1 Chronicles 26:22).

11. A leader of the tribe of Manasseh in David's time (1 Chronicles 27:20).

12. A Kohathite Levite, son of Azariah, in Hezekiah's day (2 Chronicles 29:12).

13. One of the men who were guilty of marrying foreign wives in Ezra's day (Ezra 10:43).

14. A leader of the tribe of Benjamin who had returned to Jerusalem after the exile (Nehemiah 11:9).

Johanan \Jo-hay-nan\ (Sometimes spelled Jehohanan.)

1. Josiah's oldest son, who died at a young age (1 Chronicles 3:15).

2. Son of Elioenai, a descendant of David (1 Chronicles 3:24).

3. Son of Azariah, a descendant of Aaron (1 Chronicles 6:9, 10).

4. A Benjamite who joined David at Ziklag (1 Chronicles 12:4).

5. A Gadite who joined David at Ziklag (1 Chronicles 12:12).

6. An officer who cooperated with Gedaliah as governor of Judah (2 Kings 25:22, 23).

7. See also 2 Chronicles 28:12; Ezra 8:12; 10:6; Nehemiah 6:18; 12:22.

John \Jahn\

1. Son of Zebedee and brother of James; one of the first of Jesus' disciples called to follow Jesus (Matthew 4:21; 10:2); called the disciple Jesus loved (John 13:23; 21:7, 20). He was the author of the Gospel of John, 1, 2, and 3 John, and Revelation.

2. John the Baptist, son of Zechariah and Elizabeth (Matthew 3:1-15; Luke 1:5-13, 57-66). He was arrested by Herod Antipas and later executed (Mark 6:14-29).

3. The fourth Gospel and fourth book of the New Testament, written much later than the other Gospels and including more unique information than any of them. See Books of the Bible Chart.

4. The 23rd–25th books of the New Testament (1, 2, & 3 John), fifth–seventh of the general epistles; written by the apostle John. See Books of the Bible Chart.

5. Simon Peter's father (Matthew 16:17, NLT; John 21:15-17, except KJV & NKJV), also known as Jona or Jonah (Matthew 16:17, other versions; John 21:15-17, NKJV) or Jonas (John 21:15-17, KJV).

6. A member of the family of Annas the high priest who attended the trial of Peter and John in Acts 4 (Acts 4:6).

7. John Mark, son of Mary in whose home the church met to pray for Peter (Acts 12:12). See Mark.

Jonadab \Jon-uh-dab\

David's nephew and friend of David's son Amnon; he suggested the plan by which Amnon lured his sister Tamar into his room, where Amnon raped her (2 Samuel 13:3).

Jona \Jo-nuh\

Alternate spelling for the name of the father of Peter (Matthew 16:17; John 1:42, KJV). See Jonas; John #5.

Jonah \Jo-nuh\

1. Amittai's son; prophet of Israel and author of the Old Testament book of Jonah (Jonah 1:1).

2. The 32nd book of the Old Testament, the fifth in the "minor prophets" section. The book tells of Jonah's

reluctant mission to Nineveh. See BOOKS OF THE BIBLE CHART.

3. Alternate spelling for the name of the father of Peter (Matthew 16:17, *NIV, NKJV*; John 1:42, *NKJV*). See JONAS; JOHN #5.

Jonas *Jo*-nus\
1. The Greek spelling of Jonah, found in the *King James Version* (Matthew 12:39-41; 16:4; Luke 11:29, 30, 32).
2. The apostle Peter's father (John 21:15-17, *KJV*). See JOHN #5.

Jonathan *Jon*-uh-thun\
1. Oldest son of King Saul (1 Samuel 14:49). Close friend to David (1 Samuel 18:1), he protected David when his father wanted to murder him (1 Samuel 19:1-7; 20:1-42).
2. A Levite who was a priest to Micah in Ephraim, and then the Danites during the period of the judges (Judges 17:7-13; 18:1-30).
3. Son of the high priest Abiathar; loyal to David when Absalom rebelled (2 Samuel 15:27, 36; 17:17-22).
4. Son of Shimeah, one of David's mighty men (2 Samuel 21:21).
5. See also 2 Samuel 23:32; 1 Chronicles 11:34; 1 Chronicles 2:32, 33; 1 Chronicles 27:25 (Jehonathan, *KJV*); 1 Chronicles 27:32; Ezra 8:6; 10:15; Nehemiah 12:11; Nehemiah 12:14, 35; Jeremiah 37:15, 20; 40:8).

Joppa *Jop*-uh\
A seaport town, 35 miles from Jerusalem; it was the receiving port for the logs Hiram sent from Lebanon for the building of Solomon's temple (2 Chronicles 2:16). Home of the disciple Dorcas (or Tabitha), whom Peter raised from the dead (Acts 9:36-41).

Joram *Jo*-ram\ (Also spelled Jehoram.)
1. Ninth king of Israel, Ahab's son (2 Kings 8:16; 9:14-23); he succeeded Ahaziah on the throne (2 Kings 3:1; 9:24). See KINGS OF ISRAEL AND JUDAH CHART.
2. Fifth king of Judah (2 Kings 8:21-24; 11:2; 1 Chronicles 3:11; Matthew 1:8). See KINGS OF ISRAEL AND JUDAH CHART.
3. Son of Toi, king of Hamath, who was sent to congratulate David on his victory over Hadadezer of Zobah (2 Samuel 8:9-12). He is called Hadoram in 1 Chronicles 18:10.
4. A Levite treasurer in David's time (1 Chronicles 26:25).

Jordan *Jor*-dun\
The main river of Israel; it runs from the springs of Huleh, north of the Sea of Galilee, to the Dead Sea.

Josabad *Jaws*-ah-bad\
See JOZABAD.

Josedech *Jahss*-uh-dek\ (Also spelled Jehozadak and Jozadak.)
Father of Joshua (or Jeshua) the high priest, who returned to Jerusalem with Zerubbabel (Haggai 1:1; 2:2; Zechariah 6:11; Ezra 3:2, 8; 5:2; 10:18).

Joseph *Jo*-suf\
1. Eleventh son of Jacob; the first by his beloved Rachel (Genesis 30:22-24).
2. Husband of Mary and earthly father (or stepfather) of Jesus (Matthew 1:16; Luke 2:4-7).
3. One of Jesus' brothers (Matthew 13:55).
4. Brother to James the Less (Mark 15:40).
5. A rich man from Arimathea; a disciple of Jesus, he provided the tomb for Jesus' burial (Matthew 27:57-60).
6. Given name of Barnabas, who worked with Paul in ministry (Acts 4:36, except KJV).
7. Given name of a disciple also known as Barsabas and surnamed Justus, one of two potentially chosen to take the place of Judas Iscariot. Matthias, the other, was then chosen by lot (Acts 1:23-26).
8. A son of Asaph (1 Chronicles 25:2, 9)
9. A postexilic resident of Judah who had married a foreign wife (Ezra 10:42).
10. A priest in the time of Nehemiah (Nehemiah 12:14).
11. Father of Janna and son of Matthias, in Luke's genealogy of Jesus (Luke 3:24, 25).
12. Father of Semei and son of Judah, in Luke's genealogy of Jesus (Luke 3:26, *KJV*).
13. Father of Judah and son of Jonan, in Luke's genealogy of Jesus (Luke 3:30).

Josephus \Jo-*see*-fus\
First-century Jewish military officer and historian. His writings provide insight into Jewish life and historical events in the time of Jesus and the early church.

Joses *Jo*-sez\ (Usually spelled Joseph.)
1. One of Jesus' brothers (Matthew 13:55; Mark 6:3, *KJV*).
2. Brother to James the Less (Mark 15:40).
3. Given name of Barnabas, who worked with Paul in ministry (Acts 4:36, *KJV*).

Joshua *Josh*-yew-uh\ (Also spelled Jehoshua or Jeshua.)
1. Son of Nun; assistant and successor to Moses (Joshua 1:1-5).
2. The sixth book of the Old Testament, and first in the "history" section. It tells about Joshua's leadership of the Israelites and the conquest of Canaan. SEE BOOKS OF THE BIBLE CHART.
3. Son of Josedech, high priest in the time of Nehemiah (Haggai 1:1; Zechariah 3).

Jj

JUDGES OF ISRAEL

Judge	Major Oppressor	Years as Judge
Othniel (Judges 3:8-11)	Mesopotamia (Cushan-Rishathaim)	1373–1334 BC
Ehud (Judges 3:12-30)	Moabites (Eglon)	1319–1239 BC
Shamgar (Judges 3:31)	Philistines	1300 BC
Deborah (Judges 4, 5)	Canaanites (Jabin)	1239–1199 BC
Gideon (Judges 6-8)	Midianites	1192–1152 BC
Abimelech (Judges 9)	Period of Civil War	1152–1150 BC
Tola (Judges 10:1, 2)	Ammonites	1149–1126 BC
Jair (Judges 10:3-5)	Ammonites	1126–1104 BC
Jephthah (Judges 10:6-12:7)	Ammonites	1086–1080 BC
Ibzan (Judges 12:8-10)	Philistines	1080–1075 BC
Elon (Judges 12:11, 12)	Philistines	1075–1065 BC
Abdon (Judges 12:13-15)	Philistines	1065–1058 BC
Samson (Judges 13-16)	Philistines	1075–1055 BC
Eli (1 Samuel 1-4)	Philistines	1107–1067 BC
Samuel (1 Samuel 7-9)	Philistines	1067–1043 BC

Josiah \Jo-*sigh*-uh\
Fifteenth king of Judah, son of Amon (2 Chronicles 33:25). He was righteous and destroyed idol worship in Judah (2 Chronicles 34, 35). See KINGS OF ISRAEL AND JUDAH CHART.

Jotbah *Jot*-buh\
See JUTTAH.

Jotham *Jo*-thum\
1. The youngest son of Gideon (Judges 9:5-57).
2. Tenth king of Judah, son of Uzziah (2 Chronicles 27:1-9). See KINGS OF ISRAEL AND JUDAH CHART.
3. A son of Jahdai from Caleb's clan of the tribe of Judah (1 Chronicles 2:47).

Jozabad *Jaws*-ah-bad\ (Also spelled Josabad.)
1. A man from Gederah who joined David at Ziklag (1 Chronicles 12:4).
2. The name of two men from Manasseh who joined David at Ziklag (1 Chronicles 12:20).
3. A Levite appointed by Hezekiah as an overseer (2 Chronicles 31:13).
4. See also 2 Chronicles 35:9; Ezra 8:33; 10:22, 23; Nehemiah 8:7.

Jozadak *Joz*-uh-dak\
See JOSEDECH.

Judaea \Joo-*dee*-uh\
See JUDEA.

Judah *Joo*-duh\
1. Jacob and Leah's fourth son (Genesis 29:35). Ancestor of King David (Ruth 4:18-22) and Jesus (Matthew 1:3-16).

2. One of Israel's 12 tribes, the descendants of Judah, son of Jacob.
3. Territory given to the tribe of Judah.
4. The name of five people mentioned in Ezra and Nehemiah. Three were Levites (Ezra 3:9—some versions have Hodaviah; 10:23; Nehemiah 12:8), one a Benjamite (Nehemiah 11:9), and the fifth a leader of Judah (Nehemiah 12:34).
5. An ancestor of Jesus, but not Jacob's son, is mentioned in Luke 3:30 (Juda, *KJV*).
6. The southern kingdom of Israel, comprised of the two tribes of Judah and Benjamin. Rehoboam became the first king of Judah when the tribes split after the death of Solomon (1 Kings 12:20-24).

Judaism *Joo*-duh-izz-um\ or *Joo*-day-izz-um\
The religion of the Jews.

Judaizers *Joo*-duh-*ize*-ers\ (strong accent on *Joo*)
People who believe one must become a Jew before he or she can be a Christian (Galatians 2:14).

Judas *Joo*-dus\
1. Judas Iscariot; the disciple who betrayed Jesus. Remorseful, he tried to return the money—then hanged himself (Matthew 27:3-10).
2. Another apostle of Jesus (John 14:22), the son or brother of James (Luke 6:16). See THADDAEUS.
3. One of Jesus' brothers (Matthew 13:55). Also called Jude, and author of the book of Jude (Jude 1).
4. Judas of Galilee, led the Jews in a revolt against the Romans (Acts 5:37).
5. A man who lived on Straight Street in Damascus with whom Saul of Tarsus (Paul) stayed after he met Jesus on the road; Ananias went to Saul there, restored his sight, and baptized him (Acts 9:11, 17, 18).

6. Judas Barsabas, a disciple who was sent, along with Silas, with Paul and Barnabas to Antioch after the Council of Jerusalem (Acts 15:22).

7. Judas Maccabeus, one of the sons of Mattathias Maccabeus, who led the Jews during the time between the testaments. He led the armies in many successful battles against the Syrians and Samaritans.

Jude \Jood\
1. The 26th book of the New Testament, eighth of the general epistles; written by Judas (Jude) the brother of Jesus. See Books of the Bible Chart.
2. Brother of Jesus and author of the book of Jude. See Judas #3.

Judea \Joo-*dee*-uh\ (Also spelled Judaea.)
The territory inhabited by the Jews. After the Jewish captives returned from Babylon, the name applied to the vicinity of Jerusalem (Ezra 5:8, KJV), though in the Maccabean era and later it sometimes referred to the entire land between the Jordan River and the Mediterranean Sea. In New Testament times it designated the southern portion of Israel, south of Samaria, and comprising land from what had been the tribes of Judah, Benjamin, Dan, Simeon, and part of Ephraim.

Judean \Joo-*dee*-un\
1. An inhabitant of the territory of Judea.
2. Related to Judea, as in "Judean wilderness."

Judges *Jud*-juzz\
1. Rulers of Israel in the time between the Conquest and the Monarchy. See Judges of Israel Chart.
2. The seventh book of the Old Testament, and second in the "history" section. It tells about the leaders who ruled Israel after the Conquest of Canaan and before the Monarchy. See Books of the Bible Chart.

Junia *Joo*-ni-uh\
A relative and fellow prisoner of Paul, possibly the wife of Andronicus (Romans 16:7, KJV; otherwise spelled Junias).

Junias \Joo-ni-us\
See Junia.

Jupiter *Joo*-puh-ter\
The chief god of the Roman pantheon; equivalent to the Greek god Zeus (Acts 14:12, 13).

Juttah *Jut*-ah\ (Also spelled Jotbah.)
A Levitical city located in the hill country of Judah (Joshua 15:55).

Kk

Kadesh *kay*-desh\
An oasis located 50 miles south of Beersheba. Abraham camped near there (Genesis 20:1), and Miriam was buried there (Numbers 20:1).

Kadesh Barnea *kay*-desh-*bar*-nee-uh\ (strong accent on *bar*) (Also spelled Kadeshbarnea.)
Another name for Kadesh. The Israelites sent the 12 spies to Canaan from this place (Deuteronomy 1:19-23).

kainos *(Greek)* \kye-*noss*\
Greek word for "new" (2 Corinthians 5:17). It expresses a newness in quality more than in time; *neos* suggests new in time.

kaleo *(Greek)* \Kuh-*leh*-oh\
Greek word for "call."

Kareah \Ka-*ree*-uh\
See Careah.

Karkor *Kar*-kor\
The place where Gideon captured the two Midianite kings, Zebah and Zalmunna (Judges 8:10).

Kebar *Kee*-bar\
See Chebar

Kedar *Kee*-dar\
1. Abraham's grandson; son of Ishmael (Genesis 25:13).
2. A tribe that descended from Kedar and their land. Nebuchadnezzar attacked them in the Arabian Desert (Jeremiah 49:28-33).

Kedeshnaphtali *Kee*-desh-*naf*-tuh-lye\ (strong accent on *naf*) (Also known as Kedesh in Naphtali.)
Located north of the Sea of Galilee; home of Barak, whom Deborah summoned to lead the army of Israel against Sisera of the Canaanites (Judges 4:6-10).

Kelaiah *Key*-lay-*eye*-uh\ (strong accent on *eye*)
See Kelita.

Kelita *Kel*-ih-tuh\ (Also spelled Kelaiah.)
A Levite who married a foreign woman during Ezra's time (Ezra 10:23).

Kenaanah \Kih-*nay*-uh-nah\
See Chenaanah.

Jj
Kk

Kenaz *Kee*-naz\\
1. Esau's grandson through Elephaz (Genesis 36:11, 15).
2. Father of Othniel; Caleb's younger brother (Joshua 15:17; Judges 1:13; 3:9-11).
3. A descendant of Caleb (1 Chronicles 4:15).

Kenezites *Ken*-ez-ites\\ or *Ken*-uh-zites\\
In the *King James Version*, this is the ancestral tribe of Jephunneh, Caleb's father (Numbers 32:12; Joshua 14:6, 14, *KJV*). Other versions have *Kenizzites*.

Kenites *Ken*-ites\\
One of the 10 tribes of Canaan (Genesis 15:19; Judges 4:11). Moses' father-in-law was called a Kenite in Judges 1:16.

Kenizzites *Ken*-ez-ites\\ or *Ken*-uh-zites\\
1. One of the 10 tribes of Canaan during Abraham's time (Genesis 15:19).
2. The ancestral tribe of Jephunneh, Caleb's father (Numbers 32:12; Joshua 14:6, 14, except *KJV*).

kenosis \\kuh-*no*-sus\\
Theological position that Jesus divested himself of His divine attributes (such as omnipotence and omniscience) in the incarnation. Comes from the Greek verb *kenoo,* "to empty," from Philippians 2:7.

kensos *(Greek)* *kane*-sahs\\
Greek for "tribute" or "tax" (Matthew 17:24; 22:17; Mark 12:14).

Kerioth *Kee*-rih-oath\\
1. A city of south Judah, also called Hazor (Joshua 15:25). *Iscariot* is formed from this name, so Judas was probably from there.
2. A city of Moab (Jeremiah 48:24; Amos 2:2).

Kerith *Key*-rith\\
See Cherith.

Kesil *Kess*-ill\\
See Chesil.

Keturah \\Keh-*too*-ruh\\
The second wife of Abraham; she bore him six sons (Genesis 25:1-6).

Kidron *Kid*-ron\\
A valley and brook separating Jerusalem and the Mount of Olives; David crossed this brook in his flight from Absalom (2 Samuel 15:23); Jesus crossed it the night He was betrayed (John 18:1; *KJV* has Cedron here).

Kilion *Kil*-ee-on\\
See Chilion.

Kk

Kings (1 and 2) \\kingz\\
Eleventh and twelfth books of the Old Testament, the sixth and seventh in the "history" section. They tell the history of Israel and Judah from the last years of David to the Babylonian Exile. See Books of the Bible Chart.

Kings of Israel and Judah
See chart on next page.

Kinnereth *Kin*-eh-reth\\
See Chinnereth. (Where the *KJV, ASV, NASB,* and others have *Chinnereth* or *Chinneroth* the *NIV* always has *Kinnereth.* The *NLT* also uses *Kinnereth,* but it often cites it only in a footnote and uses *Galilee* in the text.)

Kirjathjearim *Kir*-jath-*jee*-uh-rim\\ (strong accent on *jee*) or *jee*-*a*-rim\\ (strong accent on *a*) (Also spelled Kirjath-jearim, Kiriath-jearim, or Kiriath Jearim.)
A city of the Gibeonites (who tricked Joshua and the Israelites into making a treaty with them, Joshua 9). The ark of the covenant was kept there after it was returned by the Philistines (1 Samuel 7:1, 2).

Kittim *Kit*-tim\\
See Chittim.

Kishon *Kye*-shon\\
A river that flows through the valley of Jezreel. Barak and Deborah led Israel in the defeat of Sisera near this river (Judges 4, 5).

knop \\nop\\
An ornamental bulb or knob; the capital of a pillar. The term is used 16 times in the *King James Version,* usually of a feature of the golden lamp stand of the tabernacle (Exodus 25:31-36; 37:17-22). Three times it describes bulb- or gourd-shaped carvings in Solomon's temple (1 Kings 6:18; 7:24).

Kohath *Ko*-hath\\
Levi's second son (Genesis 46:11).

Kohathite *Ko*-hath-ite\\
A Levitical family, descendant of Kohath. The Kohathites cared for the sanctuary (Numbers 3:27-32).

koheleth *(Hebrew)* \\ko-*hel*-eth\\
Hebrew for "preacher" or "teacher"; it is found in Ecclesiastes but nowhere else in Scripture.

koine *(Greek)* *koy*-nay\\
The form of Greek found in the New Testament.

koinoneo *(Greek)* \\koy-no-*neh*-oh\\
Greek verb for "share," "participate," "have fellowship," or "partner."

KINGS OF ISRAEL AND JUDAH

UNITED MONARCHY
1. Saul
2. David
3. Solomon

DIVIDED MONARCHY

JUDAH (CONTINUES DAVIDIC LINE)		ISRAEL (9 SEPARATE DYNASTIES: I, II, ETC.)		
1.	Rehoboam	I	1.	Jeroboam
2.	Abijah (or Abijam)		2.	Nadab
3.	Asa	II	3.	Baasha
4.	Jehoshaphat		4.	Elah
5.	Jehoram (or Joram)	III	5.	Zimri
6.	Ahaziah	IV	6.	Omri
	Athalia (usurped throne; ruled 6 years)		7.	Ahab
7.	Joash (or Jehoash)		8.	Ahaziah
8.	Amaziah		9.	Joram (or Jehoram)
9.	Uzziah (or Azariah)	V	10.	Jehu
10.	Jotham		11.	Jehoahaz
11.	Ahaz		12.	Jehoash
12.	Hezekiah		13.	Jeroboam II
13.	Manasseh		14.	Zechariah
14.	Amon	VI	15.	Shallum
15.	Josiah	VII	16.	Menahem
16.	Jehoahaz (or Shallum)		17.	Pekahiah
17.	Jehoiakim (or Eliakim)	VIII	18.	Pekah
18.	Jehoiachin	IX	19.	Hoshea
19.	Zedekiah (or Mattaniah)			

Kk

koinonia *(Greek)* \koy-no-*nee*-uh\
Greek noun for "participation" or "fellowship."

Korah *Ko*-rah\
1. A Levite who led a rebellion against the leadership of Moses (Numbers 16).
2. Esau's son (Genesis 36:5, 14, 18; 1 Chronicles 1:35).
3. Esau's grandson (Genesis 36:16).
4. A descendant of Caleb (1 Chronicles 2:43).

Korahites *Ko*-ra-ites\ (Also spelled Korhites.)
The Levitical family descended from the rebellious Korah but faithful in service as gatekeepers and singers in the house of the Lord (1 Chronicles 9:19; 12:6; 26:1).

korinthiazesthai *(Greek)* \ko-rin-thee-*adz*-ess-thai\ (*th* as in *thin*) (Also spelled korinthiazomai.)
Verb formed from the name Corinth; literally "to act as a Corinthian." It was used in the first century to describe immoral behavior.

korinthiazomai *(Greek)* \ko-*rin*-thee-*od*-zo-my\ (*th* as in *thin*; strong accent on *od*)
See KORINTHIAZESTHAI.

kosmos *(Greek)* *kahss*-moss\
Greek for "world" or "universe" (John 3:16).

kranion *(Greek)* \kray-*nee*-on\
Greek for "skull"; used as the name of the place where Jesus was crucified (Matthew 27:33; Mark 15:22; Luke 23:33; John 19:17).

kurios *(Greek)* *koo*-re-os\
Greek for "Lord" (Philippians 2:11).

Ll

Laban *Lay*-bun\\
1. The nephew of Abraham; brother of Rebekah, who married Isaac (Genesis 24:29-31); father of Rachel and Leah, whom Jacob took as wives (Genesis 29).
2. A place near where the Israelites made camp when Moses recited the Law to them (Deuteronomy 1:1). The location is unknown.

Lachish *Lay*-kish\\
A city to the southwest of Jerusalem. The king of Lachish joined Adoni-Zedek and three other kings in an attempt to punish the Gibeonites for making a treaty with Israel (Joshua 10). Amaziah, king of Judah, fled to Lachish when a conspiracy rose against him, but the conspirators followed and killed him in Lachish (2 Kings 14:17-20).

Laish *Lay*-ish\\ (Also spelled Laishah.)
1. A city in the Jordan valley that men from Dan conquered and renamed Dan (Judges 18:7, 27-31; Isaiah 10:30).
2. The father of Phalti or Paltiel; Saul gave his daughter Michal, David's wife, to Paltiel (1 Samuel 25:44).

lama *(Aramaic)* *lah*-mah\\ (Also spelled lema.)
Part of an Aramaic expression quoted by Jesus just before He died (Matthew 27:46; Mark 15:34), meaning, "why."

Lamech *Lay*-mek\\
1. Son of Methushael; a descendant of Cain and first known polygamist (Genesis 4:18-24).
2. Methuselah's son and father of Noah (Genesis 5:25-31; 1 Chronicles 1:3).

Lamentations \\Lam-en-*tay*-shunz\\
The 25th book of the Old Testament, third in the "major prophets" section. It comprises five poems that mourn the fall of Jerusalem in 586 BC. See BOOKS OF THE BIBLE CHART.

Laodicea \\Lay-*odd*-uh-*see*-uh\\ (strong accent on *see*)
One of the seven cities in Asia Minor that was home to a church addressed in Revelation (Revelation 1:11; 3:14-18). It was located about 80 miles from Ephesus.

Laodiceans \\Lay-*odd*-uh-*see*-unz\\ (strong accent on *see*)
The inhabitants of Laodicea.

Lapidoth *Lap*-ih-doth\\ (Also spelled Lappidoth.)
The husband of Deborah the prophetess (Judges 4:4).

lasciviousness \\luh-*sih*-vee-us-nuss\\
Immorality, total disregard for decency—in public or in private.

Lasea \\Lay-*see*-uh\\
A seaport of Crete's southern coast, a stop on Paul's voyage to Rome (Acts 27:8).

Lazarus *Laz*-uh-rus\\
1. Mary and Martha's brother; Jesus raised him from the dead in the presence of many witnesses (John 11:1–12:19).
2. The name of a beggar in a parable of Jesus (Luke 16:19-31).

Lebanon *Leb*-uh-nun\\
Mountain range and country north of Israel; known for its cedars, which were used in the construction of Solomon's temple (1 Kings 5:6).

Lebbaeus \\Leh-*bee*-us\\ (Also spelled Lebbeus.)
Another name for Thaddaeus or Judas (not Judas Iscariot), one of the 12 disciples (Matthew 10:3, *KJV, NKJV*).

Lemuel *Lem*-you-el\\
A king whose sayings are recorded in Proverbs 31.

Levi *Lee*-vye\\
1. Third son of Jacob and Leah (Genesis 29:34).
2. The tribe of Levi, descendants of Levi, son of Jacob; the priestly tribe. (See LEVITES.)
3. Another name for Matthew, the disciple who had been a tax collector (compare Matthew 9:9 with Mark 2:14).
4. An ancestor of Jesus (Luke 3:24).

leviathan \\luh-*vye*-uh-thun\\
A large sea creature that is mentioned in Psalms 74:14; 104:26; Job 3:8; 41:1; and Isaiah 27:1. It has sometimes been associated with the crocodile or some kind of large serpent; some scholars see in these references biblical evidence for dinosaurs.

Levites *Lee*-vites\\
The descendants of Levi; they were blessed with priestly duties throughout Israel (Numbers 3:11-13; Deuteronomy 33:8-11).

Levitical \\Leh-*vit*-ih-kul\\
Having to do with the tribe of Levi or the services at the temple, which were provided by the Levites.

Leviticus \\Leh-*vit*-ih-kus\\
The third book of the Old Testament, and third in the "law" section. Written by Moses, it describes many of the priestly duties of the Levites. See BOOKS OF THE BIBLE CHART.

lex talionis *(Latin)* \\leks tal-ee-*oh*-niss\\
Latin term for eye-for-an-eye kind of justice. It means, roughly, "law of equal and direct retribution." For physical injury the legal punishment is the same kind of injury in

Libertines *Lib*-er-teens\
Former slaves that had been granted their freedom. (Some versions call them "Freedmen.") Philo tells of some Jews who had been captives of the Romans and, after being set free, had built a synagogue at Jerusalem. Members of this synagogue opposed the teaching of Stephen (Acts 6:9).

Libnah *Lib*-na\
1. A place where the Israelites made camp, the fifth camp-site after leaving Sinai (Numbers 33:20). The location of the site is unknown.
2. A Canaanite city that was conquered by Joshua in the southern campaign (Joshua 10:29-32; 12:15).

ligure *lih*-gyur\
A precious stone found in the high priest's breastplate (Exodus 28:19 *KJV*; other translations call it jacinth).

lintel *lint*-ul\
The horizontal beam of a doorway; one of the places on the doorframe where the Israelites were instructed to put the blood of the Passover lamb (Exodus 12:22).

Lo-Ammi \Lo-*am*-my\ (Also spelled Loammi.)
A name meaning "not my people"; one of Hosea's sons was given this name as a warning to Israel (Hosea 1:9).

logos (*Greek*) *law*-goss\
Greek for "word"; used by John to describe Jesus (John 1:1, 14; 1 John 1:1).

Lois *Lo*-is\
Timothy's maternal grandmother (2 Timothy 1:5).

Lo-Ruhamah \Lo-roo-*hah*-muh\ (strong accent on *hah*) (Also spelled Loruhamah.)
A name meaning "not pitied" or "no mercy"; Hosea's daughter was given this name as a warning to Israel (Hosea 1:6-8).

Lucifer *Loo*-sih-fur\
Another name for Satan or the devil, from a term meaning "morning star" (Isaiah 14:12, *KJV, NKJV*).

Lucius *Lew*-shus\
A man from Cyrene, one of the prophets and teachers in Antioch (Acts 13:1).

Luke \Look\ (*oo* as in *boot*)
1. Companion of the apostle Paul and author of the Gospel of Luke and the book of Acts.
2. The third Gospel and third book of the New Testament, written from a Gentile perspective, probably in about AD 60. See BOOKS OF THE BIBLE CHART.

Luxor *Luck*-sor\
Ancient Thebes, capital of Egypt's Middle and New Kingdoms; near the Valley of the Kings.

Luz \Luzz\
1. A Canaanite town that Jacob renamed Bethel (Genesis 28:19; 35:6; 48:3). Apparently the Canaanites continued to use the name Luz to the time of Joshua (Joshua 18:13).
2. A Hittite city built by a man from the Canaanite Luz; i.e., Bethel (Judges 1:22-26).

Lycaonia *Lik*-uh-*o*-ni-uh\ (strong accent on *o*)
A province of Asia Minor; the cities of Lystra, Derbe, and Iconium were in this province (Acts 14:6).

Lydda *Lid*-uh\
A town northwest of Jerusalem, where Peter healed Aeneas (Acts 9:32-35).

Lydia *Lid*-ee-uh\
A dealer in purple from Thyatira whom Paul baptized in Philippi (Acts 16:14, 15); she was the first Christian convert in Europe.

Lysanias \Lie-*say*-ne-us\
Tetrarch of Abilene, or Abila (Josephus, *Antiquities* 20:138) at the time Jesus began His ministry (Luke 3:1).

Lysias *Lis*-ee-us\
Claudius Lysias. See CLAUDIUS #2.

Lystra *Liss*-truh\
A city in the region of Lycaonia where Timothy lived (Acts 16:1).

Mm

Maacah *May*-uh-kuh\ (Also spelled Maachah.)
1. A son of Nahor by a concubine, Reumah (Genesis 22:23, 24).
2. One of David's wives, the mother of Absalom (2 Samuel 3:2, 3).
3. A city and district to the east and south of Mt. Hermon that was attacked but not conquered by Joshua in occupying the land east of the Jordan River (Joshua 13:9-13).
4. The father of Achish, king of the Philistine city Gath, to which two slaves of Shimei had fled (1 Kings 2:39).
5. The mother of King Abijah, the wife of King Rehoboam (1 Kings 15:1, 2; also spelled Michaiah).

return, according to Exodus 21:24; Leviticus 24:19, 20; and Deuteronomy 19:21.

Ll

Mm

6. A concubine of Caleb (1 Chronicles 2:48).
7. The wife of Makir, a descendant of Manasseh (1 Chronicles 7:16).
8. The wife of Jeiel, the great-grandmother of Saul (1 Chronicles 9:35, 36).
9. The mother of one of David's mighty men, Hanan (1 Chronicles 11:43).
10. The mother of Shephatiah, one of the officers over the tribe of Simeon (1 Chronicles 27:16).

Maaseiah \May-uh-*see*-yuh\
1. One of the Levitical musicians accompanying the ark from the house of Obed-Edom (1 Chronicles 15:18, 20).
2. One of the commanders of hundreds who helped place Josiah on the throne (2 Chronicles 23:1, 10, 11).
3. Officer in King Uzziah's army (2 Chronicles 26:11).
4. Son or relative of Ahaz, king of Judah, killed in war with Israel (2 Chronicles 28:7).
5. A city official appointed by King Josiah to help repair the temple (2 Chronicles 34:8).
6. Four priests with this name divorced their foreign wives after the return from captivity (Ezra 10:18, 19, 21, 22, 30).
7. Father of one of the workers helping Nehemiah to repair the walls of Jerusalem (Nehemiah 3:23).
8. One of those who stood at the right hand of Ezra while he read the Law to the people (Nehemiah 8:4).
9. One of the Levites who explained the Law as it was read by Ezra (Nehemiah 8:7).
10. A leader of the people who joined with Nehemiah in affirming the covenant (Nehemiah 10:25).
11. Son of Baruch, descendant of Perez, son of Tamar, who lived in Jerusalem after the return from captivity (Nehemiah 11:1, 5).
12. A Benjamite, the son of Ithiel, who settled in Jerusalem after the captivity (Nehemiah 11:7).
13. A priest who sang and played the trumpet at the dedication of the wall of Jerusalem (Nehemiah 12:40-42).
14. The father of a priest sent by King Zedekiah to inquire of Jeremiah concerning the Babylonians (Jeremiah 21:1, 2).
15. A son of Shallum, a doorkeeper of the temple in the time of Jeremiah (Jeremiah 35:4).

Maccabees *Mack*-uh-bees\
A family of Jewish leaders in the time between the Testaments, known especially for their resistance in the persecution under Antiochus Epiphanes, who took the Syrian throne in about 175 BC.

Macedonia \Mass-eh-*doe*-nee-uh\
A region adjacent to the northern boundary of Greece. In New Testament times it was a Roman province with familiar cities such as Philippi, Thessalonica, and Berea

(Acts 16:9). Paul went to Macedonia in response to a vision (Acts 16:9, 10).

Machir *May*-ker\ (also spelled Makir).
1. The firstborn of Manasseh, son of Joseph, whose descendants were allotted land east of the Jordan (Joshua 17:1).
2. Descendant of Machir (#1) who cared for the crippled son of Jonathan after Jonathan was killed (2 Samuel 9:3, 4).

Machpelah \Mack-*pea*-luh
A field and cave near Hebron that Abraham purchased as a burial place for Sarah (Genesis 23:17). Abraham, Isaac, Rebekah, Leah, and Jacob were also buried there (Genesis 25:9; 49:29-31; 50:13).

Magdala *Mag*-duh-luh\
The home of Mary Magdalene. It probably was a village called Magadan, about four miles north of Tiberias on the western shore of the Sea of Galilee (Matthew 15:39).

Magdalene *Mag*-duh-leen\ or \Mag-duh-*lee*-nee\
A resident of Magdala. One of the women who followed Jesus was Mary Magdalene. Jesus drove seven demons out of her (Mark 16:9; Luke 8:2). She gave support to the ministry of Jesus (Luke 8:3). She was among the women who planned to anoint the body of Jesus (Mark 16:1). She was the first to see Jesus after His resurrection (John 20:10-18). She is often portrayed as a former harlot, but the Bible nowhere supports that. Perhaps some confuse her with the sinful woman who anointed Jesus' feet at the home of Simon the Pharisee in Luke 7:36-50.

Magi *May*-jye\ or *Madge*-eye\
A group of wise men who probably were schooled in the sciences. They were guided by a star to the young child Jesus (Matthew 2:1-12).

Magnificat (Latin) \Mag-*nif*-ih-cot\
Mary's expression of praise and faith, sometimes referred to as a poem or hymn, which she uttered in response to Elizabeth's blessing (Luke 1:46-55). The title comes from the first word in the Latin translation.

Mahanaim \May-ha-*nay*-im\
Where angels of God appeared to Jacob when he was returning from Haran, prior to meeting Esau. The word means "two camps"—God's and Jacob's (Genesis 32:1).

Maher-Shalal-Hash-Baz *May*-her-*shal*-al-*hash*-bas\
(Strong accent on *hash*). (Also spelled Mahershalalhashbaz.)
A symbolic name that was given by Isaiah to his son, signifying the invasion of Syria by Assyria (Isaiah 8:1-4).

Mahlon *Mah*-lon\
One of the sons of Naomi and Elimelech. He was the

first husband of Ruth but died, along with his father and brother, in Moab (Ruth 1:2; 4:10).

Makir *May*-ker\\
See MACHIR.

Malachi *Mal*-uh-kye\\
1. Prophet and author of the last book of the Old Testament (Malachi 1:1).
2. The 39th and final book of the Old Testament, the twelfth in the "minor prophets" section. See BOOKS OF THE BIBLE CHART.

Malchiah \\Mal-*kye*-uh\\ (Also spelled Malchijah, Malkijah, and Melchiah.)
1. A Levite who served in the tabernacle in David's time (1 Chronicles 6:40).
2. Father of Pashhur (or Pashur), a messenger from King Zedekiah to Jeremiah (Jeremiah 21:1; 38:1).
3. Three of the former exiles who divorced their wives had this name (Ezra 10:25, 31).
4. Son of Recab (or Rechab) who helped repair the Dung Gate of Jerusalem (Nehemiah 3:14).
5. A goldsmith who helped repair the walls of Jerusalem after the captivity (Nehemiah 3:31).
6. He stood at the left of Ezra for the reading of the Law (Nehemiah 8:4).
7. The father of a priest who signed an agreement to keep the Law (Nehemiah 11:12; 12:42).

Malchishua *Mal*-kye-*shoe*-uh\\ (strong accent on *shoe*) (Also spelled Malchi-shua, Malkishua, Malki-Shua, and Melchishua.)
A son of Saul who died with his father on Mt. Gilboa (1 Samuel 14:49; 31:2; 1 Chronicles 8:33; 10:2).

Malchus *Mal*-kus\\
A servant of the high priest whose ear was cut off by Peter at the time of Jesus' arrest but whose ear Jesus restored (John 18:10; Luke 22:50, 51).

malefactors *mal*-ih-fac-ters\\
Wrongdoers or criminals. *The King James Version* uses this term of the two men hanging on crosses beside Jesus (Luke 23:39). Elsewhere they are referred to as thieves or robbers (Matthew 27:38; Mark 15:27).

Malki-Shua *Mal*-kye-*shoe*-uh\\ (strong accent on *shoe*)
See MALCHISHUA. This form is typical in the *New International Version*.

Malta *Mawl*-tuh\\ (Also spelled Melita.)
An island off the foot of Sicily where Paul's ship was wrecked while he was being transported to Rome as a prisoner (Acts 27:27–28:1).

Mamre *Mam*-reh\\
1. One of three Amorite brothers who assisted Abraham in rescuing Lot from the kings from the north (Genesis 14:11-13, 24).
2. A city where Abraham and Isaac made their homes (Genesis 35:27). Here it was that Abraham entertained three angels (Genesis 18:1, 2). It was located near Hebron (Genesis 23:17).

Manaen *Man*-uh-en\\
One of the prophets and teachers in the church at Antioch. It appears he was reared in the household of Herod the tetrarch (Acts 13:1).

Manasseh \\Muh-*nass*-uh\\
1. The first of Joseph's two sons who were born in Egypt (Genesis 46:20).
2. One of the 12 tribes of Israel comprised of descendants of Manasseh.
3. Territory given to the tribe of Manasseh as an inheritance; divided into two portions, one to the east of the Jordan and one to the west (Joshua 17:1, 2, 5, 7-10; 18:7).
4. Thirteenth king of Judah, son of Hezekiah. He ruled for 55 years. His reign was marked by evil practices including paganism and terrible violence (2 Kings 21). However, after being captured by the Assyrians, he turned to the Lord and was released and lived a more faithful life (2 Chronicles 33:10-13). See KINGS OF ISRAEL AND JUDAH CHART.
5. Grandfather of Jonathan, a priest in Dan who participated in idol worship (Judges 18:30, *KJV, NASB, NKJV*).
6. Two Israelite men who divorced their wives after the return from Babylonian captivity were named Manasseh (Ezra 10:30, 33).

mandrake *man*-drake\\
A plant of the nightshade family, with yellow or pale orange fruit. Its fruit was believed to act as an aphrodisiac (Genesis 30:14-16; Song of Solomon 7:13).

Maneh *may*-neh\\
A mina, a measure of weight equaling 60 shekels (Ezekiel 45:12).

Manoah \\Muh-*no*-uh\\
Father of Samson. (Judges 13:2, 3, 24).

manorah *(Hebrew)* \\muh-*nor*-uh\\
Hebrew for "lamp stand" or, as in the *King James Version*, "candlestick." Usually transliterates as "menorah."

Mara *Mah*-ruh\\
Bitterness. The name Naomi (which means "delight" or "pleasantness") gave herself on returning to Bethlehem from Moab (Ruth 1:20). The word is related to Marah, below.

Mm

Marah *Mah*-ruh\\
The bitter springs that were made sweet by the Lord after the people grumbled early on their journey in the wilderness (Exodus 15:23-25).

Marchesvan *Mar*-chez-vun\\
The eighth month of the Jewish calendar (1 Kings 6:38); known as Bul before the exile. See Calendar Chart.

Marduk *Mar*-duke\\ (Also known as Merodach.)
Chief god of Babylonian mythology (Jeremiah 50:2).

Mariamne *May*-ree-*ahm*-nee\\ (strong accent on *ahm*)
Herod the Great had two wives by this name, but neither is mentioned in Scripture. The second was the mother of Herod Philip (not the tetrarch).

Mariolatry \\Mare-ee-*ah*-luh-tree\\
The worship of Mary the mother of Jesus.

Maritima \\Mare-uh-*tee*-muh\\
By the sea. The name is sometimes added by commentators to that of Caesarea on the Mediterranean coast to distinguish it from Caesarea Philippi. The name is not found in Scripture.

Mark \\Mark\\
1. John Mark, son of Mary (Acts 12:12), cousin of Barnabas (Colossians 4:10), co-worker of Paul (2 Timothy 4:11) and Peter (1 Peter 5:13). He was also the author of the Gospel of Mark. He abandoned Paul and Barnabas's first journey (Acts 13:13), and Paul refused to accept him as a companion on the second (Acts 15:36-40). But the mention of Mark in 2 Timothy 4:11 shows he had once again won Paul's favor and trust.
2. The second Gospel and second book of the New Testament, written by John Mark. Tradition holds that Mark recorded the preaching of Peter as his Gospel. See Books of the Bible Chart.

martureo *(Greek)* \\mar-too-*reh*-oh\\
Greek for "bear witness" or "testify."

martus *(Greek)* *mar*-toose\\
Greek for "witness." It is the source of the English word *martyr* (see martyr), but the term is used in that sense in the New Testament only three times (Acts 22:20; Revelation 2:13; 17:6).

martyr *mar*-tur\\
Transliteration of the Greek *martus,* meaning witness. It has come to mean one who bears witness at the cost of his or her life, as Stephen (Acts 22:20).

Mary *May*-ry\\ or *Mer*-ry\\
1. The mother of Jesus (Matthew 1:18; Luke 1:26, 27).
2. Mary Magdalene. (See Magdalene.)

3. The sister of Lazarus (John 11:32). This Mary anointed Jesus' feet (John 12:1-8).
4. The mother of James and Joses (or Joseph). She witnessed the crucifixion (Matthew 27:56) and the open tomb (Mark 15:40).
5. The wife of Clopas (or Cleophas). She witnessed the crucifixion (John 19:25).
6. Mother of John Mark (Acts 12:12).
7. Member of the church at Rome to whom Paul sent personal greetings (Romans 16:6).

Mashal \\Muh-*shal*\\
1. A city in Asher that was given over to the Levites of the family of Gershon (1 Chronicles 6:74). Joshua 19:26 has an alternate spelling, Mishal or Misheal, *KJV.*
2. Hebrew for "proverb" or "parable."

mashiach *(Hebrew)* \\mah-*she*-ock\\
Hebrew for "anointed" or "Messiah." See Messiah.

Massah *Mass*-uh\\
A place near Rephidim where God provided water through Moses for the Israelites after they complained bitterly about the lack of water. Moses declared they were testing God and gave this name to the place of testing (Exodus 17:1-7).

Matri *May*-try\\
A clan of the tribe of Benjamin to which Saul belonged (1 Samuel 10:21).

Mattan *Mat*-an\\
1. A priest of Baal who was slain when Joash was made king of Judah (2 Kings 11:18, 19).
2. Father of Shephatiah, who counseled King Zedekiah to put Jeremiah to death (Jeremiah 38:1, 4).

Mattaniah \\Mat-uh-*nye*-uh\\
1. Earlier name of Zedekiah, who was made king of Judah and renamed Zedekiah by Nebuchadnezzar (2 Kings 24:17). See Zedekiah #2.
2. One of the sons of Heman chosen by David to provide music for the temple (1 Chronicles 25:4, 6).
3. An ancestor of Jahaziel who counseled King Jehoshaphat (2 Chronicles 20:14, 15).
4. An ancestor of a group of Levites who assisted Hezekiah in purifying the temple (2 Chronicles 29:13, 15).
5. Four Levites who divorced their wives after they returned from captivity (Ezra 10:11, 18, 26, 27, 30, 37).
6. A Levite, a descendant of Hanan, who was an assistant to the priest in charge of the storerooms of Jerusalem after the captivity (Nehemiah 13:13).

Matthew *Math*-yew\\
1. A tax collector whom Jesus called to be one of His disciples (Matthew 9:9). Mark and Luke identify him as Levi (Mark 2:14; Luke 5:27).

2. The first Gospel and first book of the New Testament, written by the apostle Matthew. See BOOKS OF THE BIBLE CHART.

Matthias \Muh-*thigh*-us\ (*th* as in *thin*)
The man chosen to be an apostle in the place of Judas Iscariot (Acts 1:15-26).

Mattithiah *Mat*-ih-thigh-uh\
1. A Levite, son of Shallum, in charge of baking bread for the temple (1 Chronicles 9:31).
2. A Levite, son of Jeduthun, one of six brothers who played the harp (1 Chronicles 25:1, 3, 21).
3. One of the men who stood by Ezra when he read the book of the Law (Nehemiah 8:4).

Mazzaroth *Maz*-uh-rahth\
The constellations (Job 38:32).

Medes \Meedz\
Inhabitants of Media. It was among these people that some of the Israelites were deported after the destruction of the northern kingdom (2 Kings 17:6; 18:11). A coalition of Medes and Persians later defeated Babylon (Daniel 5:31). Medes were also present in Jerusalem on Pentecost after Jesus' resurrection (Acts 2:9).

Media *Meed*-ee-uh\
A country north of Babylonia and east of Assyria. It became a world power when it aligned with Babylon to conquer Nineveh, thus destroying the Assyrian Empire. Later the Medes combined with the Persians to destroy Babylon and to dominate the world. Media figured prominently in the history of captive Israel (Daniel 8:20; Esther 1:3, 14, 18; 10:2).

Mediterranean *Med*-uh-tuh-*ray*-nee-un\ (strong accent on *ray*)
The large sea that separates Africa from Europe and western Asia. Also the region around this sea. Most Bible versions do not use this name (*NLT* has it 37 times), using instead such designations as the "sea of the Philistines" (Exodus 23:31), "great sea" (Numbers 34:6), "western sea" (Deuteronomy 11:24; *KJV* has "uttermost sea" here), or simply "the sea" (Numbers 13:29).

meet \meet\
Adjective meaning "appropriate, suitable" (Genesis 2:18, *KJV, ASV*).

megas *(Greek)* *meg*-oss\
Greek for "great" or "large."

Megiddo \Muh-*gid*-doe\
1. City in the tribe of Manasseh, on the southeastern slope of Mt. Carmel, where the Canaanites resisted Israelite occupation (Joshua 12:21; Judges 1:27).

2. Valley or plain near the city of Megiddo that was on a major trade route and became a strategic battle site. Here Barak and Deborah defeated Sisera (Judges 5:19); later Josiah was fatally wounded here trying to intercept Pharaoh Neco on his way to fight the Babylonians at Carchemish (2 Chronicles 35:20-24).

Melchiah \Mel-*kye*-uh\
See MALCHIAH.

Melchizedek \Mel-*kiz*-eh-dek\
A priest of God who greeted and blessed Abram after he returned from the rescue of Lot (Genesis 14:17-20; Hebrews 7:1-10). He was the prototype of Christ's infinite priesthood (Psalm 110:4; Hebrews 7:17).

Melita *Mel*-i-tuh\
See MALTA.

Melzar *Mel*-zar\
A guard who was in charge of Daniel, Shadrach, Meshach, and Abednego (Daniel 1:11, 16, *KJV*). Probably a title rather than a name.

Menahem *Men*-uh-hem\
Sixteenth king of Israel (the northern kingdom); he gained the throne by killing Shallum, the previous king. He ruled ten years, becoming a vassal to Assyria in the later years of his reign (2 Kings 15:14-22).

mene *Me*-ne\
A word meaning "numbered." It was the first word of the writing on the wall of Belshazzar's palace spelling out the end of Babylon (Daniel 5:25, 26).

Mephibosheth \Meh-*fib*-o-sheth\
1. A son of Rizpah, concubine of King Saul, who was surrendered to the Gibeonites for execution because of Saul's sin against them (2 Samuel 21:5-9).
2. A son of Jonathan and grandson of Saul who was crippled in both feet when dropped by a nurse at the news of the death of both Jonathan and Saul (2 Samuel 4:4). As an adult he was welcomed at King David's table (2 Samuel 9:1-7).

Mercurius \Mur-*koo*-ri-us\
Greek spelling of the name of the mythical god Mercury. See MERCURY.

Mercury *Mur*-kyuh-ree\
Mythical Greek/Roman god who was thought to have served as spokesman and messenger for the other gods (Acts 14:12). Greek name is *Hermes.*

Meribah *Mehr*-ih-buh\
Waters at Kadesh where Moses failed to honor God (Numbers 27:14; Deuteronomy 32:51).

Mm

Mesha *Me*-shuh\\

1. An area, probably in southwestern Arabia, where descendants of Shem settled (Genesis 10:30).
2. King of Moab who rebelled against Jehoram, king of Israel. Jehoram enlisted the help of King Jehoshaphat of Judah and defeated the Moabites (2 Kings 3:4-27). The deeds of King Mesha are inscribed on the Moabite Stone.
3. The eldest son of Caleb (1 Chronicles 2:42).
4. A son of Shaharaim, a descendant of Benjamin who lived in Moab (1 Chronicles 8:8, 9).

Meshach *Me*-shack\\

Originally called Mishael, he was one of the three companions of Daniel who were trained to enter Nebuchadnezzar's service. He was one of three who was thrown into the fiery furnace (Daniel 1:3-9; 3:12-30).

Meshullam *Me*-*shul*-am\\

1. Grandfather of a scribe appointed by King Josiah to be in charge of the money given for the repair of the temple (2 Kings 22:3, 4).
2. The eldest son of Zerubbabel (1 Chronicles 3:19).
3. One of a group of Gadites who lived in Bashan (1 Chronicles 5:13).
4. A Benjamite, descendant of Elpaal, who returned from Babylonian captivity (1 Chronicles 8:17).
5. A Benjamite, father of Sallu, who returned from Babylonian captivity (1 Chronicles 9:7; Nehemiah 11:7).
6. A Benjamite, son of Shephatiah, who returned from Babylonian captivity (1 Chronicles 9:8).
7. A priest, the son of Zadok, who returned from Babylon (1 Chronicles 9:11; Nehemiah 11:11).
8. A son of Meshillemith of the priestly tribe who moved back to Jerusalem from Babylon (1 Chronicles 9:12).
9. An ancestor of a Levite supervising work to restore the temple in the time of Josiah (2 Chronicles 34:12).
10. A Jewish leader sent by Ezra to recruit Levites who had stayed in Babylon to return to Jerusalem to serve in the temple (Ezra 8:16, 17).
11. A priest who opposed Ezra's directions for priests and Levites to divorce foreign wives (Ezra 10:15).
12. An Israelite who divorced his foreign wife after returning from Babylon (Ezra 10:29).
13. A son of Berekiah who was a worker on the wall of Jerusalem next to the Fish Gate and on another section of the wall (Nehemiah 3:4, 30).
14. The son of Besodeiah who helped in repairing the Old Gate of Jerusalem (Nehemiah 3:6).
15. One who stood on Ezra's left at the reading of the Law at the gate (Nehemiah 8:4).
16. One of the priests who signed the covenant alongside Nehemiah (Nehemiah 10:7).
17. A Levite who signed the covenant alongside Nehemiah (Nehemiah 10:20).
18. A head of Ezra's priestly family who returned from Babylon (Nehemiah 12:13).
19. A head of Iddo's priestly family who returned from Babylon (Nehemiah 12:16).
20. A gatekeeper who guarded the storerooms at the gates (Nehemiah 12:25).

Mesopotamia *Mes*-uh-puh-*tay*-me-uh\\ (strong accent on *tay*).

Literally meaning "between the rivers," this term refers to a region that includes all or part of lands otherwise known as Chaldea, Padan-Aram, and Syria. Modern Iraq occupies much of what was Mesopotamia. (See Acts 2:9; 7:2.)

Messiah \\Meh-*sigh*-uh\\

Anglicized rendering of the Hebrew *mashiach,* "anointed." Kings, priests, and prophets were referred to in the Old Testament as anointed (Leviticus 4:3; 1 Samuel 24:10; 1 Kings 19:16). The Greek equivalent to *Messiah* is *Christos* (John 1:41; 4:25).

messianic \\mess-ee-an-ick\\

Of, or related to, the Messiah. Prophecies that predict the Messiah are called messianic prophecies. Psalms about the Christ are called messianic psalms.

metamorphosis *met*-tuh-*mor*-fuh-suss\\ (strong accent on *mor*)

Change in physical form; transformation.

mete \\meet\\

Verb meaning "to measure" (Luke 6:38, *KJV, ASV).*

Methuselah \\Muh-*thoo*-zuh-luh\\ (*th* as in *thin*)

Son of Enoch, father of Lamech, grandfather of Noah. He lived 969 years, the greatest age of any person recorded in the Bible (Genesis 5:21-29; 1 Chronicles 1:3). Calculations from the genealogies in Genesis indicate that he died in the same year as the flood of Noah. Some believe he perished in the flood; others, that he died in the same year but before the flood began.

Micah *My*-kuh\\

1. A prophet of God during the reigns of Jotham, Ahaz, and Hezekiah, kings of Judah (Micah 1:1).
2. The 33rd book of the Old Testament, the sixth in the "minor prophets" section. The book deals with the judgment of God against both Judah and Israel. See Books of the Bible Chart.
3. A man in the hill country of Ephraim who set up a bogus worship center (Judges 17:1-5).
4. A descendant of Reuben, a son of Shimei (1 Chronicles 5:3-5).
5. Grandson of Merib-baal (that is, Mephibosheth), son of Jonathan (1 Chronicles 8:34).

Mm

6. The first son of Uzziel, a priest, a descendant of Levi (1 Chronicles 23:12, 20).

7. Father of Abdon (2 Chronicles 34:20).

Micaiah \My-*kay*-uh\ (Also spelled Michaiah.)

1. A true prophet of God in Israel. He disagreed with 400 sycophant prophets and warned Ahab against going to battle with a Syrian force. He was put in prison as a result (1 Kings 22:1-9).

2. Father of Achbor, who acted as a messenger for King Josiah to Huldah the prophetess (2 Kings 22:12-14).

3. The wife of King Rehoboam and mother of Abijah, who succeeded Rehoboam to the throne (2 Chronicles 12:16—13:2; see MAACAH, #5).

4. One of a group of officials of King Jehoshaphat's court sent to teach the people of Judah from the "book of the Law of the Lord" (2 Chronicles 17:7, 9).

5. A priest who was an ancestor of Zechariah who served as a musician at the dedication of the wall of Jerusalem (Nehemiah 12:35).

6. A trumpet player at the dedication of the wall of Jerusalem (Nehemiah 12:41).

7. The son of a scribe who reported some dire predictions of Jeremiah to officials of King Jehoiakim's court (Jeremiah 36:11-13).

Michal *My*-kal\

A daughter of King Saul whom he gave to David in marriage (1 Samuel 18:20, 21, 27). In the ensuing years the marriage was off again, on again, and off again (1 Samuel 19:11; 25:44; 2 Samuel 3:14, 15; 6:16).

Micmash *Mik*-mash\ (Also spelled Michmash.)

A city in the hill country of Benjamin about 20 miles north of Jerusalem. This is the site of Jonathan's great victory over the Philistines (1 Samuel 14:1-13).

Michtam (Hebrew) *Mik*-tam\

See MIKTAM.

Midian *Mid*-ee-un\

1. Abraham's fourth son by Keturah (Genesis 25:2).

2. Land to which Moses fled after killing an Egyptian (Exodus 2:15; 3:1; Acts 7:29). It lay on both sides of the eastern arm of the Red Sea. Toward the end of the wilderness wandering, leaders from Midian conspired with leaders in Moab to prevent the Israelites from passing through Moab (Numbers 22:1-7).

Midianites *Mid*-ee-un-ites\

1. The nomadic people of Midian. Jethro (Reuel), the father-in-law of Moses, was a priest of Midian (Exodus 2:18, 21). Years after Moses, Gideon defeated the Midianites in the valley of Jezreel with 300 men (Judges 6, 7, 8).

2. Merchantmen who purchased Joseph from his brothers (Genesis 37:28). These are also called Ishmaelites.

Miktam (Hebrew) *Mik*-tam\ (Also spelled Michtam.)

This Hebrew word means "writing" or "psalm." It is in the ascription of Psalms 56–60.

Milcah *Mil*-kuh\

1. Daughter of Hanan, wife of Nahor, grandmother of Rebekah (Genesis 11:29; 24:15).

2. A female descendant of Manasseh who was allocated a tract of land as her inheritance (Numbers 26:33; Joshua 17:3, 4).

Milcom *Mill*-com\ (Also known as Molech or Moloch.)

A false god of the Ammonites (1 Kings 11:5; 2 Kings 23:13). See MOLECH.

millennia \muh-*len*-ee-uh\

Plural of millennium. See MILLENNIUM.

millennium \muh-*len*-ee-um\

A period of 1000 years. "The millennium" is a reference to the reign of Christ mentioned in Revelation 20:2-7. Differing views of the millennium and of the timing of Christ's return relative to it have become the primary identifying feature of different views of end times. Premillennial theology anticipates Christ's return before the millennium. Postmillennial theology anticipates Christ's return after the millennium. Amillennial theology holds that the millennium is not a literal 1000-year reign but a figurative expression for the church age.

Mm

Miletus \My-*lee*-tus\

A city on the Aegean seacoast about 35 miles south of Ephesus. Paul met elders from the church at Ephesus here and bade them farewell (Acts 20:15-38).

Millo *Mill*-o\

1. A citadel at Shechem (Judges 9:6-20).

2. A fortification at Jerusalem (2 Samuel 5:9; 1 Kings 9:15).

Minnith *Min*-ith\

An Ammonite city about 20 miles east of the mouth of the Jordan River. Jephthah laid waste to the area because the Ammonites had made war on Israel (Judges 11:33). Some 600 years later the area was known for trading with other nations (Ezekiel 27:17).

Minotaur *Min*-o-tor\

Mythological creature that was half man and half bull.

Miriam *Meer*-ee-um\

1. The daughter of Amram and Jochebed and sister of Moses and Aaron (Numbers 26:58, 59).

2. A descendant of Caleb (1 Chronicles 4:15, 17).

Mishael *Mish*-a-el\\
1. A son of Aaron's uncle, Uzziel (Exodus 6:22).
2. One of the men who stood at Ezra's left during the reading of the Law (Nehemiah 8:4).
3. One of the three companions of Daniel in the court of Nebuchadnezzar. He was also called Meshach (Daniel 1:6).

Mishnah *Mish*-nuh\\ (Also spelled Mishna.)
Collection of Jewish traditions compiled about AD 200.

Mithredath *Mith*-re-dath\\
1. Treasurer of Cyrus, King of Persia, who transferred riches to the Jews returning to Jerusalem (Ezra 1:8).
2. A Persian official, one of several who opposed the rebuilding of Jerusalem and wrote to King Artaxerxes to that effect (Ezra 4:7, 11-16).

Mizar *My*-zar\\
An unidentified mountain from which Mt. Hermon may be viewed (Psalm 42:6).

Mizpah *Miz*-pah\\ (Also spelled Mizpeh.)
1. The place where Jacob and Laban made a covenant and declared that God was a witness to it (Genesis 31:48-53).
2. The home of Jephthah, east of the Jordan in Gilead (Judges 11:29, 34).
3. An area north of the Sea of Galilee, in the region of Mt. Hermon where Jabin's forces fled from Joshua (Joshua 11:3).
4. A town of the tribe of Judah located west of Jerusalem in the western foothills (Joshua 15:38).
5. A city in an area allotted to Benjamin (Joshua 18:26). The Israelites gathered here before the Lord, after an atrocity was committed by some Benjamites (Judges 20:1-7). Here too, Gedaliah, the governor of Judah under Nebuchadnezzar, was placed to administer the affairs of the remnant left in Judah (2 Kings 25:23).

Mizpeh *Miz*-peh\\
See Mizpah.

Moab *Mo*-ab\\
1. Lot's oldest daughter's son by Lot (Genesis 19:36, 37).
2. An area to the east of the Dead Sea, reaching to the Arabian Desert. For most of its history, the extent of its boundaries north and south was adjacent to the lower half of the Dead Sea.

Moabites *Mo*-ub-ites\\
Descendants of Moab, grandson of Lot (Genesis 19:37), or inhabitants of Moab.

Moabitess *Mo*-ub-*ite*-ess\\ (strong accent on Mo)
A female descendant of Moab. Ruth was so identified (Ruth 1:22; 2:2).

Mohammed \\Mo-*ham*-ed\\ (Also spelled Muhammad.)
Arab prophet and founder of Islam, he lived from AD 570–632.

Mohammedanism \\Moe-*ham*-ud-uh-*niz*-um\\ (strong accent on *ham*)
The teachings of Mohammed; Islam or Islamism.

Molech *Mo*-lek\\ (Also known as Milcom or Moloch.)
A pagan god of the Ammonites, who practiced the sacrifice of children (Leviticus 18:21; 20:1-5). Several kings of Israel disobeyed God and built altars to Molech (2 Kings 16:3; 2 Kings 21:6).

Moloch *Mo*-lock\\
Variation of Molech (Amos 5:26 *KJV*).

monasticism \\mah-*nas*-tuh-*sih*-zum\\ (strong accent on *nas*)
The practice of living in seclusion for religious purposes, as in a monastery.

monotheist *mon*-uh-thee-ust\\ (*th* as in *thin*)
One who believes in and worships one god. Believers in the one true God are monotheists, but not every monotheist believes in the one true God.

Morasthite *Mo*-rass-thite\\
A person from Moresheth. The prophet Micah was a Morasthite (Jeremiah 26:18; Micah 1:1, *KJV*).

Mordecai *Mor*-dih-kye\\
1. An officer in the service of King Xerxes of Persia. He was cousin to Esther, whom he helped to become queen of Persia (Esther 2:1-18). He uncovered a plot to assassinate the king for which he was belatedly honored and elevated to a place of power (Esther 2:19-23; 6:1-11).
2. A Jew who returned from Babylon with Zerubbabel (Ezra 2:2).

Moreh *Moe*-reh\\
1. A place near Shechem where Abraham stopped by a tree after leaving Haran and journeying to Canaan (Genesis 12:6). This may be the same oak tree under which Jacob later buried his household's foreign gods (Genesis 35:4). It is probably the same tree under which Joshua set up a memorial stone (Joshua 24:26) and where Abimelech was crowned king (Judges 9:6).
2. A hill in the valley of Jezreel near which Gideon, with 300 men, defeated the Midianites (Judges 7).

Moresheth *Mo*-resh-eth\\
A city a few miles west of Gath in the Philistine plain. The prophet Micah was from this city (Jeremiah 26:18; Micah 1:1).

Moriah \Mo-*rye*-uh\
1. The region to which Abraham took Isaac, his son, to sacrifice him (Genesis 22:2).
2. Mt. Moriah is the site of the threshing floor that David was instructed by God to buy from Araunah on which he was to build an altar (2 Samuel 24:18-25) and on which, later, Solomon was to build the temple (2 Chronicles 3:1, 2).

Mosaic \Mo-*zay*-ik\
Of, or related to, Moses, as the Mosaic Law.

Moses *Mo*-zes\ or *Mo*-zez\
The son of Amram and Jochebed and a brother of Aaron and Miriam, who were slaves in Egypt (Exodus 1). He led the Israelites through the wilderness to the promised land but not into it. The first five books of the Old Testament (Pentateuch) as well as Psalm 90 are attributed to Moses.

Mosheh *(Hebrew)* *Moe*-sheh\
Hebrew derivation of the Egyptian word for "drawn out"; Moses (Exodus 2:10).

Most Holy Place \Most *Hoe*-lee Plase\
A room in the tabernacle/temple in which was the ark of the covenant (Exodus 26:33, 34; Hebrews 9:2). Sometimes called the Holy of Holies.

Murrain *murr*-un\
A plague not clearly identified but highly infectious (Exodus 9:3).

muthos *(Greek)* *moo*-thawss\
Greek for story, saying, myth, or fable. While the word can mean a true story or a false one, the term is used in the New Testament (five times) only in the sense of myth or fable (1 Timothy 1:4; 4:7; 2 Timothy 4:4; Titus 1:14; 2 Peter 1:16).

Myra *My*-ruh\
A city in Lycia near a seaport where Paul transferred to a ship sailing directly to Rome (Acts 27:5, 6).

Myrrh \mur\
A gum-like resin used to make perfume and to be used in the preparation of a body for burial. It was one of the gifts given to the baby Jesus (Matthew 2:11).

Mysia *Mish*-ee-uh\
A Roman province at the northwest corner of Asia Minor. This was one of the areas in which Paul was forbidden to preach the gospel on the second missionary journey. Instead, the Holy Spirit directed him to Troas where he saw a man in a vision beckoning him to come to Macedonia (Acts 16:6-10).

Nn

Naamah *Nay*-uh-muh\
1. Daughter of Lamech and sister of Tubal-Cain (Genesis 4:22).
2. An Ammonite woman, wife of Solomon and mother of Rehoboam (1 Kings 14:21, 31; 2 Chronicles 12:13).
3. A town in the western foothills given to Judah as an inheritance (Joshua 15:41).

Naaman *Nay*-uh-mun\
1. Syrian (Aramean) army commander under Ben-Hadad. He was a valiant soldier, but he had leprosy (2 Kings 5:1). He sought help from Elisha, who told him to wash himself seven times in the Jordan River. When he complied, he was healed (2 Kings 5:2-14).
2. A son of Benjamin who accompanied Jacob into Egypt (Genesis 46:5, 21).

Naamathite *Nay*-uh-muth-ite\
A title or designation for Zophar, one of the friends of Joab (Job 2:11; 11:1).

Nabal *Nay*-bull\
A rich, churlish man who rebuffed David, who then set out to eliminate him and his men. Abigail, Nabal's wife, intervened. Nabal, upon learning of his near execution, had a heart attack and died. David married the widow, Abigail (1 Samuel 25:1-42).

Nabateans *Nab*-uh-*tee*-unz\ (strong accent on *tee*)
Arabian tribe that conquered Edom in about 325 bc. Aretas of Damascus (2 Corinthians 11:32) was a Nabatean.

Nabonidus \Nab-uh-*nye*-dus\
Last king of the Babylonian Empire. His son Belshazzar was reigning as regent in his father's absence when Babylon fell to the Medes and Persians (Daniel 5).

Naboth *Nay*-bawth\
An owner of a vineyard in Jezreel that King Ahab coveted. Ahab's wife Jezebel conspired to falsely accuse Naboth of cursing God and the king. Naboth was stoned to death and his was vineyard given to Ahab (1 Kings 21:1-16).

Nachor *Nay*-kor\
Alternate spelling of Nahor in Joshua 24:2; Luke 3:34 (*KJV*). See NAHOR.

Nadab *Nay*-dab\
1. Son of Aaron and one of the first priests of Israel. With his brother Abihu, he improperly offered incense in

Mm
Nn

the tabernacle; the two were struck dead (Exodus 6:23; Leviticus 10:1, 2).

2. The son of Jeroboam who succeeded him as second king of the northern kingdom. His reign was evil like his father's. He was assassinated two years later by Baasha, who became king (1 Kings 15:25-28). See KINGS OF ISRAEL AND JUDAH CHART.

3. Identified as the son of Shammai of the tribe of Judah. He had two sons (1 Chronicles 2:28, 30).

4. A son of Jeiel of the tribe of Benjamin (1 Chronicles 8:29; 9:35, 36).

Nahor \Nay-hor\ (Also spelled Nachor.)
1. Father of Terah; grandfather of Abraham (Genesis 11:22-25; Luke 3:34).
2. Brother of Abraham, grandfather of Rebekah (Genesis 11:26; Joshua 24:2; Genesis 22:20-23).
3. The town to which Abraham sent his servant to find a wife for Isaac (Genesis 24:10).

Nahshon \Nah-shahn\
A leader in the wilderness wanderings. He was brother-in-law of Aaron (Exodus 6:23). He was an ancestor of Christ (Matthew 1:4; Luke 3:32).

Nahum \Nay-hum\
1. A prophet of God who pronounced God's judgment on Nineveh.
2. The 34th book of the Old Testament, the seventh in the "minor prophets" section. See BOOKS OF THE BIBLE CHART.
3. An ancestor of Jesus (Luke 3:25; spelled Naum in the *King James Version*).

Nannar \Nah-nar\
Supposed deity in Ur of the Chaldees and Haran in the time of Abraham.

Naomi \Nay-oh-me\
She was the widow of Elimelech and the mother of Mahlon and Chilion and the mother-in-law of Ruth and Orpah. The two sons died (Ruth 1:1-5).

Naphtali \Naf-tuh-lye\
1. The sixth son of Jacob and the second born to Bilhah, maidservant of Rachel (Genesis 30:7, 8; 35:25).
2. One of the 12 tribes of Israel.
3. The land containing the Jordan Valley above the Sea of Galilee and the mountains to the west that was the inheritance of the tribe of Naphtali (Joshua 19:32-39).

Nathan \Nay-thun\ (th as in *thin*)
1. Son of King David by Bathsheba (1 Chronicles 3:5). He was an ancestor of Jesus (Luke 3:31).
2. A prophet during the reigns of David and Solomon. He reproved David for his sin involving Bathsheba and

Uriah (2 Samuel 12:1-14). He assisted in the succession of Solomon to David's throne (1 Kings 1:7-30).

3. The father of Igal, one of David's mighty men from Zobah in northern Syria (2 Samuel 23:8, 36).

4. The father of two of David's advisers (1 Kings 4:5).

5. A descendant of Judah, the son of Attai (1 Chronicles 2:3, 36).

6. A leader under Ezra who helped in the preparations for the return to Jerusalem from Babylon (Ezra 8:15-17).

Nathanael \Nuh-than-yull\ (th as in *thin*) (Also spelled Nathaniel.)
A disciple of Jesus from Cana in Galilee (John 1:43-50; John 21:2). See BAR-THOLAMI.

Nathaniel \Nuh-than-yull\ (th as in *thin*)
See NATHANAEL.

Nazarene \Naz-uh-reen\
An inhabitant of Nazareth. Jesus was called a Nazarene (Matthew 2:23; Mark 14:67; 16:6). The followers of Jesus were so called (Acts 24:5).

Nazareth \Naz-uh-reth\
The home of Mary and Joseph (Luke 1:26; 2:39). It was located about 15 miles due west of the southern tip of the Sea of Galilee. Because Jesus grew to manhood there, He was sometimes called Jesus of Nazareth (Luke 2:51, 52; 4:16; 18:37; 24:19).

Nazarite \Naz-uh-rite\
See NAZIRITE.

Nazirite \Naz-uh-rite\ (Also spelled Nazarite.)
A person who makes a vow for a fixed period of time to be set apart for service to God. Such a person is to abstain from eating grapes or products of the vine and abstain from cutting his hair or touching a dead body. At the completion of the vow, he was required to make special offerings (Numbers 6:1-21).

Neapolis \Nee-ap-o-lis\
The seaport town where Paul first landed on European soil. From there he went inland about 10 miles to Philippi (Acts 16:11, 12).

Nebat \Nee-bat\
A man of the tribe of Ephraim; father of Jeroboam, who became the first king of the northern kingdom (1 Kings 11:26).

Nebo \Nee-bo\
1. A town bordering both Reuben and Gad about 15 miles east of the mouth of the Jordan River (Numbers 32:1-3). The town was rebuilt by the tribe of Reuben (Numbers 32:37, 38).

Nn

2. The mountain overlooking the promised land. Moses climbed Mt. Nebo and died there. The mountain was opposite the head of the Dead Sea (Deuteronomy 32:48-50).

3. An ancestor of some men of Israel who returned with Ezra to Jerusalem (Ezra 2:29; 10:43).

4. A false god of Babylon (Isaiah 46:1).

Nebuchadnezzar *Neb*-yuh-kud-*nez*-er\\ (strong accent on *nez*) (Also spelled Nebuchadrezzar.)
Strong king of Babylon who carried the people of Judah into captivity (2 Chronicles 36:15-21).

Nebuchadrezzar *Neb*-uh-kad-*rez*-er\\ (strong accent on *rez*)
A variation of *Nebuchadnezzar* in portions of Jeremiah and in Ezekiel. Some translations (as *NIV, NASB,* and *NLT*) render it with the more familiar spelling when it occurs.

Nebuzaradan *Neb*-you-zar-*a*-dun\\ (strong accent on *a*)
The commander of Nebuchadnezzar's imperial guard who laid waste to Jerusalem and who oversaw the transportation of the people to Babylon (Jeremiah 52:12-16). He was also given protective charge of Jeremiah (Jeremiah 39:11-14).

Nefertiti \\Nef-er-*tee*-tee\\
Egyptian queen, wife of Akhenaten. Some believe she was the Pharaoh's daughter who adopted Moses (Exodus 2:5-10), but this is unlikely.

Negeb *Neg*-eb\\
See NEGEV.

Negev *Neg*-ev\\ (Sometimes spelled Negeb.)
Southern part of Israel (Judah), near the border of Edom (Joshua 15:21). The word is the Hebrew word for "south," and many versions simply render it "the south" rather than as a proper noun.

Nehemiah *Nee*-huh-*my*-uh\\ (strong accent on *my*)
1. The son of Hacaliah, cupbearer to Artaxerxes (Nehemiah 2:1), appointed to be governor in the land of Judah after the return from Babylon (Nehemiah 5:14). His ministry is recorded in the book bearing his name.

2. A leader among the captive Israelites who returned to Jerusalem with Zerubbabel (Ezra 2:2).

3. A helper in building the walls of Jerusalem (Nehemiah 3:16).

4. The 16th book of the Old Testament, the 11th in the "history" section. It recounts the events of Nehemiah's service in building the city walls and in reestablishing life and worship among the people who returned from Babylon. See BOOKS OF THE BIBLE CHART.

Nehushta \\Ne-*hush*-tah\\
Mother of Jehoiachin. She was taken captive with her son by Nebuchadnezzar (2 Kings 24:8, 15).

Nehushtan \\Nee-*hush*-tun\\
The name given to Moses' bronze snake, which the people of Israel had been worshiping in the time of Hezekiah (2 Kings 18:4).

Neos *(Greek)* *Neh*-os\\
Greek for "new" or "young."

Nephesh *(Hebrew)* *Nef*-esh\\
Hebrew for "spirit," "soul," or "life."

Nephilim *Nef*-ih-*leem*\\
The term appears twice in the Old Testament to refer to a race of large people before (Genesis 6:4) and after the flood (Numbers 13:33). The term is rendered "giants" in some versions (as *KJV, NKJV,* and *NLT*).

Nephthalim *Nef*-thuh-lim\\ (*th* as in *thin*)
Reference to the area allotted to the tribe of Naphtali (Matthew 4:13, *KJV*).

Neriah \\Ne-*rye*-uh\\
The father of Baruch, the scribe who helped Jeremiah (Jeremiah 32:12).

Nethaneel \\Nih-*than*-e-el\\ (*th* as in *thin*)
See NETHANEL.

Nethanel \\Nih-*than*-el\\ (*th* as in *thin*) (Spelled Nethaneel in the *King James Version*.)
1. Man of the tribe of Issachar chosen to assist Moses in the census (Numbers 1:8; 2:5).

2. Son of Jesse and older brother of David (1 Chronicles 2:14).

3. One of the trumpeters chosen to participate in bringing the ark of the covenant into Jerusalem (1 Chronicles 15:24).

4. The father of the Levite scribe who recorded the various divisions of Levites in David's time (1 Chronicles 24:6).

5. Son of Obed-Edom and a gatekeeper at the tent David pitched for the ark of the covenant (1 Chronicles 26:4).

6. One of the officials sent by Jehoshaphat to teach the law in the cities of Judah (2 Chronicles 17:7).

7. One of Josiah's officials who contributed animals for the Passover sacrifice (2 Chronicles 35:9).

8. One of the Levites guilty of marrying a foreign wife in Ezra's day (Ezra 10:22).

9. A priest in Jerusalem after the exile (Nehemiah 12:21).

10. One of the musicians on the newly rebuilt wall of Jerusalem at the dedication (Nehemiah 12:36).

Nn

Nethinim *Neth*-ih-nim\
Some Bible versions, as *KJV, ASV,* and *NKJV,* use this term for temple servants after the Exile (Ezra 7:24).

Nicanor \Nye-*cay*-nor\
One of seven men chosen to administer the distribution of food to Grecian widows in the church in Jerusalem (Acts 6:1-5).

Nicea \Ny-*see*-uh\
City in France and site of ecumenical council in AD 325 that formally recognized the New Testament canon.

Nicodemus *Nick*-uh-*dee*-mus\ (strong accent on *dee*)
A member of the Sanhedrin (John 3:1). He met with Jesus one night (John 3:2-21). Later he spoke up for Jesus in a council meeting (John 7:50, 51). He assisted Joseph of Arimathea in preparing the body of Jesus for burial (John 19:38-42).

Nicolaitans \Nik-o-*lay*-ih-tunz\
A sect in the churches at Ephesus and Pergamum condemned by Jesus (Revelation 2:6, 12-15).

Nicolas *Nick*-uh-lus\
One of the seven men chosen in the Jerusalem church to look out for the Grecian widows (Acts 6:5).

Niger *Nye*-jer\
Another name for Simeon, a prophet or teacher in the church in Antioch (Acts 13:1).

Nimshi *Wim*-shy\
The grandfather of Jehu, king of the northern kingdom (2 Kings 9:2, 14).

Nineveh *Nin*-uh-vuh\
Capital city of the Assyrian Empire (2 Kings 19:36). God sent Jonah to Nineveh to warn the people to repent. Both Nahum and Zephaniah predicted its downfall (Nahum 2, 3; Zephaniah 2:13-15).

Nipto *(Greek)* *Nip*-toe\
Greek for "to wash."

Ninevites *Nin*-uh-vites\
Peoples of Nineveh (Matthew 12:41; Luke 11:30).

Nisan *Nye*-san\
The first month of the Jewish year, roughly equivalent to Mid-March to Mid-April (Nehemiah 2:1; Esther 3:7). It was called Abib before the exile. See CALENDAR CHART.

Non *None*\
Alternate spelling of Nun in 1 Chronicles 7:27 *(KJV)*.

Numbers *Num*-berz\
The fourth book of the Old Testament, and fourth in the "law" section. Written by Moses, it tells of the wilderness wanderings of the Israelites after the exodus from Egypt. See BOOKS OF THE BIBLE CHART.

Nun *None*\
  1. The father of Joshua, a member of the tribe of Ephraim (Exodus 33:11; Numbers 13:8).
  2. Fourteenth letter of the Hebrew alphabet (Psalm 119:105).

Nunc Dimittis *(Latin)* \Nunk Dih-*mit*-us\
The song of Simeon upon seeing the baby Jesus (Luke 2:29-32). The title, "Nunc Dimittis," is Latin for "Now may he [your servant] depart."

Oo

Obadiah \O-buh-*dye*-uh\
  1. The prophet who wrote the book bearing his name, an oracle against Edom (Obadiah 1:1).
  2. A devout servant of God in charge of Ahab's palace. He hid 100 prophets from Jezebel and later served as a messenger for Elijah (1 Kings 18:2-16).
  3. A descendant of David (1 Chronicles 3:21).
  4. A descendant of Issachar (1 Chronicles 7:3).
  5. A descendant of Saul (1 Chronicles 8:33, 38).
  6. A Levite (1 Chronicles 9:16) and a gatekeeper who guarded the storerooms (Nehemiah 12:25).
  7. A brave Gadite warrior in service to David (1 Chronicles 12:8, 9).
  8. The father of an officer over the tribe of Zebulun in King David's service (1 Chronicles 27:19).
  9. An official in the court of Jehoshaphat who was selected to teach the book of the Law in the towns of Judah (2 Chronicles 17:7, 9).
  10. A supervisor of work being done on the temple in Josiah's time (2 Chronicles 34:12).
  11. A descendant of Joab who accompanied Ezra to Jerusalem (Ezra 8:9).
  12. A priest who witnessed the covenant with Nehemiah (Nehemiah 10:5).
  13. The 31st book of the Old Testament, the fourth in the "minor prophets" section. See BOOKS OF THE BIBLE CHART.

Obed *O*-bed\
The son of Ruth and Boaz; grandfather of David (Ruth 4:17) and an ancestor of Jesus (Matthew 1:5).

Obed-Edom \O-bed-*ee*-dum\ (strong accent on *ee*) (Also spelled Obededom.)
1. The man into whose care the ark of the covenant was entrusted after the death of Uzzah (1 Chronicles 13:14).
2. One of several Levites appointed to play harps in the house of the Lord (1 Chronicles 15:21). This is possibly the same Obed-Edom as #1.
3. The son of Jeduthun, one of many who were appointed by David to minister before the ark (1 Chronicles 16:38).
4. A gatekeeper in the temple (1 Chronicles 26:1, 4, 5).
5. A man who was entrusted with the care of gold and silver articles in the temple (2 Chronicles 25:24).

Oded \O-dead\
A prophet who reprimanded the army of Israel for taking captive many wives and children of Judah (2 Chronicles 28:8-11).

oikos *(Greek)* \oy-koss\
Greek for "house" or "household."

oinos *(Greek)* \oy-noss\
Greek for "wine."

Olivet \Ol-ih-vet\
Mount of Olives, the hill to the east of Jerusalem (2 Samuel 15:30, *KJV*; Acts 1:12). The term does not appear in the *NIV, NLT,* or *NCV.*

omega *(Greek)* \oh-*may*-guh\ or \oh-*mee*-guh\
The last letter of the Greek alphabet, used to denote that which is last. When *omega* is used with *alpha* ("alpha and omega"), it refers to "the beginning and the end"; used to explain God (Revelation 1:8; 21:6; 22:13).

omnipotence \ahm-*nih*-poh-tense\
Having all power; ability to do anything. Only God is onmipotent (Matthew 19:26; Mark 10:27; Luke 1:37).

omnipresence \ahm-nih-*prez*-ence\ (strong accent on *prez*).
Present at all times in all places. Only God is omnipresent (Psalm 139:7-12).

omniscience \ahm-*nish*-unts\
Knowing all things. Only God is onmiscient (Psalm 139:1-4, 17-24).

Omri *Ahm*-rye\
Sixth king of the northern kingdom; he became king by defeating Zimri, who had killed the previous king a week earlier, and Tibni, who emerged as a rival after the death of Zimri (1 Kings 16:9-22). He built the city of Samaria, which became the capital of the northern kingdom (1 Kings 16:24). See KINGS OF ISRAEL AND JUDAH CHART.

Onesimus \O-*ness*-ih-muss\
A slave who had fled from his master, Philemon, and for whom Paul sought reconciliation (Philemon 10).

Onesiphorus \Ahn-uh-*sif*-oh-ruhs\ (strong accent on *sif*)
A Christian man in Ephesus who was of assistance to Paul when he ministered there. Onesiphorus visited Paul when Paul was imprisoned in Rome (2 Timothy 1:16, 17).

Ono *Oh*-no\
A town in the tribal area of Benjamin. The surrounding area is known as the plain of Ono (Nehemiah 6:2).

onyx *ahn*-iks\
A crystalline quartz gemstone with parallel layers of different colors; a type of chalcedony (Genesis 2:12; Exodus 25:7; 8:20; 35:9, 27; some versions, including *NCV* and *NLT,* include it in Revelation 21:20).

Ophel *Oh*-fell\
A mountain ridge that is the southern extension of Mt. Moriah on which Solomon built God's temple (2 Chronicles 3:1; 27:3; 33:14).

Ophir *Oh*-fur\
1. A region in southwest Arabia that was a source of fine gold (1 Kings 9:28; 1 Chronicles 29:4; 2 Chronicles 8:18; Job 28:16; Psalm 45:9; Isaiah 13:12).
2. Son of Joktam, a descendant of Shem (Genesis 10:29; 1 Chronicles 1:23).

Ophrah *Ahf*-ruh\
1. A city allotted to the tribe of Benjamin (Joshua 18:21, 23).
2. The home of Gideon. There the angel of the Lord challenged him to deliver Israel from the Midianites (Judges 6:11-14).
3. A descendant of Othniel (1 Chronicles 4:13, 14). See EPHRON.

Orion \O-*rye*-un\
A constellation mentioned in Job (Job 9:9; 38:31).

Ornan *Or*-nahn\
See ARAUNAH.

Orontes \Aw-*rahn*-teez\
River in Turkey and Syria that flows into the Mediterranean Sea. The ancient city of Antioch was situated on the Orontes.

Orpah *Or*-pah\
Naomi's daughter-in-law and Ruth's sister-in-law (Ruth 1:4, 14, 15).

Oo

Oshea \O-*shay*-uh\
See Hoshea #2.

Othniel *Oth*-ni-el\
A nephew of Caleb, who won a victory over an enemy city and as a reward married Caleb's daughter (Joshua 15:15-17). Later, Othniel was called to be a judge in Israel (Judges 3:7-11). See Judges of Israel Chart.

Pp

Paddan Aram *Pay*-dan-*a*-ram\ (Also spelled Padanaram.)
An area in northwest Mesopotamia. It was to Paddan Aram that Abraham's servant was sent to gain a wife for Isaac (Genesis 24:3, 4; 25:20) and where Jacob earned wives from Laban (Genesis 29:15-30).

pais *(Greek)* \pice\
Greek for "child" or, in some cases, "servant."

Pamphylia \Pam-*fill*-ee-uh\
A region on the southern coast of Asia Minor northwest of Cyprus. Paul landed there on his first missionary journey (Acts 13:13).

Paphos *Pay*-fus\
A city on the western shore of Cyprus where Paul converted the proconsul, Sergius Paulus. (Acts 13:6-12).

Paraclete *Pair*-uh-kleet\
Transliteration of the Greek *parakletos,* one called alongside. Used in this form, it generally designates the Holy Spirit. The term is found in commentaries and theology books, but does not appear in the common Bible translations. (Except the *NLT* has it three times in footnotes, at John 14:16; 15:26; 16:7.)

paraklesis *(Greek)* \par-*ahh*-clay-sis\
Greek for "comfort," "encouragement," or "summons." It is a calling alongside another for help. Barnabas was the "son of paraklesis" in Acts 4:36.

parakletos *(Greek)* \par-*ahh*-clay-tahs\
Greek for "one called alongside." It is typically translated "comforter," "helper," or "advocate." It is used only five times in the New Testament. Four times it refers to the Holy Spirit (John 14:16, 26; 15:26; 16:7) and once to Jesus (1 John 2:1).

Paran *Pair*-un\
A desert area on the east-central part of the Sinai Peninsula. Ishmael lived in the Desert of Paran (Genesis 21:21). Moses and the Israelites encamped there (Numbers 10:12; 12:16). It was from the Desert of Paran that Moses sent spies into Canaan (Numbers 13:1-3).

Parmenas *Par*-meh-nas\
One of the seven men chosen to care for the Grecian widows in the church at Jerusalem (Acts 6:1-6).

Parousia *(Greek)* \Par-*oo*-see-uh\
Greek for "coming" or "appearing." About two-thirds of the 24 times the term appears in the Greek New Testament, it refers to the second coming of Christ, so theologians have adopted the term to refer specifically to that.

parsin *par*-sun\
See Peres.

Parthenon *Par*-thuh-non\ (*th* as in *thin*)
The famous temple in Athens, a shrine to Athena, the virgin goddess of Greek mythology.

parthenos *(Greek)* \par-*then*-ahss\ (*th* as in *thin*)
Greek word for virgin (Matthew 1:23).

Patara *Pat*-uh-ruh\
A city on the western shore of Lycia (Acts 21:1).

Pathros *Path*-ros\
A region in Egypt, south of the capital Memphis. Here a remnant of the Jews fled after the destruction of Jerusalem (Isaiah 11:11; Jeremiah 44:1, 15; Ezekiel 29:14; 30:14). The *New International Version* has Upper Egypt.

Patmos *Pat*-muss\
The island to which the apostle John was banished for preaching the Word of Christ (Revelation 1:9). It was a rocky island about 80 miles southwest of Ephesus.

patriarchs *pay*-tree-arks\
Usually they were the fathers of tribes. The New Testament classifies Abraham (Hebrews 7:4), the sons of Jacob (Acts 7:8), and David (Acts 2:29) as patriarchs.

Pedaiah \Peh-*day*-yuh\
1. Grandfather of Jehoiakim, king of Judah (2 Kings 23:36).
2. A descendant of Jehoiachin and father of Zerubbabel (1 Chronicles 3:16-19).
3. Father of Joel, an officer in David's army who had been placed over the half tribe of Manasseh west of the Jordan (1 Chronicles 27:20, 21).

Oo

Pp

4. A worker under Nehemiah who helped repair the wall of Jerusalem (Nehemiah 3:25, 26).

5. One who stood to the left of Ezra as he read the Law to the people (Nehemiah 8:4).

6. Descendant of Benjamin and ancestor of one of the exiles who returned to Jerusalem (Nehemiah 11:7).

7. A Levite, with others, entrusted with the temple storerooms' security and the distribution of supplies to the people (Nehemiah 13:13).

Pekah *Peek*-uh\\

The 18th king of the northern kingdom of Israel. He was an officer in the service of Pekahiah. Pekah conspired against Pekahiah, killed him, and then assumed the throne. He reigned for 20 years and then was assassinated by his successor, Hoshea, who became the last king of Israel (2 Kings 15:25, 27-31).

Pekahiah \\Pek-uh-*hi*-uh\\

The 17th king of the northern kingdom, Israel. He succeeded his father Menaham to the throne, but was assassinated after two years by Pekah, an officer in his service (2 Kings 15:23-26). See KINGS OF ISRAEL AND JUDAH CHART.

Pelaiah \\Pe-*lay*-yuh\\ or \\Pe-*lye*-uh\\

1. A descendant of King Jehoiachin, one of the Jews who returned from Babylon (1 Chronicles 3:17, 24).

2. An assistant to Ezra as an instructor in the Law (Nehemiah 8:7).

Pelethites *Pel*-uh-thites\\

A group of David's fighting men under the command of Benaiah (2 Samuel 8:18; 15:18).

Peloponnesus *Pel*-uh-puh-*nee*-us\\ (strong accent on *nee*)

The peninsula that is the southern part of Greece. In New Testament times it was essentially the same as Achaia.

Peniel \\Peh-*nye*-el\\ (Also spelled Penuel.)

The place where Jacob wrestled with God (Genesis 32:22-32). It was near the River Jabbok, east of the Jordan River.

Peninnah \\Peh-*nin*-uh\\

The second wife of Elkanah (1 Samuel 1:1, 2).

Pentateuch *Pen*-ta-teuk\\

The first five books of the Old Testament; also called the books of law or the books of Moses.

Pentecost *Pent*-ih-kost\\

A day set aside by God for sacred assembly of the Hebrew people, 50 days after the Sabbath of the Passover (Leviticus 23:15-21); also called Feast of Weeks (Exodus 34:22; Deuteronomy 16:9, 10). It was the occasion of the first gospel sermon and the beginning of the church (Acts 2:1).

Penuel \\Pih-*nu*-el\\

See PENIEL.

Perea \\Peh-*ree*-uh\\

The eastern side of the Jordan River (in New Testament times).

peres *pair*-ess\\

Singular form of *parsin*, one of the words written on the palace wall of Belshazzar, the king of Babylon. (*KJV* and others have *upharsin*, which means "and parsin.") (Daniel 5:25). In explaining the writing, Daniel used the singular form, *peres*, which means "divided" (Daniel 5:28).

Perez *Pair*-ezz\\ (Also spelled Phares or Pharez.)

Son of Judah by his daughter-in-law Tamar. He was an ancestor of Jesus (Genesis 38:13-30; Matthew 1:3). *The King James Version* uses this spelling only three times; typically it uses *Pharez* in Old Testament references and *Phares* in the New Testament.

Perga *Per*-gah\\

Paul's port of entry into Asia Minor on his first missionary journey. It was the capital of the province of Pamphylia. John Mark left the missionary party here (Acts 13:13, 14).

Pergamos *Per*-guh-mus\\ (Also spelled Pergamum.)

One of the seven cities in Asia Minor that was home to a church addressed in Revelation (Revelation 1:11; 2:12). It is located roughly halfway between Troas and Ephesus.

Pergamum *Per*-guh-mum\\

See PERGAMOS.

Pericles *Pair*-ih-kleez\\

The leader of Athens at the height of its splendor and influence in the fifth century BC. He was the ruler who commissioned the building of the Parthenon, as well as many of the other spectacular structures in Athens.

Perizzites *Pair*-ih-zites\\

A group of people who dwelt in the land of Canaan before the conquest (Joshua 3:10; 9:1).

Persepolis *Per*-*sep*-puh-lis\\

The capital of Persia in the time of Nehemiah. It was northeast of the modern city of Shiraz in what today is Iran.

Persia *Per*-zhuh\\

A great world empire that assumed dominance at the fall of Babylon. Cyrus, king of Persia, allowed the return of the Jews from Babylon to Jerusalem. Esther, a Jew, became queen of Persia (Ezra 1:1-4; Esther 1:19; 2:17).

Pp

Peter *Pea*-ter\\
1. One of the 12 apostles, also known as Simon (Matthew 10:2) and Cephas (John 1:42). He was a fisherman before Jesus called him; his brother was Andrew (Matthew 4:18). He preached on Pentecost (Acts 2:14) and wrote the two epistles we call 1 and 2 Peter.
2. The 21st and 22nd books of the New Testament (1 & 2 Peter), third and fourth of the general epistles; written by the apostle Peter. See BOOKS OF THE BIBLE CHART.

Pethor *Pea*-thor\\
The home of Balaam. It was located on the shore of the upper Euphrates River (Numbers 22:5).

Pethuel \\Peth-*you*-el\\
Father of the prophet Joel (Joel 1:1).

Petra *Pet*-rah\\
1. A fortress carved into the rock cliffs in Edom by the Nabateans.
2. Greek word for "rock," as in "bedrock," not a mere stone (Matthew 16:18).

Phanuel \\Fuh-*nyoo*-el\\
Father of Anna, the prophetess (Luke 2:36).

Pharaoh *Fair*-o\\ or *Fay*-roe\\
Kings of Egypt, one of which figured prominently in the life of Joseph (Genesis 39–50) and another in the life of Moses (Exodus 2:1-10).

Pharaoh Neco *Fay*-ro *Nee*-ko\\ (Also spelled Pharaoh-nechoh and Pharaoh Necho.)
The king of Egypt who killed Josiah, king of Judah, in a battle at Megiddo (2 Kings 23:29, 30).

Pharez *Fay*-reez\\ or *Fair*-ez\\ (Also spelled Phares.)
See PEREZ.

Pharisees *Fair*-ih-seez\\
One of two major religious parties (Sadducees, the other) of the Jews that developed after the captivity in Babylon. Major differences between the two parties concerned the resurrection, angels, and spirits (Acts 23:7, 8). The Pharisees were much more concerned with keeping the Mosaic law than the more politically minded Sadducees.

Pharpar *Far*-par\\
One of two rivers in Damascus that Naaman favored over the Jordan (2 Kings 5:11, 12).

Phebe *Fee*-be\\
See PHOEBE.

Phenice \\Fih-*nye*-see\\
See PHOENICIA.

Phichol *Fye*-kahl\\
Commander of the Philistine forces who, along with Abimelech, entered into an agreement with Abraham for the use of a well Abraham had dug at Beersheba (Genesis 21:22-32).

Philadelphia *Fill*-uh-*dell*-fee-uh\\ (strong accent on *dell*.)
One of the seven cities in Asia Minor that was home to a church addressed in Revelation (Revelation 1:11; 3:7). It was located about 50 miles from Ephesus.

philarguros *(Greek)* \\fil-*ar*-goo-ross\\
Greek for "money-loving" or "covetous"; it is a combination of the Greek words for "love" and "silver."

Philemon \\Fih-*lee*-mun\\ or \\Fye-*lee*-mun\\
1. The owner of the slave Onesimus who had fled to Rome. Philemon was a member of the church in Colosse whom Paul had brought to the Lord.
2. The 18th book of the New Testament, the fourth of the prison epistles. It was written by Paul to Philemon on behalf of Onesimus (Philemon 1-21). See BOOKS OF THE BIBLE CHART.

phileo *(Greek)* \\fih-*leh*-oh\\
One of the Greek verbs for "love." See PHILIA.

philia *(Greek)* \\fil-*ee*-uh\\
Greek word for "love" (the noun). It describes a goodwill toward another that is based on or deepened by a response. (Where *agape* is described as love "in spite of," *philia* may be called love "because of.")

Philip *Fil*-ip\\
1. One of the 12 apostles, from the town of Bethsaida and probably a fisherman before being called to follow Jesus (Matthew 10:3; Mark 3:18; Luke 6:14; John 1:43-48; 6:5-7; 14:8, 9).
2. One of seven men chosen to care for the Grecian widows in Acts 6. He became an evangelist and had four daughters who were prophetesses (Acts 6:5; 8:5-12, 26-40; 21:8, 9).
3. Herod Philip, son of Herod the Great (who murdered the infants of Bethlehem) and brother to Herod Antipas (who murdered John the Baptist). He was the first husband of Herodias, who left him to marry Antipas (Matthew 14:3; Mark 6:17).
4. Philip the Tetrarch. He also was a son of Herod the Great (by a different mother than Herod Philip's) and, upon Herod's death, became tetrarch of Iturea and Traconitis, northeast of Galilee (Luke 3:1).

Philippi \\Fih-*lip*-pie\\ or *Fil*-ih-pie\\
A Macedonian city off the northern coast of the Aegean Sea. Paul founded a church there that faithfully supported

Pp

him in his ministry and in his imprisonment (Acts 16:9-12, Philippians 1:1-8).

Philippians \Fih-*lip*-ee-unz\
1. Residents of Philippi.
2. The 11th book of the New Testament, second of the prison epistles; a letter from Paul to the church in Philippi, encouraging the believers there to remain faithful and to thank them for their continuing support of his ministry (Philippians 1:1). See Books of the Bible Chart.

Philistia \Fuh-*liss*-tee-uh\
The land bordering the Mediterranean Sea from south of Joppa to the city of Gaza. The home of the Philistines.

Philistines \Fuh-*liss*-teenz\ or *Fill*-us-teenz\
The inhabitants of Philistia, descended from Ham. In the days of the judges and kings of Israel and Judah they were very warlike. Five fortified cities provided their strength as a nation: Gaza, Ekron, Ashdod, Ashkelon, and Gath. The Philistines were among the nations left by Joshua at the direction of God in the conquest of the promised land (Judges 2:23–3:4).

Philo *Fie*-low\
First-century Jewish philosopher from Alexandria. Copies of some of his writings survive to the present and provide insight into life at the time of Christ.

philos *(Greek)* *fill*-oss\
Greek for "friend" or "one who loves."

Phinehas *Fin*-ee-us\
1. Grandson of Aaron (Exodus 6:25). He was commended by God for his action in ending an affair between an Israelite man and a Midianite woman (Numbers 25:6-13).
2. The second son of Eli (1 Samuel 1:3; 4:1-11).
3. Father of Eleazar who assisted Uriah, the priest, in caring for the sacred articles of the temple (Ezra 8:33).

Phoebe *Fee*-be\ (Also spelled Phebe.)
A Christian woman from the church at Cenchrea whom Paul commended to the church in Rome (Romans 16:1, 2).

phobeo *(Greek)* \fo-*beh*-oh\
Greek verb for "fear."

Phoenicia \Fuh-*nish*-uh\ (Also spelled Phenice.)
Country consisting of the narrow coastland of the Mediterranean Sea bordering the hills of Galilee on the south. Two of its most famous cities were Tyre and Sidon.

Phoenicians \Fuh-*nish*-unz\
Canaanite people living in Phoenicia (Genesis 10:13, 15). Tyre, their strong city, withstood the armies of nations

until the time of Alexander the Great. Hiram of Tyre provided Solomon with building material for many years (1 Kings 5:1-18).

phone *(Greek)* \foe-*nay*\
Greek for "sound" or "noise."

phos *(Greek)* \fohss\
Greek for "light."

Photina *Fo*-ti-na\
Supposedly a name given by Jesus to the Samaritan woman He met by Jacob's well. She is venerated as a saint in both the Roman and Greek churches.

Phrygia *Frij*-e-uh\
A Roman province in Asia Minor where Paul preached before going to Troas (Acts 16:6-8).

phylacteries \fih-*lak*-ter-eez\
Little boxes worn by Jewish men to remind them to keep the decrees and commands of God (Deuteronomy 6:4-9). The boxes contained Scriptures and were secured by straps around the forehead and arm. To draw attention to themselves, the Pharisees made their phylacteries wide (Matthew 23:5).

Pi Hahiroth \Pie Ha-*hi*-roth\ (Also spelled Pihahiroth.)
Stopping place for the Israelites on the third night of their exodus from Egypt (Numbers 33:5-7).

Pilate *Pie*-lut\
See Pontius Pilate.

Pisgah *Piz*-guh\
Mountain from which Moses viewed the promised land before Israel, under the leadership of Joshua, crossed into that land. Mount Nebo is a summit near Pisgah or possibly part of it, as both names are used of the place where Moses went to view the land (Deuteronomy 34:1).

Pishon *Pie*-shahn\
One of the four rivers running from the Garden of Eden (Genesis 2:8-14).

Pisidia \Pih-*sid*-ee-uh\
A Roman district in Asia Minor (Acts 13:14; 14:24).

Pisidian Antioch \Puh-*sid*-ee-un *An*-tee-ock\
See Antioch, #2.

Pithom *Py*-thum\
One of two storage cities built by the enslaved Hebrews for Pharaoh (Exodus 1:11).

Pp

Pleiades *Plee*-uh-deez\\
One of the constellations mentioned in Job (Job 9:9; 38:31).

pneuma *(Greek)* \\noo-muh\\
Greek for "spirit" or "wind."

poimaino *(Greek)* \\poy-*my*-no\\
To act as a shepherd or to rule.

polis *(Greek)* *pol*-iss\\ or *pahl*-iss\\
Greek for "city."

polites *(Greek)* \\pol-*ee*-tace\\
Based on *polis,* above, it means "citizen" or "resident of a city" (Luke 15:15; 19:14; Acts 21:39).

politeuma *(Greek)* \\pol-it-*too*-ma\\
Citizenship or the conduct of a citizen. The only New Testament use of the Greek word is in Philippians 3:20.

Pollux *Pol*-uks\\
A figurehead on the ship bearing Paul to Rome to appear before Caesar. Pollux was one of the false gods of Rome (Acts 28:11).

Polybius \\Puh-*lib*-ee-us\\
Greek historian of the second century BC. Copies of his writings survive to the present and provide insight into life in that period.

Pp

polytheism *pohl*-ih-thee-iz-um\\
The worship of multiple gods, which are usually represented by idols.

pomegranate *pom*-ih-gran-it\\
A fruit to be eaten or made into wine (Song of Solomon 4:3; 8:2). Representations of the fruit were used in priestly robes and carvings that decorated the robes of the priests and Solomon's temple (Exodus 28:31-34; 2 Chronicles 3:16).

Pontius Pilate *Pon*-shus\\ or *Pon*-ti-us *Pie*-lut\\
Roman procurator of Judea before whom Jesus was tried and condemned (John 18:28–19:22). He gave permission to Joseph of Arimathea to remove the body of Jesus for burial (John 19:38). Pilate ordered Jesus' tomb be secured (Matthew 27:62-66). (See also 1 Timothy 6:13).

Pontus *Pon*-tuss\\
A Roman province along the north coast of Asia Minor in which many Jewish people lived. Jews from Pontus were in Jerusalem when Peter preached on Pentecost (Acts 2:9). Aquila, husband of Priscilla, was a native of Pontus (Acts 18:2).

Porcius Festus *Por*-she-us *Fess*-tus\\
Roman governor before whom Paul appeared to answer charges made against him by some Jews. At this hearing Paul appealed to Caesar. Consequently, Festus sent him to Rome (Acts 24:27; 25:1-27).

porneia *(Greek)* \\por-*nigh*-uh\\ or \\por-*nay*-uh\\
Greek word for "sexual immorality" or "fornication" (Mark 7:21; Acts 15:20, 29; 1 Corinthians 5:1; 6:13, 18; 7:2; Galatians 5:19; Colossians 3:5). This is the root word for the English word *pornography.*

Potiphar *Pot*-ih-far\\
An Egyptian official in Pharaoh's service who purchased Joseph from the Midianite merchants. Potiphar was impressed with Joseph's service and elevated Joseph to be in charge of Potiphar's estate. After Potiphar's wife falsely accused Joseph, Potiphar had Joseph put in prison (Genesis 39:1-20).

Potipherah *Pot*-i-*fee*-ruh\\ (strong accent on *fee*) (Also spelled Potiphera.)
An Egyptian priest and the father-in-law of Joseph. (Genesis 41:45).

potsherd *pot*-sherd\\
A broken piece of pottery (Psalm 22:15; Proverbs 26:23; Isaiah 45:9). Job scraped his sores with one (Job 2:8).

Prisca *Pris*-kuh\\
See Priscilla. *Prisca* is a variant of *Priscilla* used three times in the New Testament (Romans 16:3; 1 Corinthians 16:19; 2 Timothy 4:19), but not all the translations distinguish between the two forms. *The New International Version* never uses *Prisca;* the *King James* does just once.

Priscilla \\Prih-*sil*-uh\\ (Also called Prisca.)
The wife of Aquila and a helper of Paul as well as a teacher of Apollos (Acts 18:2, 18, 26). A church met in the home of Priscilla and Aquila (1 Corinthians 16:19).

privily *prih*-vuh-lee\\
Older term (used in the *KJV* and *ASV*) for "privately" or "secretly," usually with a sinister motive implied (as in Psalm 10:8; 31:4; Proverbs 1:11; Galatians 2:4). However, the sinister motive is not always present (e.g., Matthew 1:19).

Prochorus *Prock*-uh-rus\\
See Procorus.

Procorus *Prock*-uh-rus\\ (Also spelled Prochorus.)
One of seven men chosen by the apostles to minister to Grecian widows (Acts 6:5).

propitiation \\pro-*pih*-she-*ay*-shun\\ (strong accent on *ay*).
The atoning sacrifice for sin (1 John 2:2).

proselyte *prahss*-uh-light\\
A Gentile convert to Judaism (Matthew 23:15; Acts 2:10; 6:5; 13:43). The term is never used in the *NIV* or the *NLT*.

proskuneo *(Greek)* \\prahss-koo-*neh*-oh\\
Greek for "worship."

Proverbs *Prah*-verbz\\
The 20th book of the Old Testament, third in the "poetry" section. Written mostly by Solomon, it contains practical wisdom for ethics, business, child-rearing, wholesome speech, and more. See BOOKS OF THE BIBLE CHART.

psalmist *sahl*-mist\\
Writer or singer of psalms (songs). David is called the "sweet psalmist of Israel" (2 Samuel 23:1, *KJV, NASB, NLT*, and others).

Psalms \\Sahlmz\\
The 19th book of the Old Testament, second in the "poetry" section. It is a collection of songs used in Jewish worship. Several writers wrote individual psalms, but David wrote more than any other single writer. See BOOKS OF THE BIBLE CHART.

Ptolemais \\Toll-uh-*may*-us\\
A city located at the north end of the Bay of Acre, about 10 miles north of Mt. Carmel. Paul landed at the city on his return from his third missionary journey (Acts 21:7).

Puah *Peu*-uh\\
1. A midwife who was instructed by the king of Egypt to kill newborn Hebrew baby boys (Exodus 1:15, 16).
2. A son of Issachar (1 Chronicles 7:1).
3. The father of Tola, a judge who succeeded Abimelech as judge in Israel (Judges 10:1, 2).

Purim *Pew*-rim\\
A Jewish festival celebrating the preservation of the Jewish people in Persia (Esther 9:23-28).

Puteoli \\Pew-*tee*-o-li\\
A harbor near Rome where Paul disembarked from the ship carrying him to Rome to appear before Caesar (Acts 28:13).

Pythagoras \\Pi-*thag*-o-rus\\
Greek philosopher and mathematician of the sixth century BC.

Qq

Qohelet *(Hebrew)* \\Koe-*hel*-it\\
Hebrew for "preacher" or "teacher." It is found seven times in the book of Ecclesiastes.

Quarantania \\Kwar-an-*tan*-i-uh\\
A 1200 foot mountain about seven miles northwest of Jericho, believed by some to be the site of Jesus' temptation in the wilderness (Matthew 4:8).

quaternions \\kwa-*ter*-nee-unz\\
The term is used only once in the New Testament, in Acts 12:4 (*KJV, ASV*). It describes the "squads of four soldiers each" used to guard Peter in prison.

Quartus *Kwor*-tus\\
A believer in Corinth who sent greetings in Paul's letter to the Romans (Romans 16:23). His name means "fourth"; possibly he was a former slave whose master gave him a mere number instead of a name.

Quirinius \\Kwy-*rin*-ee-us\\ (Also called Cyrenius.)
Governor of Syria, identifying the time of the census decreed by Caesar Augustus that required Joseph and Mary to register in Bethlehem (Luke 2:1-5).

Qumran \\Koom-*rahn*\\
Region along the northwest shore of the Dead Sea, including some caves in which were found ancient biblical manuscripts now known as the Dead Sea Scrolls.

Rr

Raamses \\Ray-*am*-seez\\
See RAMESES.

Rabbah *Rab*-buh\\ (Also spelled Rabbath.)
1. A city east of the Jordan in the land of the Ammonites (Deuteronomy 3:11). The tribe of Gad was given land east of the Jordan that bordered Rabbah (Joshua 13:24, 25). The city figured in the history of Israel through the kings and down to the fall of Jerusalem (Ezekiel 21:20).
2. A town associated with Kiriath Jearim some seven miles west of Jerusalem (Joshua 15:60).

Rabbath *Rab*-buth|
See RABBAH.

Rabbi *Rab*-eye\
A title of respect accorded to teachers (John 1:38; 3:26; 6:25).

rabbinical \ruh-*bin*-ih-kul\
Related to a rabbi or group of rabbis.

Rabboni \Rab-*o*-nye\
Another form of Rabbi (John 20:16).

Rabshakeh \Rab-she-keh\ or \Rab-*shay*-ke\
A high-ranking Assyrian officer (2 Kings 18:17). Possibly a title rather than a name. Not found in *NIV* or *NLT.*

raca *ray*-kuh\ or \ray-*kah*\
A term of derision and contempt (Matthew 5:22).

Rachab *Ray*-kab\
See Rahab. This spelling is found only in Matthew 1:5 (*KJV*).

Rahab *Ray*-hab\ (Also spelled Rachab.)
1. A prostitute in Jericho who hid two of Joshua's spies and was later rewarded by Joshua by sparing her family (Joshua 2:1-14; 6:22, 23). She is listed in the genealogy of Christ (Matthew 1:5).
2. A large sea creature, either real or mythological, that is mentioned in symbolic language to describe the power of God over evil (Job 9:13; 26:12; Isaiah 51:9) or as a reference to Egypt (Isaiah 30:7; see also Psalm 87:4; 89:10). *The New International Version* uses the name Rahab in each of the passages cited above; the *King James Version* does so only in the Psalms and Isaiah 51:9. Other versions vary on when to use the name as a proper noun and when to render it "strength" or "proud" or even "Egypt."

Rr

Ramah *Ray*-muh\ (Sometimes spelled Ramoth or Ramath.)
1. A town in Asher near the city of Tyre (Joshua 19:29).
2. A city allotted to the tribe of Benjamin. It was grouped with Gibeon and Jerusalem (Joshua 18:21-25). Later the city was fortified by Baasha, king of Israel, to prevent any Israelites from entering Judah (1 Kings 15:16, 17).
3. A city of Gilead (2 Kings 8:29).
4. One of the fortified cities of Naphtali (Joshua 19:35, 36). Its association with Hazor places it about 20 miles north, northwest of the Sea of Galilee.
5. The home of Hannah and Elkanah. The village was about seven miles north of Jerusalem (1 Samuel 1:1-19). This village is also called Ramathaim or Ramathain-Zophim.
6. A village in the desert land of Simeon (Joshua 19:8).

Ramath *Ray*-muth\
See Ramah.

Ramathaim-zophim *Ray*-muh-*thay*-im-*zo*-fim\ (strong accents on *thay* and *zo*).
The village where the prophet Samuel was born (1 Samuel 1:1, 19, 20). The village was often called Ramah. It is where Samuel lived (1 Samuel 7:17) and where he was buried (1 Samuel 25:1).

Rameses *Ram*-ih-seez\ (Also spelled Raamses or Ramses.)
1. A district in the eastern delta region of the Nile River where the Israelites lived (Genesis 47:11).
2. One of two storage cities built by the enslaved Hebrews for Pharaoh (Exodus 1:11).
3. Extra-biblical sources list 11 Egyptian kings by that name.

Ramoth *Ray*-muth\
See Ramah.

Ramoth Gilead *Ray*-muth-*gil*-ee-ud\ (strong accent on *gil*) (Also spelled Ramothgilead.)
One of the chief cities of the tribe of Gad to the east of the Jordan River and about 20 miles north of the Dead Sea. It was designated a city of refuge (Deuteronomy 4:42, 43). It figured in the history of the kings (1 Kings 4:13; 22:29-40; 2 Kings 8:28).

rapere *(Latin)* \rap-*ear*\
To snatch, drag off, or seize. The word appears in the Latin translation of 1 Thessalonians 4:17 ("caught up" in most English translations) and is the source of the term *rapture* as it is used in theological circles.

Rebekah \Reh-*bek*-uh\
Daughter of Bethuel, nephew of Abraham. Rebekah became the wife of Isaac (Genesis 22:20-23; 24:67) and the mother of Jacob and Esau (Genesis 25:21-26).

Rechab *Ree*-kab\
1. One of the Israelites who killed Ish-Bosheth, son of Saul, and, in reporting it to David to seek favor, was himself slain (2 Samuel 4:5-12).
2. Father of Jehonadab who assisted Jehu in destroying Ahab's family (2 Kings 10:15-17). He was an ancestor of the Rechabites (Jeremiah 35:6).

Rechabites *Reck*-uh-bites\
Descendants of Rechab in Jeremiah's day who, in their mode of living (Jeremiah 35:6-10), were similar to the Nazirites. God used them as an illustration of obedience in contrast to the disobedience of the people of Jerusalem (Jeremiah 35:13-16).

Rehoboam \Ree-huh-*boe*-um\
Son of Solomon (1 Kings 14:21). His stubborn resistance to reform led to the division of the kingdom. He remained king of the southern part, known as Judah, and Jeroboam

became king of the northern part, called Israel (1 Kings 11:42–12:20). See Kings of Israel and Judah Chart.

Rehoboth \Re-*ho*-bahth\

1. One of the centers of Nimrod's kingdom in Assyria (Genesis 10:8-11).
2. A well dug by Isaac in an area near Beersheba (Genesis 26:19-22).
3. A city in Edom from which King Shaul came (Genesis 36:37).

Remaliah \Rem-uh-*lye*-uh\

The father of Pekah. His son Pekah became king of Israel after killing the ruling king, Pekahiah (2 Kings 15:25).

Rephidim *Ref*-ih-dim\

A camping site for the Israelites. They complained about the lack of water. God instructed Moses to strike a rock with his staff. He did and water came forth (Exodus 17:1-7). Here also the Israelites were attacked by the Amalekites. Hur and Aaron held Moses' hands aloft during the battle and the Amalekites were overcome (Exodus 17:8-13).

Reuben *Roo*-ben\

1. The eldest son of Jacob by Leah (Genesis 29:32).
2. One of the 12 tribes of Israel.
3. The area allotted to the tribe of Reuben, which lay to the east of the Dead Sea from the River Arnon (about halfway up the sea) to opposite the mouth of the Jordan River (Joshua 13:15-23).

Reubenites *Roo*-ben-ites\

The descendants of Reuben.

Reuel *Roo*-el\

1. A son of Esau, ancestor of the chiefs of Edom (Genesis 36:10, 17).
2. A priest of Midian, whose daughter married Moses after Moses fled from Egypt (Exodus 2:15-21). He was also known as Jethro (Exodus 3:1) and Raguel (Numbers 10:29, *KJV*). See Jethro; Hobab.
3. Father of Eliasaph, a leader of Gad during the wilderness wandering (Numbers 2:14, *KJV* and others; *NIV* and others have "Deuel").
4. Ancestor of a Benjamite who returned to Jerusalem after the Babylonian captivity (1 Chronicles 9:1-8).

Revelation \Rev-uh-*lay*-shun\

1. Divine impartation of knowledge. Paul's gospel was received by revelation, not by human teaching (Galatians 1:11, 12).
2. The final book of the Bible, an apocalyptic (see Apocalypse) description of the final victory of Christ over the forces of Satan, culminating in the new heavens and new earth. See Books of the Bible Chart.

Rezin *Ree*-zin\

The king of Syria (or Aram) with whom Pekah, king of Israel, allied to resist Babylon. They attempted to pressure Judah into joining the alliance (2 Kings 15:37; 16:5, 6; Isaiah 7:1-6).

Rezon *Ree*-zun\

A Syrian king who was an adversary of Solomon (1 Kings 11:23-25).

Rhegium *Ree*-ji-um\

A city located on the toe of the boot of Italy where Paul landed after leaving Syracuse of Sicily on his way to Rome (Acts 28:12, 13).

Rheims \Reemz\

City in France about 90 miles east of Paris where the Latin Vulgate New Testament was translated into English.

Riblah *Rib*-luh\

1. A landmark on the northeast corner of the area designated as the promised land. It is just north of the Sea of Galilee (Numbers 34:1, 11).
2. A city in Syria, some 60 miles north of Damascus, where Pharaoh Neco placed Jehoahaz, king of Judah, in chains (2 Kings 23:33). It was also where Nebuchadnezzar camped while his army besieged Jerusalem (2 Kings 25:1, 6, 20, 21; Jeremiah 39:5, 6).

Romans *Roe*-munz\

1. Inhabitants or residents of Rome, either the city or the empire.
2. Sixth book of the New Testament and first of the epistles; a letter written by Paul to the church at Rome. See Books of the Bible Chart.

ruah *(Hebrew)* *rue*-ah\

Hebrew for "wind," "breath," or "spirit" (Ezekiel 37:9, 10).

ruby *roo*-be\

A red gemstone (Exodus 28:17; 39:10; Ezekiel 28:13, *NIV, NASB, NCV*). See sardius. (See also Job 28:18; Proverbs 3:15.)

Rufus *Roo*-fus\

A son of the Simon of Cyrene who carried the cross of Christ (Mark 15:21). This may be the same Rufus to whom Paul sent greetings in Rome (Romans 16:13).

Ruhamah *Roo*-hah-muh\

A symbolic name given to Israel meaning "you have obtained mercy" (Hosea 2:1, *KJV, NLT*).

Ruth \Rooth\

1. Moabitess who returned to Bethlehem from Moab with her mother-in-law, Naomi, and became the wife of Boaz

Rr

and an ancestress of Christ. The book of Ruth tells her story.

2. The eighth book of the Old Testament, and third in the "history" section. It tells about Ruth the Moabitess, above. See BOOKS OF THE BIBLE CHART.

Ss

sabachthani *(Aramaic)* \suh-*back*-thuh-nee or –nie\
Part of an Aramaic expression quoted by Jesus just before He died (Matthew 27:46; Mark 15:34), meaning, "you have forsaken me."

Sabaoth *Sab*-a-oth\
A term used only twice in the New Testament (Romans 9:29; James 5:4) and only in some translations (e.g., *KJV, NASB, ASV, NKJV*). Other versions have "Lord Almighty" or "Lord of hosts" where these have "Lord of Sabaoth."

Sabeans \Suh-*be*-unz\
An Arab tribe of people, nomadic in Job's day, but more settled and commercial in Solomon's—the Sheba of 1 Kings 10:1 is thought to be the country of the Sabeans (Job 1:15; Isaiah 45:14; Ezekiel 23:42; Joel 3:8).

sachar *(Hebrew)* \sah-*har*\
"Wages" or "reward." It is the root of the name Issachar (Genesis 30:18)

sacrilege *sack*-rih-lij\
Irreverence toward a sacred person, place, or object.

Sadducees *Sad*-you-seez\
One of two major religious parties of the Jews—the Pharisees being the other—that arose after the Babylon captivity. The Sadducees differed from the Pharisees in that they did not believe in a resurrection from the dead or of angels and spirits (Acts 23:7, 8). Indications suggest that the Sadducees were more politically motivated than spiritual.

Salamis *Sal*-uh-mis\
A major city on Cyprus. It was located at the eastern end of the island and was the first city visited by Paul on his first missionary journey (Acts 13:1-5).

Salathiel \Sul-*lath*-ee-el\
See SHEALTIEL.

Salem *Say*-lum\
The home of Melchizedek (Genesis 14:18; Psalm 76:2; Hebrews 7:1, 2).

Salim *Say*-lim\
A place in the Jordan valley near where John the Baptist was baptizing at Aenon (John 3:23).

Salma *Sal*-muh\
See SALMON.

Salmon *Sal*-mun\ (Also spelled Salma.)
The father of Boaz and an ancestor of David (Ruth 4:21, 22; 1 Chronicles 2:11, 12; Matthew 1:5, 6; Luke 3:31, 32).

Salome \Suh-*lo*-me\
One of the women who followed Jesus in His ministry and cared for His needs (Mark 15:40, 41). She was among the women who came to Jesus' tomb to anoint His body (Mark 16:1).

Samaria \Suh-*mare*-ee-uh\
1. A region that was part of the 10 rebellious tribes that separated themselves from the kingdom of Israel after the death of Solomon (1 Kings 13:32). The northern kingdom was sometimes referred to as both Israel and Samaria (Hosea 8:2, 5).
2. The capital city of the northern kingdom. The city was built by Omri (1 Kings 16:2, 3, 21-24). It was a strong fortified city that withstood the Syrian army twice (1 Kings 20:1-21; 2 Kings 6:24 –7:16).
3. In the New Testament, a region between Judea and Galilee (John 4:3, 4).

Samaritans \Suh-*mare*-uh-tunz\
The inhabitants of the city or region of Samaria. After the exile the people of this area were of mixed race and mixed religion and were not accepted by the Jews who returned from Babylon (Ezra 4:1-5; Nehemiah 6:1-8). Animosity arose, and it still existed in the time of Christ (John 4:8, 9; Luke 9:51-56).

Samothrace \Sam-o-*thrase*\ (Also spelled Samothracia.)
An island in the Aegean Sea where Paul spent a night before proceeding to Macedonia on his second missionary journey (Acts 16:11).

Samothracia \Sam-o-*thray*-shuh\
See SAMOTHRACE.

Samuel *Sam*-you-el\
1. Son of Hannah and Elkanah (1 Samuel 1:1-20). He was reared and trained by Eli the priest and was accepted by the people as a prophet (1 Samuel 3:20). After the ark of the covenant had been returned to the house of God (following 20 years of neglect), Samuel assumed leadership (1 Samuel 7:2-6). He continued as judge all the days of his life (1 Samuel 7:15). Samuel anointed Saul as king (1 Samuel 10:1, 24) and David to be king (1 Samuel 16:1, 13).

Rr
Ss

2. Names of two books of the Bible (1 and 2 Samuel): the ninth and tenth books of the Old Testament, fourth and fifth in the "history" section. They give the history of Israel from the close of the period of the judges to David's purchase of the threshing floor of Araunah. See BOOKS OF THE BIBLE CHART.

Sanballat \San-*bal*-ut\
An official in Samaria who opposed the Jews who were returning to Jerusalem (Nehemiah 2:10; 4:1, 2; 6:1-7).

Sanhedrin *San*-huh-drun\ or \San-*heed*-run\
A council of the Jews consisting of the high priest, elders, and teachers of the Law (Mark 14:53; Matthew 26:57, 59). The council was made up of 70 elders and teachers, in addition to the high priest. It was in charge of the internal government. The Sanhedrin accepted false witnesses against Jesus (Mark 14:55, 56) and condemned Him to death (Matthew 27:1).

Sapphira \Suh-*fye*-ruh\
The wife of Ananias who, together with him, lied to the Holy Spirit about their gift to the church that was to be distributed to the needy. She, like her husband, died because of her sin (Acts 5:1, 2, 7-10).

sapphire *sa*-fire\ (*sa* as in *sat*)
A precious stone, blue in color and transparent or translucent. It is found in the high priest's breastplate (Exodus 28:18) and in the foundation of the New Jerusalem (Revelation 21:19).

Sarah *Say*-ruh\ (Also known as Sarai.)
The wife of Abraham. Her name was Sarai until changed by God to signify she would be the mother of nations (Genesis 17:15, 16). She was the mother of Isaac (Genesis 21:1-3). Sarah died at the age of 127 and was buried in Machpelah (Genesis 23:1-19).

Sarai *Seh*-rye\
See SARAH.

Sarapis \Suh-*rap*-is\ (also spelled Serapis.)
Egyptian god invented in the third century BC in a mixing of Greek and Egyptian religion under the Ptolemies.

sardine \sar-*deen*\
A type of gemstone in Revelation 4:3 (*KJV*), from the Greek *sardinos*. The Greek word is related to the one translated "sardius" or "carnelian" in Revelation 21:20, and probably refers to the same gem. See SARDIUS.

Sardis *Sar*-dis\
One of the seven cities in Asia Minor that was home to a church addressed in Revelation (Revelation 1:11; 3:1-6). The city was about 45 miles northeast of Ephesus.

sardius *Sard*-ee-us\
A precious gemstone, red in color, associated with divine glory. It is sometimes called a ruby or carnelian (Exodus 28:17; 39:10; Ezekiel 28:13; Revelation 4:3; 21:20). The *New International Version* and the *New Living Translation* do not use this term.

sardonyx \sar-*dahn*-iks\
A precious stone; a type of onyx with layers of sard— a reddish brown chalcedony (Revelation 21:20).

Sargon *Sar*-gon\
One of the great kings of Assyria to whom Israel, the northern kingdom, fell. Isaiah 20:1-6 speaks of Sargon's victory over Egypt. Inscriptions of Sargon confirm the record in 2 Kings 17:5, 6, which speaks of the defeat of the northern kingdom by Sargon, who had succeeded Shalmaneser, and of the deportation of the people.

sarim *(Hebrew)* \sah-*reem*\
A general Hebrew term for leaders (the word is plural; *sar* is the singular). It is translated "leaders," "princes," "captains," and in other ways (Genesis 12:15; Numbers 31:48).

Saron *Say*-ron\ (Also spelled Sharon.)
See SHARON (this spelling found only at Acts 9:35, *KJV*).

Satan *Say*-tun\
A created heavenly being who was cast out of Heaven (Luke 10:18). He was the serpent to Adam and Eve (Genesis 3:1-15). He is the prince of demons (Matthew 9:34), the devil (Matthew 13:39), the dragon, and the old serpent (Revelation 20:1, 2). He is doomed to destruction (Revelation 20:10).

Sceva *See*-vuh\
The father of seven sons in Ephesus who attempted to use the names of Jesus and Paul in exorcising evil spirits but were beaten as a result (Acts 19:13-16).

Scythians \Sith-ee-unz\
People of Scythia, a region assumed to be north of the Black Sea. Extra-biblical sources state they were allied with the Babylonians and Medes in the overthrow of Nineveh. Paul refers to them probably as an example of a barbaric people (Colossians 3:11).

seah *seh*-ah\
A dry measure; a little over a half bushel (Genesis 18:6).

Seba *See*-buh\
1. The eldest son of Cush, a grandson of Ham (Genesis 10:6, 7).
2. A subservient people to Solomon (Psalm 72:10).

Ss

Sebaste \Seh-*bas*-tee\

The rebuilt city Samaria, rebuilt by Herod the Great. Some believe it was the Samaritan city where Philip the Evangelist went to preach (Acts 8:5-14).

Secundus \See-*kun*-duss\

A man of Thessalonica who traveled with Paul (Acts 20:4). His name means "second"; possibly he was a former slave whose master gave him a mere number instead of a name.

seder *say*-der\

The Jewish ceremony that includes the Passover meal.

Seir *See*-ir\

1. The father of sons who lived in the land of Seir (1 Chronicles 1:38).
2. A land that occupied what became Edom, south and east of the Dead Sea, bordering the Arabian Desert (Genesis 32:3).
3. Mt. Seir is a range of mountains that runs south from the Dead Sea on the east side of the great valley (Arabah) to the gulf (Aqaba). This area was given to Esau; the Israelites were not to violate it (Deuteronomy 2:1-5).

Sela Hammahlekoth *See*-lah Ham-*mawl*-lee-koth\

The place where Saul nearly captured David but had to abandon the pursuit because the Philistines had raided the land (1 Samuel 23:26-28).

selah *(Hebrew)* *see*-luh\

Perhaps a musical notation that is used in many of the psalms.

Seleucia \Sih-*lew*-shuh\

The seaport of Antioch of Syria on the Orontes River. Paul sailed from there on his first missionary journey (Acts 13:4).

Seleucids \Suh-*loo*-kids\

Rulers of Asia Minor and Syria after the death of Alexander the Great and before the Maccabees secured Jewish independence. See ANTIOCHUS.

Seleucus \Suh-*loo*-kuss\

The name of several rulers of the Seleucid dynasty. See SELEUCIDS.

Seneca *Sen*-uh-kuh\

First-century Roman statesman and philosopher. Copies of some of his writings survive to the present and provide insight into life in the time of Christ and the early church.

Sennacherib \Sen-*nack*-er-ib\

The son of Sargon, whom he succeeded as ruler of the Assyrian empire. In the 14th year of Hezekiah, Sennacherib attacked Judah (2 Kings 18:13) and later besieged Jerusalem but was defeated by the intervention of God (2 Kings 18:17–19:36).

Sepharvaim \Sef-ar-*vay*-im\

A city in the Assyrian empire from which people were taken and settled in the towns of Samaria after the captivity by Sargon (2 Kings 17:24).

Sephoris *Sef*-oh-ris\

A major city in Nazareth, some four miles northwest of Nazareth, Herod Antipas's capital in Galilee.

Septuagint \Sep-*too*-ih-jent\

Greek translation of the Hebrew Old Testament, dating to the third century BC. The name comes from the Greek word for seventy, a reference to the seventy (actually seventy-two) Jewish translators involved in the work. (In many scholarly works the Roman numeral LXX is used to designate the Septuagint.)

sepulchre *sep*-ul-kur\

A tomb in a cave or an excavation (Matthew 27:66).

Seraiah \Se-*ray*-yuh\ or \Se-*rye*-uh\

1. A scribe of David (2 Samuel 8:17).
2. A chief priest taken prisoner by a guard under Nebuchadnezzar (2 Kings 25:18-22). He was executed at Riblah (Jeremiah 52:24-27).
3. A Judean army officer who sought assurances from Gedaliah, governor of Judah (2 Kings 25:23, 24).
4. Father of Joab (1 Chronicles 4:13, 14).
5. A man of the tribe of Simeon, son of Asiel (1 Chronicles 4:35).
6. A priest who returned from captivity with Zerubbabel (Nehemiah 12:1). He was probably the one who signed the covenant (Nehemiah 10:2).
7. Son of Aziel sent to arrest Jeremiah and Baruch (Jeremiah 36:26).
8. A staff officer who went to Babylon with King Zedekiah. He was given a special mission by Jeremiah (Jeremiah 51:59-64).

seraphim *sair*-uh-fim\

Celestial beings seen by Isaiah in a vision. They were singing praises to God. One of them touched the lips of Isaiah, cleansing them (Isaiah 6:2-7).

Sergius Paulus *Ser*-jih-us *Paul*-us\

A proconsul in Paphos, Cyprus, who sent for Paul to hear Paul preach about Christ. Sergius Paulus was converted to Christ (Acts 13:7, 12).

Shabbethai *Shab*-ee-thigh\

A Levite who opposed the order for Jews returning from Babylon to divorce their foreign wives (Ezra 10:2-15).

Ss

Shadrach *Shay*-drack\ or *Shad*-rack\
Originally called Hananiah, he was one of Daniel's three friends whom God saved from Nebuchadnezzar's fiery furnace (Daniel 1:6, 7, 19; 3:13-30).

Shalem *Shay*-lum\
A place associated with Shechem, where Jacob settled when he returned to Canaan (Genesis 33:18, *KJV*).

Shallum *Shall*-um\
1. Fifteenth king of Israel, he had acquired the throne by conspiring against and killing King Zechariah. Shallum reigned just one month before he suffered the same fate as Zechariah (2 Kings 15:8-14). See Kings of Israel and Judah Chart.
2. Husband of Huldah, the prophetess (2 Kings 22:14).
3. A descendant of Judah, the father of Jekamiah (1 Chronicles 2:40, 41).
4. Sixteenth king of Judah, after Josiah, his father. He is most often called Jehoahaz (2 Kings 23:30; Jeremiah 22:11). See Kings of Israel and Judah Chart.
5. A descendant of Simeon and son of Shaul (1 Chronicles 4:24, 25).
6. A son of Zadok, the priest (Ezra 7:2-4).
7. A son of Naphtali (1 Chronicles 7:13).
8. Name of one or more who returned from Babylon to Jerusalem following the captivity (1 Chronicles 9:1, 17, 19; Ezra 10:24, 42; Nehemiah 3:12, 15).
9. Father of Jehizkiah from Israel who opposed taking prisoners of war from Judah (2 Chronicles 28:8-13).
10. The father of a doorkeeper who was on duty when Jeremiah brought the Rechabites into Jerusalem (Jeremiah 35:4).
11. An uncle of Jeremiah (Jeremiah 32:6, 7).

Shalmaneser *Shal*-mun-*ee*-zer\
King of Assyria who put Hoshea, king of Israel, in prison and laid siege to Samaria, the capital of Israel. The siege of Samaria lasted three years at which time Shalmaneser died and Sargon ascended the throne to complete the conquest and to take the people of Israel into captivity in Assyria (2 Kings 17:3-6). See Sargon.

shalom *(Hebrew)* \shah-*lome*\
Hebrew for "peace." The word describes more than simply the absence of conflict, but an all-encompassing wholeness for a person and/or society.

Shamer *Shay*-mer\
See Shemer.

Shamgar *Sham*-gar\
He became a judge of Israel after Ehud. He lifted the oppression of the Philistines by killing 600 with an ox goad (Judges 3:31). See Judges of Israel Chart.

Shammai *Sham*-eye\
1. A son of Onan, a descendant of Judah (1 Chronicles 2:3, 28).
2. A son of Rekem a descendant of Judah (1 Chronicles 2:44).
3. A son of Mered, a descendant of Caleb, the son of Jephunneh (1 Chronicles 4:15, 17).

Shaphan *Shay*-fan\
A scribe who was in charge of the workmen who were repairing the temple in the days of Josiah (2 Chronicles 34:8-11) and who, when the book of the Law was found, carried it to King Josiah (2 Chronicles 34:14-18).

Shaphat *Shay*-fat\
1. One of the 12 spies sent by Moses to explore the land of Canaan (Numbers 13:1, 2, 5).
2. The father of Elisha the prophet (1 Kings 19:19).
3. Son of Shemaiah, descendant of King Jehoiakim (1 Chronicles 3:17, 22).
4. Chief of the Gadites in Bashan (1 Chronicles 5:11, 12).
5. A herdsman of David's cattle (1 Chronicles 27:29).

Sharon *Share*-on\ (Also spelled Saron.)
A plain between the Mediterranean Sea and the hill country west of Jerusalem (1 Chronicles 5:16; 27:29; Song of Solomon 2:1; Isaiah 33:9; Acts 9:35).

Shealtiel \She-*al*-tee-el\ (Also spelled Salathiel.)
The son of King Jehoiachin (1 Chronicles 3:17) and the father of Zerubbabel (Ezra 3:2). He was an ancestor of Christ (Luke 3:27).

Shear-Jashub \She-are-*yay*-shub\ (strong accent on *yay*) (Also spelled Shearjashub.)
A symbolic name given to a son of Isaiah to denote that a remnant would return from the conflict with Syria (Isaiah 7:3).

Sheba \She-buh\
1. A son of Raamah, grandson of Cush, who was a son of Ham (Genesis 10:6, 7).
2. A descendant of Shem (Genesis 10:21, 28).
3. The grandson of Keturah, Abraham's wife (Genesis 25:1-3).
4. Following the death of Absalom, Sheba carried on the insurrection against David (2 Samuel 20:1-22).
5. A leader of the Gadites who lived in Bashan (1 Chronicles 5:11-13).
6. The Queen of Sheba visited Solomon to confirm what she had heard (1 Kings 10:1-13). The kingdom is thought to have been located on the Arabian peninsula.

Shebat \Sheh-*baht*\
Eleventh month on the Jewish calendar, roughly equivalent to mid-January to mid-February. See Calendar Chart.

Ss

Shebna \Sheb-nuh\

An official in Hezekiah's court (Isaiah 22:15). He also acted as a secretary (2 Kings 19:1, 2).

Shechaniah \Shek-uh-*nye*-uh\ (Also spelled Shecaniah.)

1. A descendant of David who lived after the exile (1 Chronicles 3:21).
2. One or two men whose descendants accompanied Ezra to Jerusalem (Ezra 8:3, 5).
3. A son of Jehiel who divorced his foreign wife when he returned to Jerusalem (Ezra 10:2).
4. Father of Shemaiah who repaired the walls of Jerusalem and was a keeper of the East Gate (Nehemiah 3:29).
5. The father-in-law of Tobiah who was in opposition to Nehemiah (Nehemiah 6:17, 18).
6. A priest who accompanied Zerubbabel to Jerusalem (Nehemiah 12:1, 3).

Shechem *Shee*-kem\ or *Shek*-em\ (Also spelled Sichem.)

1. A city in Samaria at the base of Mt. Gerizim where Abraham built an altar to the Lord shortly after his arrival in Canaan (Genesis 12:6, 7). Jacob also stopped here after his stay in Paddan Aram. He purchased some land and pitched a tent (Genesis 33:18). Joseph was brought from Egypt and buried on the plot of land purchased by Jacob (Joshua 24:32). Here Joshua gathered all Israel for his farewell address (Joshua 24:1–15).
2. Son of Hamor who molested Dinah, the daughter of Jacob (Genesis 34:2).
3. A descendant of Manasseh (Numbers 26:31).

Shekinah *(Hebrew)* \Sheh-*kye*-nuh\

Not found in the Bible, the term describes the glory of God, usually in some visible manifestation as smoke and fire (Exodus 19:18; 2 Chronicles 7:1-3).

Shelemiah \Shel-e-*my*-uh\

1. A gatekeeper for the East Gate of the tabernacle (1 Chronicles 26:14).
2. Descendants of Binnui, a priest, who had returned from Babylon (Ezra 10:38-41).
3. The father of Hananiah who worked on the wall of Jerusalem after the return from Babylon (Nehemiah 3:30).
4. A priest whom Nehemiah put in charge of the storerooms holding the tithes of grain (Nehemiah 13:13).
5. One of the officers sent by Jehoiakim to arrest Baruch and Jeremiah (Jeremiah 36:26).
6. The father of Jehucal who was sent to Jeremiah requesting prayers for the king (Jeremiah 37:3).
7. The father of Irijah, an officer sent to arrest Jeremiah (Jeremiah 37:13).

Shem \Shem\

Son of Noah, brother of Ham and Japheth (Genesis 5:32). He was an ancestor of Abraham (Genesis 11:10-26). A table of nations (Genesis 10:21-31) suggests that Shem's descendants inhabited the lands east of Canaan.

Shema *She*-muh\ (proper noun, not the verb).

1. A son of Hebron of the clans of Caleb (1 Chronicles 2:42-44).
2. A descendant of Joel of the tribe of Reuben (1 Chronicles 5:4, 8).
3. The head of a family in Aijalon who helped drive out the inhabitants of Gath (1 Chronicles 8:12, 13).
4. One of the men who stood at the right hand of Ezra while he read the book of the Law (Nehemiah 8:4).
5. One of the towns listed as being southernmost in the land allotted to the tribe of Judah (Joshua 15:21, 26).

shema *(Hebrew)* \shih-*mah*\

Hebrew verb for "hear." Deuteronomy 6:4, 5, which begins "Hear, O Israel," is called the *shema*.

Shemaiah \She-*may*-yuh\ or \She-*my*-uh\

1. A prophet in the time of Rehoboam who warned him against making war against Israel (1 Kings 12:22-24; 2 Chronicles 11:1-4). Later he called the king and the nation to repentance when Shishak of Egypt attacked Jerusalem (2 Chronicles 12:5-8, 15).
2. A leader who, with 200 relatives, helped carry the ark to the tabernacle David had erected in Jerusalem (1 Chronicles 15:1, 2, 8, 11-15).
3. A scribe who recorded the names of the priests as they were divided by David into 24 divisions for ministry in the temple (1 Chronicles 24:6, 18).
4. The son of Obed-Edom. He was one in a division of gatekeepers for the temple (1 Chronicles 26:4-7, 12).
5. A Levite, one of the teachers sent by Jehoshaphat to tour Judah to teach the people from the book of the Law (2 Chronicles 17:7-9).
6. A Levite who assisted in the purification of the temple in the days of Hezekiah (2 Chronicles 29:14).
7. A Levite who assisted in the distribution of the Levites' portion of the freewill offerings in the days of Hezekiah (2 Chronicles 31:14, 15). Possibly the same as #6.
8. A liberal contributor of offerings to be used in Josiah's Passover celebration (2 Chronicles 35:1, 9).
9. The father of Urijah (or Uriah), a contemporary prophet with Jeremiah who prophesied against Jerusalem (Jeremiah 26:20).
10. A false prophet in Jeremiah's time (Jeremiah 29:24-32).
11. Father of Delaiah, one of the officials of King Jehoiakim who heard Baruch read the scroll dictated by Jeremiah (Jeremiah 36:11-15).
12. A descendant of King Jehoiachin; a member of the royal family after the exile (1 Chronicles 3:17-22).
13. A descendant of Simeon; the father of Shimri (1 Chronicles 4:24, 37).
14. A son of Joel; a descendant of Reuben (1 Chronicles 5:4).

15. A son of Hasshub; a Levite who was one of the first to return to Jerusalem after the Exile (1 Chronicles 9:14; Nehemiah 11:3, 15).
16. The father of Obadiah, a Levite who was one of the first to return after the Exile (1 Chronicles 9:16).
17. One of three brothers who brought 60 men as they joined Ezra on the return to Jerusalem (Ezra 8:13).
18. A Levite, among many who were summoned by Ezra to help obtain ministers to serve in the temple (Ezra 8:16, 17).
19. A priest, a descendant of Harim, who divorced his foreign wife when he returned to Jerusalem from captivity (Ezra 10:18-21, 31).
20. A guard at the East Gate of Jerusalem and one who helped rebuild the walls of Jerusalem (Nehemiah 3:28, 29).
21. A traitor, bribed by Tobiah and Sanballat, to mislead Nehemiah (Nehemiah 6:10-13).
22. A head of a priestly family who returned to Jerusalem with Zerubbabel (Nehemiah 12:4, 18).
23. The name of one or more members of the choir that sang at the dedication of the wall of Jerusalem and the father of a trumpet player at the same occasion (Nehemiah 12:31, 34-36, 42).

Shemer *Shee*-mer\\ (Also spelled Shamer or Shomer.)
1. The owner of the hill Omri bought and on which he built Samaria (1 Kings 16:23, 24).
2. A Levite; the son of Mahli who served before the tabernacle in the early days of the nation of Israel (1 Chronicles 6:46-49).
3. A son of Heber of the tribe of Asher (1 Chronicles 7:32, 34).

Sheol *(Hebrew)* *She*-ol\\
The grave; the abode of the dead. The Greek equivalent is *Hades.*

Sherebiah *Sher*-ee-*bye*-uh\\ (strong accent on *bye*)
1. A Levite who returned to Judah with Zerubbabel (Nehemiah 12:1, 8).
2. A descendant of Mahli, son of Levi, who was brought with his sons and brothers to accompany Ezra to Jerusalem (Ezra 8:17, 18).
3. One of the Levites who assisted in the reading of the Law (Nehemiah 8:5-8). Possibly the same as #1 or #2.

Sheshbazzar \\Shesh-*baz*-ar\\
A man who laid the foundations of the temple (Ezra 5:16).

Shetharboznai *She*-thar-*boz*-nye\\ (strong accent on *boz*) (Also spelled Shethar-Bozenai.)
An official of a Persian province who went with the governor to question Ezra about rebuilding the temple (Ezra 5:3), and who, having received clearance from Darius, king of Persia, allowed the work to proceed (Ezra 6:1, 6, 7, 13).

Shiloh *Shy*-low\\
1. The site where the tabernacle was set up by Joshua. It was on a mountain in Ephraim about eight miles north of Bethel. The ark was in Shiloh when Samuel came to serve Eli there (1 Samuel 1).
2. Some versions, such as *King James Version, New American Standard Bible,* and *New Century Version,* have this term as a title for the Messiah in Genesis 49:10.

Shilonite *Shy*-lo-nite\\
1. Ahijah, a prophet, was identified as the Shilonite in the days of Jeroboam (1 Kings 12:15).
2. People taken into captivity, probably from the area of Shiloh, who returned to Jerusalem (1 Chronicles 9:5).

Shimeah *Shim*-ee-uh\\
See Shimei.

Shimei *Shim*-e-i\\ (Also spelled Shimi or Shimeah.)
1. A son of Gershon, a son of Levi (Exodus 6:13, 17), who shared in the Exodus.
2. A man of Saul's clan in the tribe of Benjamin who cursed King David when David fled Absalom (2 Samuel 16:5-13).
3. A brother of David (2 Samuel 21:21).
4. An official under Solomon in the tribe of Benjamin (1 Kings 4:7, 18).
5. A son of Pedaiah and brother of Zerubbabel (1 Chronicles 3:19).
6. The father of 16 sons and 6 daughters of the tribe of Simeon (1 Chronicles 4:26, 27).
7. A man of the tribe of Reuben, father of Micah (1 Chronicles 5:3-5).
8. The son of Jahath who served in the tabernacle (1 Chronicles 6:42, 43; 2 Chronicles 34:12).
9. A Benjamite, father of nine sons (1 Chronicles 8:19-21).
10. The head of a group of singers in the temple (1 Chronicles 25:1, 17).
11. Head of David's vineyards (1 Chronicles 27:27).
12. An ancestor of some who assisted in the purification of the temple in the days of Hezekiah (2 Chronicles 29:14, 18).
13. A Levite who assisted his brother in caring for the offerings in the temple under Hezekiah (2 Chronicles 31:12, 13).
14. A Levite who had married a foreign woman (Ezra 10:19, 23).
15. A descendant of Hashum who had married a foreign wife and divorced her by the orders of Ezra (Ezra 10:19, 33).
16. Another Levite, descendant of Binnui, who divorced his foreign wife (Ezra 10:19, 38).
17. A Benjamite, the grandfather of Mordecai (Esther 2:5).

Shimi *Shim*-ee\\
See Shimei.

Ss

Shinar *Shye*-nar\\
An area in the southern part of Babylonia (Genesis 10:8-10). Tower of Babel (Genesis 11:1-6).

Shiphrah *Shif*-ruh\\
One of two midwives who disobeyed Pharaoh to preserve the Hebrew baby boys' lives (Exodus 1:15-22).

Shishak *Shy*-shak\\
Egyptian king who raided Jerusalem in the fifth year of King Rehoboam, son of Solomon. He carried off the treasures of the temple and palace (1 Kings 14:25, 26).

Shittim *Shih-teem*\\
The last camping place of the Israelites before entering the promised land. It is where many Israelite men committed adultery with Moabite women and were induced to worship idols (Numbers 25:1-3).

Shochoh *Show*-ko\\
See SOCOH.

Shoco *Show*-ko\\
See SOCOH.

Shomer *Show*-mer\\
See SHEMER.

shofar *show*-far\\
A trumpet made from the horn of a ram.

Shuah *Shoe*-uh\\
The sixth son of Keturah by Abraham (Genesis 25:1, 2).

Shuhite *Shoe*-hite\\
A designation of Bildad, one of Job's friends who came to comfort him (Job 2:11; 18:1, etc.).

Shunem *Shoo*-nem\\
A village in lower Galilee, near the Esdraelon Plain, where the Philistines gathered before the battle in which Saul was killed (1 Samuel 28:4). It was the home of Abishag who cared for David in his old age (1 Kings 1:3, 4). It was also the home of the woman who was hospitable to Elisha (2 Kings 4:8-37).

Shushan *Shoo*-shan\\
See SUSA.

Sichem *Sigh*-kem\\
Alternate spelling of Shechem (Genesis 12:6, *KJV*).

Sidon *Sigh*-dun\\ (Also spelled Zidon.)
An ancient Phoenician seacoast city about 20 miles north of Tyre. It figured prominently in ancient history. It marked the northern border of the territory of the tribe of Asher (Joshua 19:24, 28). Jezebel was the daughter of the king of Sidon (1 Kings 16:31). The city is still flourishing today as a part of Lebanon.

Sidonians *Sigh*-doe-nee-uns\\ (Also known as Zidonians.)
Inhabitants of the city of Sidon. In Solomon's day the men were skilled in felling timber (1 Kings 5:6-9). The Sidonians worshiped idols. Solomon married Sidonian women and accepted some of their gods as worthy of worship (1 Kings 11:5, 6).

Sihon *Sigh*-hun\\
A king of the Amorites. He ruled a land that lay beyond the Jordan opposite the lower part of the river. Prior to Moses and the Israelites' appearance in the area, he conquered Moab. He then refused permission for the Israelites to cross his land. In the ensuing battle, his forces were destroyed (Numbers 21:21-26).

sikarioi *(Greek)* \\sih-*kah*-rih-oy\\
Greek for "murderers" or "assassins." It occurs only once in the Greek New Testament (Acts 21:38), where the *New International Version* renders it "terrorists."

Silas *Sigh*-luss\\ (Also called Silvanus.)
One of two church leaders sent by the apostles with Paul and Barnabas to Antioch to deliver a letter from the church council (Acts 15:22, 23). Later he joined Paul in his missionary endeavors (Acts 15:37-40; 16:9-40; 17:10, 14; 18:5). He assisted Peter in writing his first epistle (1 Peter 5:12).

Siloam \\Sigh-*lo*-um\\
A pool of water that was located on the western base of Mt. Ophel. It was to this pool that Jesus sent a blind man to be healed (John 9:1-7). Jesus referred to a tower at Siloam that collapsed on 18 workers, killing them (Luke 13:4).

Silvanus \\Sil-*vay*-nus\\
Greek variant of *Silas.* (2 Corinthians 1:19; 1 Thessalonians 1:1; 2 Thessalonians 1:1; 1 Peter 5:12). See SILAS.

Simeon *Sim*-ee-un\\ (Sometimes spelled Symeon.)
1. Second son of Jacob and Leah (Genesis 29:33).
2. One of the 12 tribes of Israel.
3. The area assigned to the tribe of Simeon as its inheritance in the promised land (Joshua 19:1, 9).
4. A righteous and devout man who blessed the baby Jesus and Mary and Joseph when they brought Jesus to the temple for His presentation to the Lord (Luke 2:22-35).
5. Ancestor in the lineage of Jesus (Luke 3:30).
6. A prophet in the church at Antioch of Syria who was called Niger (Acts 13:1).
7. The apostle Peter (Acts 15:14, *KJV, NASB,* others, but not *NIV,* "Simon," or *NLT,* "Peter").

Ss

Simon *Sigh*-mun\\
1. The apostle Peter, brother of Andrew (Matthew 4:18-20).
2. One of the 12 apostles who was designated as the Zealot (Luke 6:15; Acts 1:13; note that "Zelotes" in *KJV* and other versions means "Zealot").
3. A leper in the city of Bethany who gave a dinner for Jesus (Matthew 26:6-13).
4. A man of Cyrene who carried the cross of Jesus (Matthew 27:32).
5. A Pharisee who invited Jesus to a dinner at his house. During that meal, a woman washed Jesus' feet with her tears and wiped them with her hair (Luke 7:36-47).
6. A sorcerer who sought to buy the gift of the Holy Spirit from Peter and John (Acts 8:18-23).
7. The father of Judas Iscariot (John 6:71).
8. A tanner, at whose house Peter lodged when he had the vision that led him to visit Cornelius (Acts 9:43; 10:6, 22, 32).

Simon Barjona *Sigh*-mun Bar-*joe*-nuh\\
Another name for the apostle Peter (Matthew 16:16, 17 *KJV, NASB*). Other versions call Simon "son of Jonah" or "son of John." See BARJONA.

Sinai *Sigh*-nye\\ or *Sigh*-nay-eye\\
1. A mountainous area located in the southern part of the land mass between the two arms of the Red Sea. The people of the exodus reached the area three months after leaving Egypt (Exodus 19:1, 2).
2. The mountain on which Moses talked with the Lord and received instructions, including the Ten Commandments (Exodus 19:3–20:17).

Sirach *Sigh*-rak\\
Supposed author of the book of the Apocrypha known as Ecclesiasticus or The Wisdom of Sirach.

Sisera *Sis*-er-uh\\
1. A Canaanite commander of an army under Jabin, who with 900 chariots opposed Deborah and Barak but was routed (Judges 4:2, 12-16). He fled to a Kenite woman who killed him (Judges 4:17-21).
2. Temple servant who returned from Babylonian captivity with Zerubbabel (Ezra 2:2, 53; Nehemiah 7:55).

Sitnah *Sit*-nuh\\
The name of a second well Isaac's servants dug as a result of a clash with the Philistines (Genesis 26:19-21). It means "opposition" or "hatred."

Sivan *See*-vun\\
Third month on the Jewish calendar, roughly equivalent to May–June. See CALENDAR CHART.

Smyrna *Smur*-nuh\\
One of the seven cities in Asia Minor that was home to a church addressed in Revelation (Revelation 1:11; 2:8). It was located about 40 miles north of Ephesus.

Socoh *So*-ko\\ (Also spelled Shoco, Shochoh, Soco, and Sochoh.)
1. The son of Heber, a descendant of Caleb (1 Chronicles 4:15, 18).
2. A city in the country of Judah (Joshua 15:21, 35) and fortified by Rehoboam (2 Chronicles 11:5, 7). It was here that Goliath and the Philistines were encamped (1 Samuel 17:1).

Sodom *Sod*-um\\
The city to which Lot was attracted when he separated from Abraham (Genesis 13:11, 12). The men of Sodom were wicked and were the cause of God's judgment against it. The city was destroyed with Gomorrah. Lot and his family escaped (Genesis 19:16, 24, 25, 30).

Solomon *Sol*-o-mun\\
The son of David and Bathsheba (2 Samuel 12:24). He succeeded David as king and became the richest and wisest of the kings of the earth (2 Chronicles 9:22). He built the temple (2 Chronicles 8:16). Solomon's many wives and concubines led him to worship false gods (1 Kings 11:1-3). Because of his unfaithfulness to God, his kingdom was divided after his death (1 Kings 11:9-13).

soma *(Greek)* *so*-muh\\
Greek for "body."

Song of Solomon \\Song uv *Sol*-o-mun\\ (Also called Song of Songs and Canticles.)
The 22nd book of the Old Testament, fifth in the "poetry" section. Written by Solomon, it describes the beauty of marital love. See BOOKS OF THE BIBLE CHART.

Sopater *So*-puh-ter\\
Son of Pyrrhus, a man of Berea who traveled with Paul (Acts 20:4).

Sorek *So*-rek\\
A valley in the Philistine country where Delilah lived (Judges 16:4).

Sosthenes *Soss*-thuh-neez\\
1. A ruler of a synagogue in Corinth who was beaten by a mob of Greek Jews after the charges he had made against Paul had been dismissed (Act 18:12-17).
2. A believer known to the church in Corinth (possibly the same as #1) who sent greetings with Paul's first letter (1 Corinthians 1:1).

Ss

splagchna (Greek) \splangkh-nah\
Greek for "bowels," not only in the literal sense, but figuratively as the seat of human emotion. In fact, of the 11 uses in the Greek New Testament, only once does it refer to the literal intestines (Acts 1:18).

Stephanas \Stef-uh-nass\
An early Christian convert in Corinth (1 Corinthians 1:15; 16:15).

Stephen \Ste-ven\
One of the seven men chosen to minister to the Greek Christian widows (Acts 6:1, 3, 5). He was said to be "full of God's grace and power" (Acts 6:8, NIV). The Jews could not rebut his teaching, so they stoned him to death (Acts 6:9–7:60).

Stoic \stoe-ik\ (Also spelled Stoick.)
One of a group of philosophers who disputed with Paul (Acts 17:18). Their main characteristic was the absence of emotion—no joy, happiness, pain, or sorrow.

Stoicism \Stoe-uh-siz-um\ (strong accent on Stoe).
The philosophy of the Stoics; the practice of showing no pleasure, pain, sorrow or other emotion no matter what the circumstance.

Succoth \Soo-kawth\
1. A city to the east of the Jordan River. After meeting with Esau and becoming reconciled with him, Jacob moved his family and livestock to Succoth where he made shelters for the cattle (Genesis 33:16,17).
2. The first stop for the Israelites after leaving Egypt (Exodus 12:37).

Suetonius \Soo-toe-nee-us\
First- and second-century Roman biographer and historian. Copies of some of his writings survive to the present and provide insight into life in the Roman empire in the time of the early church.

Susa \Soo-suh\ (Also spelled Shushan.)
A capital city of the Persians which lies on a river parallel but east of the Tigris River, about 150 miles north of the Persian Gulf. Both Nehemiah and Esther lived in Susa (Nehemiah 1:1; Esther 2:8).

Sychar \Sigh-kar\
A village on the eastern slope of Mt. Ebal. It is about two miles from Shechem to the southwest and about one-half mile north of Jacob's well, where Jesus had an encounter with a Samaritan woman (John 4:4-6).

Symeon \Sim-ee-un\
Alternate spelling of Simeon in ASV: Luke 3:30; Acts 13:1; 15:14. See SIMEON #5, 6, 7.

synagogue \sin-uh-gog\
A meeting place for instruction in the Scripture and for public worship. It appears that synagogues came into being after the Babylonian captivity. Wherever a group of 10 Jewish families could assemble, they could have a synagogue. Usually, Paul used synagogues as his first preaching point when he entered a city (Acts 17:1-3).

Syntyche \Sin-tih-key\
A Christian woman of Philippi whom Paul urged to be reconciled to Euodias (Philippians 4:2, 3).

Syria \Sear-ee-uh\ (Also known as Aram.)
Country to the north and east of Israel. Damascus was its capital.

Syriac \Sear-ee-ak\
An Aramaic language of western Mesopotamia. The Bible was translated into Syriac in the earliest centuries of the church, and some manuscripts dating as early as the sixth century survive today.

Syrians \Sear-ee-unz\
Residents of or people from Syria.

Syrophenician \Sigh-roe-fih-nish-un\ (strong accent on nish) (Also spelled Syrophoenician.)
A term used to identify a person of Phoenicia in the Roman province of Syria as opposed to Libyo-Phoenicia in North Africa. The Greek woman who asked Jesus to help her daughter and expressed a faith that was willing to take the crumbs from the table (Mark 7:24-30) was so identified.

Tt

Tabeal \Tay-be-ul\
See TABEEL.

Tabeel \Tay-be-el\ (Also spelled Tabeal.)
1. Father of a would-be usurper of the throne of Judah supported by Israel and Syria (Isaiah 7:6; KJV has Tabeal).
2. One of the officials who wrote to Artaxerxes to oppose the construction of the walls of Jerusalem (Ezra 4:7).

tabernacle \ta-ber-na-kul\ (strong accent on ta)
1. Usually this term refers to the tent that Moses built in the wilderness to house the sanctuary, including the ark of the covenant, the altar of incense, the lampstand, table of showbread, and altar of burnt offerings (Exodus 25:9; 26:1-37).

Ss

Tt

2. The term simply means "tent," and it is sometimes used for a tent other than the sanctuary tent, as in references to the Feast of Tabernacles—sometimes called the Feast of Booths (Deuteronomy 16:13).

3. Sometimes the term is used specifically of the Most Holy Place, the inner sanctuary of the tabernacle/temple (Hebrews 9:3, *KJV, ASV, NASB, NKJV*).

Tabitha *Tab*-ih-thuh\\
A Christian woman (*Dorcas* in Greek) living in Joppa who died but whom Peter restored to life (Acts 9:36-41).

Tabor *Tay*-ber\\
A conical mountain about 1800 feet high, about six miles east of Nazareth. It was where Barak gathered his forces and mounted an attack on a Canaanite force under Sisera (Judges 4:2-16). Gideon's battle against the Midianites extended to Tabor (Judges 8:18).

Tacitus *Tass*-ih-tuss\\
First- and early second-century Roman historian. Copies of some of his writings survive to the present and provide insight into life in the Roman Empire in the days of the early church.

Tahpanhes *Tah*-pan-heez\\ (Also spelled Tehaphnehes).
A city in Egypt where some of the remnant of Judah fled after the Babylonian deportations (Jeremiah 2:16; 43:7-9; 44:1; 46:14; Ezekiel 30:18).

talitha cumi *(Aramaic)* *tal*-i-thuh-*koo*-my\\ or \\tuh-*lee*-thuh-*koo*-me\\ (Strong accent on *koo*.) (Also spelled Talitha Koum, -Kum, or -Cum in various translations.)
The Aramaic words spoken by Jesus to Jairus's daughter, telling her to arise (Mark 5:41).

Talmud *Tahl*-mood\\ or *Tal*-mud\\
The Mishnah, accompanying commentary (the Gemara), and some additional information not in the Mishna but contemporaneous to it (the beraitot), the authoritative body of Jewish tradition. See MISHNAH. A Palestinian Talmud was completed in about AD 400. A Babylonian Talmud was completed in the sixth century and is the more common Talmud in use in modern Judaism.

Tamar *Tay*-mer\\
1. The wife of Er and then Onan, sons of Judah. When both died, Judah asked Tamar to live as a widow until the next oldest son grew up. Later Tamar tricked Judah into an incestuous relationship (Genesis 38:6-19).
2. A daughter of David and a sister of Absalom who was raped by Amnon, son of David by another wife, Ahinoam. Amnon then spurned her and turned her out of his house. Tamar then was taken to live with Absalom, who later avenged her (2 Samuel 13:1-20; 13:23-33).

3. Daughter of Absalom (2 Samuel 14:27).
4. A place marking the southern border of the land area that the Jews were receiving after returning from Babylon (Ezekiel 47:13, 19).

Tammuz \\Tuh-*mooz*\\
Fourth month on the Jewish calendar, roughly equivalent to June–July. See CALENDAR CHART.

Tarshish *Tar*-shish\\ (Also spelled Tharshish.)
1. A seaport, a great distance from Israel. Jonah headed for Tarshish when God told him to go to Nineveh (Jonah 1:2, 3).
2. A son of Javan, a descendant of Japheth (Genesis 10:1-4).
3. A son of Bilhan, a descendant of Benjamin (1 Chronicles 7:6, 10).
4. An official in the court of the Persian king Xerxes (Esther 1:13, 14).

Tarsus *Tar*-sus\\
A city in Cilicia, near the northeast edge of the Mediterranean Sea. The birthplace of Saul who was later named Paul (Acts 22:3).

Tartarus *Tar*-tuh-rus\\
A name for the place of punishment for angelic beings who sinned (2 Peter 2:4), though nearly all Bible versions use the term *Hell* in this verse. The term does not appear as a noun in the Greek text, but the verb *tartareo* does appear, and the verb is rendered "cast (or sent or threw) into Hell." Tartarus is believed by many to be a part of Hell, particularly for the angelic beings, while Hades is for humans only. Others see it as a separate place that will be cast into Hell, the lake of fire of Revelation 20:14, at the end.

Tartessus \\Tar-*tess*-us\\
A location in Spain often considered the same as the ancient city of Tarshish, to which Jonah attempted to flee (Jonah 1:3).

Tatnai *Tat*-nye\\
See TATTENAI.

Tt

Tattenai *Tat*-nye\\ or *Tat*-eh-nye\\ (Also spelled Tatnai.)
A governor of one of the provinces near Judea. Upon seeing that construction had begun on the temple by Zerubbabel, he challenged Zerubbabel's right to build (Ezra 5:3).

Tebeth \\Teh-*beth*\\
Tenth month on the Jewish calendar, roughly corresponding to mid-December to mid-January. See CALENDAR CHART.

Tehaphnehes \\Tuh-*haff*-nuh-heez\\
Alternate spelling of Tahpanhes in Ezekiel 30:18 (*KJV, NASB, NKJV*, and others). See TAHPANHES.

tekel *tee*-kel\\
One of three words written on the wall of Belshazzar's palace; it means, "you have been weighed and found wanting" (Daniel 5:5, 27).

Tekoa \\Tih-*ko*-uh\\ (Also spelled Tekoah.)
A village about six miles south of Bethlehem and home of the prophet Amos (Amos 1:1). It was the home of a wise woman whom Joab engaged to convince David into restoring Absalom to favor (2 Samuel 14:1-33), one of David's mighty men (2 Samuel 23:8, 26), and some of the people who helped in rebuilding the walls of Jerusalem (Nehemiah 3:5).

Tel Abib \\Tell-*ah*-bib\\ (Also spelled Telabib, Tel-abib.)
Town near the Kebar River. Ezekiel, the prophet, visited some exiles who were living there (Ezekiel 3:15).

Tel-Aviv \\Tell-ah-*veev*\\
City of modern Israel near where the biblical Joppa stood.

telos (*Greek*) \\tell-awss\\
Greek noun for "end," "goal," or "finish."

Teman *Tee*-mun\\
1. A son of Eliphaz, grandson of Esau (Genesis 36:10, 11). He was a chief of the Edomites (Genesis 36:15).
2. A region in Edom where there was a stronghold. When doom was pronounced upon Edom, Teman was the focal point for destruction (Ezekiel 25:12, 13; Obadiah 9).

Temanite *Tee*-mun-ite\\
An inhabitant of, or a person from, Teman (Genesis 36:34; 1 Chronicles 1:45; Job 2:11; 4:1). *The King James Version* has Temani as the plural in Genesis 36:34.

Terah *Tair*-uh\\
The father of Abram, Nahor, and Haran. Terah accompanied Abram as far as Haran but did not accompany Abram to Canaan (Genesis 11:26-32).

terebinth *ter*-uh-binth\\
A large deciduous tree, similar to an oak (*KJV*), under which people of Israel sacrificed to idols (Hosea 4:13).

Tertius *Tur*-shih-us\\
The man who penned Paul's letter to the Romans (Romans 16:22). His name means "third"; possibly he was a slave or former slave whose master gave him a mere number instead of a name.

Tertullian \\Tur-*tull*-yun\\
Third-century church father from Carthage.

Tertullus \\Ter-*tull*-us\\
A lawyer, retained by the high priest, Ananias, to try to make a case against Paul before Felix, the governor of Judea (Acts 24:1-8).

tetrarch *teh*-trark\\ or *tee*-trark\\
A title attached to the ruler of a fourth of a particular province or region. Sometimes the term is used of a ruler of any small or divided province, even if there are not four parts (Luke 3:1).

tetrarchy *teh*-trar-key\\ or *tee*-trar-key\\
Government by tetrarch or the area and people governed by a tetrarch.

Thaddaeus \\Tha-*dee*-us\\
One of the 12 apostles. In Matthew 10:3 and Mark 3:18, he is called Thaddaeus. In Luke 6:16 and Acts 1:13, he is called Judas the son (or brother) of James. He is sometimes also called Lebbaeus.

Tharshish *Thar*-shish\\ (*th* as in *thin*)
Alternate spelling of Tarshish in 1 Kings 10:22; 22:48; 1 Chronicles 7:10, *KJV, NKJV*. See TARSHISH.

Theophilus \\Thee-*ahf*-ih-luss\\ (*th* as in *thin*)
A person to whom Luke addressed his Gospel and the book of Acts (Luke 1:3; Acts 1:1).

Thessalonians *Thess*-uh-*lo*-nee-unz\\ (strong accent on *lo*; *th* as in *thin*)
1. Residents of Thessalonica.
2. The 13th and 14th books of the New Testament (1 & 2 Thessalonians) written by Paul to the church in Thessalonica (1 Thessalonians 1:1; 2 Thessalonians 1:1). They are probably the earliest of all of Paul's letters. See BOOKS OF THE BIBLE CHART.

Thessalonica *Thess*-uh-lo-*nye*-kuh\\ (strong accent on *nye*; *th* as in *thin*)
An important Roman city that was a major seaport of Macedonia. It is about 85 miles southwest of Philippi and is located on an important highway leading to Rome. Paul and Silas started a church there during Paul's second missionary journey (Acts 17:1-4).

Thomas *Tom*-us\\
One of the twelve apostles. He is also called Didymus, which means twin, though it is not likely that Thomas's twin was one of the Twelve (Matthew 10:1, 3; Mark 3:18; John 11:16; John 21:1, 2).

Theudas *Thoo*-dus\\
A revolutionist whom Gamaliel referred to as coming to nothing when he rebelled and gathered a following of 400 men (Acts 5:34-36).

Tt

Thummim \ *Thum*-im\ (*th* as in *thin*)
See URIM.

Thyatira \ *Thy*-uh-*tie*-ruh\ (strong accent on *tie*; *th* as in *thin*)
One of the seven cities in Asia Minor that was home to a church addressed in Revelation (Revelation 1:11; 2:18). It was located about 60 miles north of Ephesus and was the home of Lydia (Acts 16:14).

Tiberias \Tie-*beer*-ee-us\
1. City on the southwestern shore of the Sea of Galilee (John 6:23). It was built by Herod Antipas and named in honor of the reigning Caesar, Tiberius.
2. Sea of Tiberias, another name for the Sea of Galilee (John 6:1; 21:1).

Tiberius Caesar \Tie-*beer*-ee-us *See*-zur\
Successor to Caesar Augustus, the first Roman emperor. His name is used by Luke to help fix the date of the beginning of Jesus' ministry (Luke 3:1).

Tibni \ *Tib*-nye\
Tibni and Omri were rivals seeking to succeed Zimri as king of Israel. Omri's forces killed Tibni (1 Kings 16:21, 22).

Tiglath-Pileser \ *Tig*-lath-pih-*lee*-zer\ (Also spelled Tilgathpileser, Tilgathpilneser, and Tilgath-pilneser; also known as Pul.)
One of the great rulers of Assyria who came to power in the closing years of the northern kingdom (2 Kings 15:19, 20, 29; 1 Chronicles 5:6, 26).

Tigris \ *Tie*-griss\ (See HIDDEKEL.)
1. One of the major rivers of Mesopotamia. The river runs south, paralleling the Euphrates and then turning to flow into it before entering the Persian Gulf. Daniel spoke of it as the great river. (Daniel 10:4).
2. One of the four rivers running from the Garden of Eden (Genesis 2:8-14). It may or may not have been at or near the same location as the modern Tigris as the flood doubtless altered world geography.

Tikvah \ *Tick*-vuh\
1. The father-in-law of Huldah the prophetess (2 Kings 22:14).
2. The father of one of the men who opposed Ezra when Ezra insisted that men who had married foreign wives should divorce them (Ezra 10:14, 15).

Tilgathpilneser \ *Til*-gath-*pil*-ness-er\ (strong accent on *pil*)
See TIGLATH-PILESER. This spelling is common in the *KJV*.

Timaeus \Tie-*me*-us\ (Also spelled Timeus.)
Father of the Bartimaeus, whom Jesus healed of blindness in Jericho (Mark 10:46-52).

Timnath Heres \ *Tim*-nath-*hee*-reez\ (strong accent on *hee*) (Also spelled Timnathheres. Also known as Timnath Serah or Timnathserah.)
This town was the inheritance of Joshua in the country of Ephraim. (Joshua 19:50). It became Joshua's burial place (Joshua 24:30; Judges 2:9).

Timon \ *Ty*-mon\
One of the seven men appointed to minister to the Grecian Jewish widows in Jerusalem (Acts 6:1, 3, 5).

Timotheus \Ti-*mo*-the-us\ (*th* as in *thin*)
Another form of Timothy (used 17 times in *KJV*). See TIMOTHY.

Timothy \ *Tim*-o-thee\ (*th* as in *thin*)
1. The son of a Jewish Christian woman named Eunice and a Greek father (Acts 16:1). On Paul's second missionary journey through Asia Minor, Timothy joined Paul's missionary party (Acts 16:1-4) and was set apart for this work (1 Timothy 4:14). He accompanied Paul on many of his journeys and was with him in Rome when Paul wrote some epistles from prison (Philippians 1:1; Colossians 1:1; Philemon 1).
2. The 15th and 16th books of the New Testament (1 & 2 Timothy), the first and second of the pastoral epistles. They were written by Paul to Timothy. The second is probably the last epistle written by Paul before his death. See BOOKS OF THE BIBLE CHART.

Tiphsah \ *Tif*-suh\
A city marking the eastern limit of Solomon's kingdom (1 Kings 4:24).

Tirshatha \Tur-*shay*-thuh\
Term for a regional government official in the Persian empire. Nehemiah was called a Tirshatha (Nehemiah 8:9; 10:1 *KJV*). Most versions translate the term "governor" (Ezra 2:63; Nehemiah 7:65, 70 except *KJV*).

Tirzah \ *Tur*-zuh\
1. A capital of Israel until Omri built Samaria and moved the capital (1 Kings 16:23, 24). Solomon referred to it as beautiful (Song of Solomon 6:4). It was one of the ancient Canaanite cities west of the Jordan conquered by Joshua (Joshua 12:7, 24).
2. One of five daughters of Zelophehad (Numbers 26:33). The daughters petitioned Joshua that an inheritance be granted them as God had instructed Moses (Joshua 17:3, 4).

Tishbe \ *Tish*-be\ (Also spelled Tishbi or Thisbi.)
Birthplace of Elijah (1 Kings 17:1 *NIV, ESV, NLT,* and others). Apparently located in Gilead, although the apocryphal book Tobit (1:2) identifies it as a place in the tribal area of Naphtali.

Tt

Tishbite \ *Tish*-bite\
The name was applied to Elijah (1 Kings 17:1) to identify him as being a native of Tishbe.

Tishri \ *Tish*-ree\
Postexilic name of the seventh month on the Jewish calendar, roughly equivalent to mid-September to mid-October. Known as Ethanim before the Exile (1 Kings 8:2). See CALENDAR CHART.

Titus \ *Ty*-tus\
1. A companion of Paul on some of his journeys (Galatians 2:1). He seems to have had a special relationship with the Corinthians (2 Corinthians 2:13; 7:6, 13-15; 8:16-24).
2. The 17th book of the New Testament, the third of the pastoral epistles. It was written by Paul to Titus, advising him as to how he should encourage the believers in their faith and daily lives (Titus 1:1). See BOOKS OF THE BIBLE CHART.

Tobiah \Toe-*bye*-uh\
1. An ancestor of some men who returned to Jerusalem from Babylon (Ezra 2:1, 60).
2. An Ammonite, who had become a political force in the Persian court (Nehemiah 6:17-19). He tried, on a number of occasions, to stop the work on the walls of Jerusalem (Nehemiah 2:10, 19, 20; 4:7, 8; 6:1-3).

Tohu \ *Toe*-hew\
An ancestor of Elkanah, the father of Samuel (1 Samuel 1:1).

Toi \ *Tow*-eye\ (Also spelled Tou.)
A king of Hamath, a city in northern Syria, who sent a gift and a congratulatory note to David when he defeated an army of Syria (2 Samuel 8:9, 10).

Tola \ *Toe*-luh\
1. A man of the tribe of Issachar who became judge of Israel after Abimelech (Judges 10:1, 2). See JUDGES OF ISRAEL CHART.
2. A son of Issachar (Genesis 46:13; 1 Chronicles 7:1, 2).

topaz \ *toe*-paz\
A yellow to brownish yellow translucent to nearly transparent gemstone. It was included in the high priest's breastplate (Exodus 28:17; 39:10) and in the foundation of the New Jerusalem (Revelation 21:20).

Tophet \ *Toe*-fet\ (Also spelled Topheth.)
A high place where children were sacrificed by fire on an altar (Jeremiah 7:31). It was located to the south of the city of Jerusalem in the Valley of Hinnom (Jeremiah 19:6).

Tou \ *Too*\
See TOI.

Traconitis \ *Trak*-o-nye-tus\ (Also spelled Trachonitis.)
The area south of Damascus and east of the Sea of Galilee. It was a part of the tetrarchy of Philip (Luke 3:1).

Troas \ *Tro*-az\
A seaport city in Mysia, the Roman province in the northwest corner of Asia Minor, fronting the Aegean Sea. Paul preached there (Acts 16:7-12; 20:4-12).

Trophimus \ *Troff*-ih-muss\
A man from the province of Asia who accompanied Paul on his third journey (Acts 20:4). Later, when Paul and his group were in Jerusalem, Trophimus was the reason for a riot and the arrest of Paul (Acts 21:27-33).

turquoise \ *tur*-koys\
A blue to blue green gemstone. It appears six times in the *New International Version* (Exodus 28:18; 39:11; 1 Chronicles 29:2; Isaiah 54:11; Ezekiel 27:16; 28:13) but never in the *King James Version*. Other versions also have it, but most of them not as often as the *NIV*.

Tychicus \ *Tick*-ih-cuss\
A companion of Paul along with Trophimus (Acts 20:4, 5). He was from the province of Asia. Paul sent Tychicus from Rome to Ephesus (Colossians 4:7; Ephesians 6:21, 22; 2 Timothy 4:12).

Tyndale \ *Tin*-dale\ or \ *Tin*-dul\
William Tyndale, 1494-1536. English reformer and Bible translator. Exiled from England, Tyndale translated and printed New Testaments in Germany and had them smuggled into England. He was condemned by the church as a heretic and executed.

Tyrannus \Ty-*ran*-nus\
The owner of a lecture hall in Ephesus. Paul taught for two years in the lecture hall of Tyrannus after he encountered opposition in the synagogue (Acts 19:8-10).

Tyre \Tire\
An important city on the Phoenician seacoast about 20 miles south of Sidon. It was important to worldly trade (Isaiah 23:8), but it also figured prominently in the history of Israel. (See 2 Samuel 5:11; 1 Kings 5:1, 10; 2 Chronicles 2:7-14; Ezekiel 26–28.) Amicable relations were present in the New Testament times: Jesus visited Tyre (Matthew 15:21); Paul stayed there with some Christians for seven days (Acts 21:3, 4).

Uu

Ulai *You*-lye\ or *You*-luh-eye\
A river or canal in central Persia that travels south through the city of Susa, the capital city and on south to the Persian Gulf (Daniel 8:1, 2, 16).

upharsin \you-*far*-sin\
See PERES.

Ur \Er\
1. The father of Eliphal, one of David's mighty men (1 Chronicles 11:10, 35).
2. A great city of Mesopotamia. This was Abram's home city, from which God called him to a different land. (Genesis 11:27—12:5).

Uri *U*-rye\
1. The father of Bezaleel, whom God had blessed with skills used in building the tabernacle (Exodus 35:30-35).
2. The father of Geber, whom Solomon chose to be a governor in Israel (1 Kings 4:7, 19).
3. A gatekeeper after the exile (Ezra 10:11, 12, 24).

Uriah \Yu-*rye*-uh\ (Sometimes spelled Urijah.)
1. A faithful Hittite soldier in David's service. His wife, Bathsheba, entered into an adulterous affair with David. Failing to cover up his sin through trickery, David arranged for Uriah to be killed in battle (2 Samuel 11:2-17).
2. A priest who witnessed Isaiah's prophetic writing of the name of a son Maher-Shalel-Hash-Baz, which signified the downfall of Israel (Isaiah 8:1-4). He may be the same priest who built an idolatrous altar for King Ahaz (2 Kings 16:10-16).
3. A man who stood beside Ezra at the reading of the Law (Nehemiah 8:4).
4. A prophet who prophesied the fall of Jerusalem in the days of King Jehoiakim. The king condemned him to death. Uriah fled but was caught and put to death (Jeremiah 26:20-23).

Urijah \Yu-*rye*-juh\
See URIAH.

Urim *You*-rim\ (combined with THUMMIM)
The means by which the will of God was made known. God gave Moses instructions to put the Urim and Thummim in the breastplate to be worn by the high priest when he entered the Most Holy Place in the tabernacle (Exodus 28:30; Numbers 27:21).

Uzzah *Uz*-zuh\ (Also spelled Uzza.)
1. One of two sons of Abinadab driving oxen pulling a cart bearing the ark of the covenant. When the oxen stumbled, Uzzah put out his hand to steady the ark. He was instantly killed (2 Samuel 6:3-7). God had specifically declared that only the Kohathites were to carry things pertaining to the tabernacle (Numbers 4:15).
2. A son of Shimei, a descendant of Levi (1 Chronicles 6:29).

Uzziah \Uh-*zye*-uh\
1. Ninth king of Judah, after his father Amaziah. He reigned 52 years and did what was right (2 Kings 15:1, 2; 2 Chronicles 26:1-4). Also known as Azariah (2 Kings 14:21). See KINGS OF ISRAEL AND JUDAH CHART.
2. Son of Uriel, a descendant of Kohath, a son of Levi (1 Chronicles 6:16, 24).
3. A descendant of Judah and the father of a resident in Jerusalem who had returned from captivity (Nehemiah 11:4).
4. A priest who had intermarried with a Gentile woman while in captivity (Ezra 10:18-21).

Vv

Vashni *Vash*-nigh\
The oldest son of Samuel (1 Chronicles 6:28, *KJV*); he is otherwise known as Joel (1 Samuel 8:2; 1 Chronicles 8:33).

Vashti *Vash*-tie\
Queen of Persia, wife of Xerxes, who refused to display herself at a royal banquet before many noble guests. Because she refused to obey the king's command she was deposed. Esther was made queen in her place (Esther 1:9-21; 2:17).

Vesuvius \Veh-*soo*-vee-us\
A volcano in Italy that erupted in AD 79, burying the city of Pompeii. That city has since proved to be a rich archaeological site.

victuals *vih*-tulz\
Supplies of food; provisions.

Ww

wadi *wah*-dee\
A river that flows in the rainy season but becomes dry in the dry season.

Wycliffe *Wick*-lif\\
John Wycliffe, 1330-1384; English preacher and professor at Oxford university. Two centuries before the Protestant Reformation, he criticized abuses in the church and translated the first English Bible.

Xx

xenos *(Greek)* *zeen*-os\\
Stranger, foreigner (Matthew 25:35, 38, 43, 44; 27:7; Acts 17:21). The term is also used for one who hosts strangers (Romans 16:23).

Xerxes *Zerk*-seez\\ (Also known as Ahasuerus.)
A Persian king, husband of Esther (Esther 2:1, 16). His kingdom was extended from India to Cush (Ethiopia, *KJV*). It was early in his reign that an accusation was lodged against the Jews for building the temple (Ezra 4:1, 6). Political intrigue and confusion delayed the completion of the temple for about 60 years. In the 12th year of Xerxes' reign, Haman tricked the king into signing the death warrant of all Jews (Esther 3:8-13). Esther worked out a plan to save them, and Xerxes so ordered it (Esther 5–8:8).

Yy

Yahweh *(Hebrew)* *Yah*-weh\\
The personal name for God, often cited as YHWH; it appears more than 6500 times in the Old Testament, the first in Genesis 4:26. In most Bibles this is the Old Testament word behind the translation "Lord" (note the capital letters). Jewish people of ancient times substituted the word *Lord (adonai)* for *Yahweh* because they considered the name too sacred to say aloud. *The King James Version* translates it "Jehovah" in Exodus 6:3; Psalm 83:18; Isaiah 12:2; 26:4. *The American Standard Version* typically translates it "Jehovah."

Yeshua \\Yeh-*shoo*-uh\\
Alternate spelling for *Joshua*. This pronunciation is more like that of the ancient Hebrews and the Jews of Jesus' day. It is also more like the way Jesus' own name would have been pronounced, as *Jesus* is transliterated from the Greek equivalent of the Hebrew *Yeshua (Joshua)*.

Zz

Zabulon *Zab*-you-lon\\
See Zebulun.

Zacchaeus \\Zack-*key*-us\\ (Also spelled Zaccheus.)
A tax official, short in stature, who climbed a tree to see Jesus, who was passing through Jericho. He served as host to Jesus and, at that time, pledged to make restitution to all whom he had defrauded (Luke 19:1-10).

Zachariah \\Zack-uh-*rye*-uh\\ (Also spelled Zechariah and Zacharias.)
See Zechariah.

Zacharias \\Zack-uh-*rye*-us\\ (Also spelled Zechariah.)
This spelling is found only in the New Testament and applied to two men. The *NIV* never uses this spelling.
1. A priest, the husband of Elizabeth and father of John the Baptist (Luke 1:5-25, 57-64, *KJV*).
2. Son of Barachias; he was murdered "between the temple and the altar" (Matthew 23:35; Luke 11:51, *KJV*).

Zadok *Zay*-dok\\
1. A descendant of Levi, a priest who joined David after Saul's death (1 Chronicles 12:28). He was a leader of one of the divisions of the family of Eleazar (1 Chronicles 24:1-6). He remained true to David when Absalom revolted (2 Samuel 15:25-29). He was asked by David to anoint Solomon as king (1 Kings 1:32-40).
2. The grandfather of Jotham, king of Judah (2 Chronicles 27:1).
3. One who helped to repair the walls of Jerusalem (Nehemiah 3:4).
4. The son of Immer. Zadok was a priest who repaired the wall of Jerusalem opposite his house (Nehemiah 3:29).
5. One of three men, a scribe, whom Nehemiah put in charge of storerooms (Nehemiah 13:13).

Zarah *Zair*-uh\\ (Also spelled Zerah.)
See Zerah.

Zarephath *Zair*-uh-fath\\
The town to which Elijah the prophet was sent by God to find hospitality during the drought inflicted on Israel by God (1 Kings 17:7-16; Luke 4:26).

Zaretan *Zair*-uh-tan\\ (Also spelled Zarethan.)
A place near the city of Adam, to which the waters of Jordan backed up when Joshua led the Israelites across the riverbed (Joshua 3:16).

Zealots *Zel*-uts\\
A group of somewhat fanatical Jewish patriots to which the apostle Simon belonged and was so designated (Luke 6:15; Acts 1:13).

Zebadiah *Zeb*-uh-*dye*-uh\\ (strong accent on *dye*)
1. A son of a Benjamite, Beriah (1 Chronicles 8:15, 16).
2. A son of a Benjamite, Elpaal (1 Chronicles 8:17, 18).
3. One of David's warriors (1 Chronicles 12:7).
4. A gatekeeper of the temple under David (1 Chronicles 26:2).
5. A nephew of Joab who was in charge of a division of David's army (1 Chronicles 27:7).

Zebedee *Zeb*-eh-dee\\
A Galilean fisherman, the father of the two apostles James and John (Matthew 4:21) and probably the husband of Salome (compare Matthew 27:56 with Mark 15:40).

Zebidah *Zeb*-ih-duh\\ (Also spelled Zebudah.)
The mother of King Jehoiakim of Judah (2 Kings 23:36).

Zeboim \\Zeh-*bo*-im\\
A valley running east from Micmash, about 10 miles north, northeast of Jerusalem, into the Jordan valley, toward Jericho and Gilgal (1 Samuel 13:16-18).

Zebudah *Zeb*-uh-duh\\
Alternate spelling of Zebidah (2 Kings 23:36 *KJV*).

Zebul *Zee*-bul\\
Governor of Shechem when Abimelech succeeded Gideon as judge of Israel. After three years of Abimelech's judgeship, the men of Shechem revolted. Zebul helped Abimelech ambush the rebels and overthrow them (Judges 9:30-41).

Zebulun *Zeb*-you-lun\\ (Also spelled Zabulon.)
1. The tenth son of Jacob; the sixth by Leah (Genesis 30:19, 20; 35:23).
2. One of the 12 tribes of Israel.
3. A tribal area just west of the Sea of Galilee and bordering the east boundary of Asher (Joshua 19:10-16). Nazareth and Cana were located in the area (Matthew 4:12-16).

Zechariah *Zek*-uh-*rye*-uh\\ (strong accent on *rye*) (Also spelled Zachariah or Zacharias.)
1. A prophet, son of Berekiah, son of Iddo, who was called to prophesy in the second year of Darius's reign in Persia, author of the book of Zechariah in the Old Testament (Zechariah 1:1, 7; Nehemiah 12:12, 16). He was contemporary with Haggai in Judah and Jerusalem (Ezra 5:1).
2. The 38th book of the Old Testament, the eleventh in the "minor prophets" section. See Books of the Bible Chart.
3. Fourteenth king of Israel, he reigned only six months. His actions were evil in God's sight. He was assassinated by Shallum, who succeeded him (2 Kings 15:8-10). See Kings of Israel and Judah Chart.
4. A son of Jehoiada, the high priest, who prophesied against Joash, king of Judah. The king had Zechariah stoned (2 Chronicles 24:20-22).
5. A prophet during the reign of Uzziah, king of Judah (2 Chronicles 26:5).
6. A witness to Isaiah's naming of his son Maher-Shalal-Hash-Baz (Isaiah 8:1, 2). Possibly the same as #5.
7. A descendant of Reuben and an official during the closing years of the northern kingdom's history (1 Chronicles 5:6, 7).
8. A gatekeeper of the tabernacle and a "wise counselor" (1 Chronicles 9:21; 26:14).
9. A brother of Kish, the father of King Saul (1 Chronicles 9:35-37).
10. A Levite appointed by David to play a lyre in the tent prepared to house the ark of the covenant (1 Chronicles 15:1, 16-18, 20).
11. A priest who was to play a trumpet while accompanying the ark to Jerusalem (1 Chronicles 15:24).
12. One of the Levites. He was one of many who were to serve at the temple (1 Chronicles 24:25, 31).
13. A gatekeeper of the tent (temple), the fourth son of Hosah (1 Chronicles 26:1, 10, 11).
14. Father of Iddo, chief of the half tribe of Manasseh east of the Jordan (1 Chronicles 27:21).
15. One of the men Jehoshaphat sent into Judah to teach the Law of the Lord (2 Chronicles 17:7, 9).
16. The father of Jahaziel, a Levite, who counseled and encouraged Jehoshaphat in his war with the Moabites (2 Chronicles 20:14-17).
17. A son of Jehoshaphat (2 Chronicles 21:2).
18. The father of King Hezekiah's mother (2 Chronicles 29:1).
19. A Levite who assisted in the purification of the temple at the instruction of King Hezekiah (2 Chronicles 29:13, 15).
20. A descendant of Kohath who oversaw the repair of the temple in the days of Josiah (2 Chronicles 34:12).
21. An administrator of God's temple in the days of Josiah (2 Chronicles 35:8).
22. A leader of 150 men who accompanied Ezra to Jerusalem in the days of King Artaxerxes (Ezra 8:1, 3).
23. A leader of 28 men who accompanied Ezra to Jerusalem (Ezra 8:11).
24. A Levite summoned by Ezra to seek men who would be attendants for the house of God when they got to Jerusalem (Ezra 8:15-17).
25. An Israelite guilty of marrying a foreign woman (Ezra 10:18, 26).

Zz

26. Ancestors of two residents who lived in Jerusalem after the return from captivity (Nehemiah 11:3-6).
27. An ancestor of a priest, Adaiah, who chose to live in Jerusalem (Nehemiah 11:12).
28. One of the priests who played a musical instrument at the dedication of the wall of Jerusalem (Nehemiah 12:27, 35, 36).

Zedekiah \Zed-uh-*kye*-uh\
1. A false prophet, son of Kenaanah; he made a favorable but false report to King Ahab and was reproved by God's prophet, Micaiah (1 Kings 22:6-25).
2. The last king of Judah, a son of Josiah (1 Chronicles 3:15). His name had been Mattaniah but was changed by Nebuchadnezzar (2 Kings 24:17; 1 Chronicles 3:15, 16). See KINGS OF ISRAEL AND JUDAH CHART.
3. A false prophet, son of Maaseiah; he and Ahab (See AHAB #2) deceived the Israelites in Babylon and whom the king of Babylon executed by burning (Jeremiah 29:20-23).
4. One of the officials in the royal court who heard Jeremiah's report to Jehoiakim, as read by Baruch, and who advised Baruch and Jeremiah to hide from the king (Jeremiah 36:11-19).

Zelophehad \Zeh-*low*-feh-had\
Son of Hepher of the tribe of Manasseh. He had no sons, so his inheritance went to his daughters (Numbers 26:33; 27:1-11; Joshua 17:3, 4).

Zelotes \Zeh-*low*-teez\
Surname for Simon, one of the Twelve, that means "Zealot" (Luke 6:15; Acts 1:13; *KJV*). See ZEALOTS.

Zephaniah \Zef-uh-*nye*-uh\
1. A son of Cushi who prophesied during the reign of Josiah (Zephaniah 1:1).
2. The 36th book of the Old Testament, the ninth in the "minor prophets" section. See BOOKS OF THE BIBLE CHART.
3. A Kohathite Levite, one of many who were in charge of the music in the house of the Lord (1 Chronicles 6:31, 32, 36).
4. A priest in the days of Jeremiah (Jeremiah 21:1). King Zedekiah sent him to Jeremiah to ask him to pray for Israel in the face of the Babylonian threat (Jeremiah 37:3, 6, 8).
5. The father of Josiah, who was made high priest after the exiles returned from Babylon (Zechariah 6:9-11).

Zerah \Zair-uh\ (Also spelled Zara and Zarah.)
1. Grandson of Esau, son of Reuel (Genesis 36:13). A chief among the Edomites (Genesis 36:17).
2. One of the twin sons of Tamar and Judah (Genesis 38:11-30).

3. A descendant of Simeon (1 Chronicles 4:24).
4. A Levite, a descendant of Gershon (1 Chronicles 6:21).
5. An Ethiopian king who invaded Judah when Asa was king. Zerah had 300 chariots and a vast army. But God helped Asa prevail (2 Chronicles 14:8-15).

Zeror *Zee*-ror\
The grandfather of Kish, the father of Saul (1 Samuel 9:1, 2).

Zerubbabel \Zeh-*rub*-uh-bul\
One of the men who led the exiles home from Babylon to Jerusalem (Ezra 2:1, 2). He served as governor in Judah and was listed in the genealogy of Jesus as the son of Shealtiel and father of Abiud (Matthew 1:12, 13; Luke 3:27).

Zeruiah *Zer*-oo-*eye*-uh\ (strong accent on *eye*)
A sister of David and mother of three of his strong men: Abishai, Joab, and Asahel (1 Chronicles 2:13-16; 11:6, 20, 26).

Zeus \Zoose\
Chief god of Greek mythology, parallel to Jupiter in Roman mythology. The people of Lystra took Paul and Barnabas for Mercury and Zeus and attempted to offer sacrifices to them (Acts 14:8-13).

Zibiah *Zib*-ee-uh\
The mother of King Joash (2 Kings 12:1, 2; 2 Chronicles 24:1).

Zidon *Zye*-dun\
See SIDON.

Zidonians \Zye-*doe*-nee-uns\
See SIDONIANS.

Zif \Zeef\
Alternate spelling of Ziv (1 Kings 6:1, 37 *KJV*). See ZIV.

ziggurat *zigg*-oo-rat\
Ancient Mesopotamian tower temple; some believe the tower built at Babel was a ziggurat.

Ziklag *Zik*-lag\
One of the southernmost towns of Judah, about halfway between Gaza and Beersheba (Joshua 15:21, 31). David lived here for a time when he was avoiding Saul (1 Samuel 27:1, 6). David received news of Saul's death while at Ziklag (2 Samuel 4:10).

Zilpah *Zil*-pa\
A maidservant of Leah who gave her to Jacob as a wife (Genesis 29:24; 30:9). Zilpah bore two sons for Jacob: Gad and Asher (Genesis 35:26).

Zz

Zimri *Zim*-rye\\

1. Fifth king of Israel, he reigned only seven days. He had killed King Elah and had taken the throne (1 Kings 16:10, 15) and then killed the royal family (1 Kings 16:11). But when the people of Israel learned of the murder of the royal family, they crowned Omri king. Omri then moved against Zimri. Zimri then committed suicide (1 Kings 16:15-18). See Kings of Israel and Judah Chart.
2. An Israelite who was killed for having sexual relations with a Midianite woman (Numbers 25:1, 6-9, 14, 15).
3. A descendant of Judah whose father was Zerah (1 Chronicles 2:6).
4. A descendant of King Saul. He was the son of Jareh (or Jadah) and the father of Moza (1 Chronicles 9:42).

Zion *Zi*-un\\

The hill on which the Jebusites had built a fortress. After David captured it, he called it the City of David (2 Samuel 5:6, 7; 1 Chronicles 11:4, 5). The name later applied to the whole city of Jerusalem (Psalm 126:1). The writer of Hebrews declares Mt. Zion to be the heavenly Jerusalem (Hebrews 12:22).

Ziph \\Zif\\

1. A descendant of Judah, the son of Jehalellel (1 Chronicles 4:1, 16).
2. A town listed as one of the southernmost towns of the tribe of Judah (Joshua 15:21, 24).
3. A town in the hill country in the area of Hebron (Joshua 15:54, 55). Rehoboam fortified the town (2 Chronicles 11:5, 8).
4. A desert area near the town of Ziph to which David fled when Saul was pursuing him (1 Samuel 23:14, 15). The Ziphites betrayed David to Saul (1 Samuel 26:1, 2).

Ziphites *Zif*-ites\\

The inhabitants of Ziph (1 Samuel 23:19).

Zippor *Zip*-or\\

The father of Balak, king of Moab (Numbers 22:1-6).

Zipporah \\Zi-*po*-ruh\\

The daughter of Jethro (Reuel) who married Moses and bore him two sons (Exodus 2:18, 21; 18:2-4).

Ziv \\Zeev\\

Pre-exilic name of the second month on the Jewish calendar, roughly equivalent to mid-April to mid-May. Called Iyyar after the exile. See Calendar Chart.

Zoar *Zo*-er\\

One of a group of five cities that lay at the southern end of the Dead Sea. The cities were subject to a confederation of kings from the north (Genesis 14:1-4) but the kings were defeated by Abraham (Genesis 14:17). Lot fled to Zoar when Sodom and Gomorrah were destroyed (Genesis 19:20-22, 29).

Zophar *Zo*-far\\

One of Job's three friends who counseled him in his distress. His advice to Job was flawed as was the advice of the other two friends, and the Lord chided them for it (Job 2:11; 42:7-9).

Zorah *Zo*-ruh\\

A town located about 15 miles due west of Jerusalem and on the southern boundary of Dan's tribal lands overlooking the Philistine plains. The birthplace of Samson (Judges 13:2-5, 24, 25). Samson was buried near Zorah (Judges 16:31).

Zuph \\Zuf\\

1. An ancestor of Elkanah, the father of Samuel. He lived in the hill country of Ephraim (1 Samuel 1:1).
2. A district to which Saul went to find some runaway donkeys belonging to his father, Kish. There Saul encountered Samuel, who anointed him king of Israel (1 Samuel 9:1–10:1).

Zz